# GRE® GENERAL TEST
## VOCABULARY FLASHCARDS

**Premium TestWare® Edition**

Vocabulary Building Games

PLUS Word Builder Chart
For Windows

By The Staff of REA

**Research & Education Association**
Visit our website at: www.rea.com

***Research & Education Association***
61 Ethel Road West
Piscataway, New Jersey 08854
E-mail: info@rea.com

**Vocabulary Flashcard Book
for the GRE® General Test
Premium TestWare® Edition
with CD-ROM**

Printed in the United States of America

ISBN-13: 978-0-7386-0841-9
ISBN-10: 0-7386-0841-6

Apple®, iPhone®, and iPod touch® are registered trademarks of Apple, Inc.

Windows® is a registered trademark of Microsoft Corporation.

REA®, INTERACTIVE FLASHCARDS® and TestWare® are registered trademarks of Research & Education Association, Inc.

C10-0101

# GRE Vocabulary Flashcards— About This Premium Edition with CD-ROM

GRE test experts all agree that building a powerful GRE-specific vocabulary is the single most important way you can raise your score on the Verbal Ability and Analytical Writing sections of the test.

This **Premium CD Edition** of REA's best-selling book contains 900 flashcards with the most frequently used words on the GRE General Test, as well as **Verbal Building Software and a Vocabulary Enhancer Chart on CD.** The software presents games and exercises designed to challenge your flashcard study and improve your GRE reading and vocabulary skills.

Learning and remembering 900 words is not an easy task, especially if many of these words are new to you. This unique flashcard book is designed to help you in your quest. Each page presents the flashcard word with space to write in your definition of the word. On the flip side of each page you'll find the correct definition of the word, its part of speech (adjective, verb, etc.), and sample sentences using the word in context.

It's a three-step learning process:
1. See the word.
2. Write in your definition.
3. Turn the page and compare your definition to the correct one.

You will also find that flashcards in a book have several advantages over flashcards in a box. You don't have to cope with hundreds of loose cards. Whenever you want to study, you can just open the book and get going.

Take this book along with you everywhere since there are a lot of words to study and the book is ready to use whenever— and wherever— you are. **With our unique iPhone® vocabulary App, you'll have access to instant test prep anywhere you go! Visit *www.rea.com/GRE* to learn more.**

**Best to start studying now — test day is drawing near!**

# *Questions*

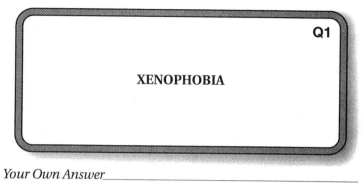

**Q1**

**XENOPHOBIA**

*Your Own Answer*_____

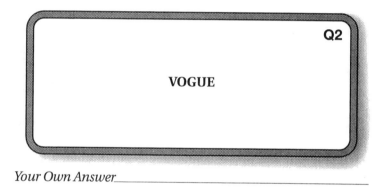

**Q2**

**VOGUE**

*Your Own Answer*_____

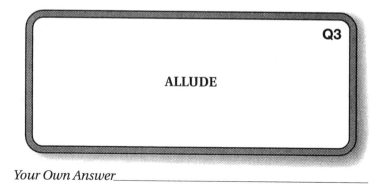

**Q3**

**ALLUDE**

*Your Own Answer*_____

# *Correct Answers*

**A1**

n.—fear of foreigners

**Xenophobia** kept the townspeople from encouraging any immigrants to move into the neighborhood.

**A2**

n.—modern fashion

Women's magazines advertise the clothing they believe to be in **vogue**.

**A3**

v.—to refer indirectly to something

Without stating that the defendant was an ex-convict, the prosecutor **alluded** to the fact by mentioning his length of unemployment.

# *Questions*

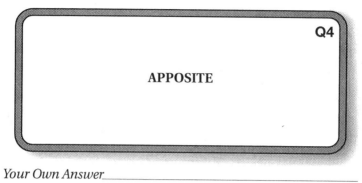

**Q4**

**APPOSITE**

*Your Own Answer*_____

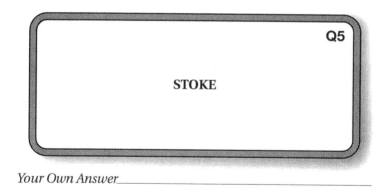

**Q5**

**STOKE**

*Your Own Answer*_____

**Q6**

**GUFFAW**

*Your Own Answer*_____

# *Correct Answers*

**A4**

adj.—suitable; apt; relevant

Without reenacting the entire scenario, the situation can be understood if **apposite** information is given.

**A5**

v.—to feed fuel to; especially a fire

With the last embers dying, he **stoked** the fire one more time.

**A6**

n.—boisterous laughter

With the **guffaw** of the boisterous crowd, the comedian was assured of his success.

# *Questions*

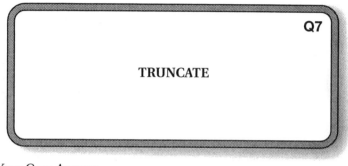

**Q7**

**TRUNCATE**

*Your Own Answer*_____

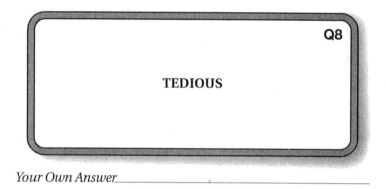

**Q8**

**TEDIOUS**

*Your Own Answer*_____

**Q9**

**REDUNDANT**

*Your Own Answer*_____

# Correct Answers

**A7**

v.—to shorten by cutting

With the football game going into overtime, the show scheduled to follow it had to be **truncated**.

**A8**

adj.—time-consuming; burdensome; uninteresting

Counting all the rubber bands in the box proves to be a **tedious** affair.

**A9**

adj.—superfluous; exceeding what is needed

With millions of transactions at stake, the bank built a **redundant** processing center on a separate power grid.

# *Questions*

Q10

**RELEGATE**

*Your Own Answer*_____

Q11

**CALLOW**

*Your Own Answer*_____

Q12

**ECONOMICAL**

*Your Own Answer*_____

# *Correct Answers*

**A10**

v.—to banish; to put to a lower position

With Internal Affairs launching an investigation into charges that Officer Wicker had harassed a suspect, the officer was **relegated** to desk duty.

**A11**

adj.—being young or immature

With his **callow** remark, the young man demonstrated he wasn't up to the job.

**A12**

adj.—not wasteful; thrifty

With her **economical** sense, she was able to save the company thousands of dollars.

# *Questions*

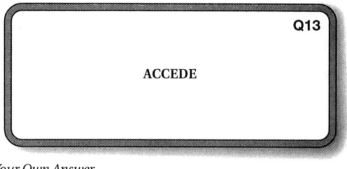

**Q13**

**ACCEDE**

*Your Own Answer*_____

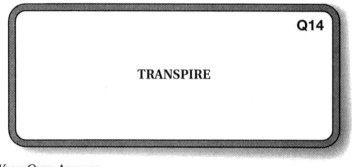

**Q14**

**TRANSPIRE**

*Your Own Answer*_____

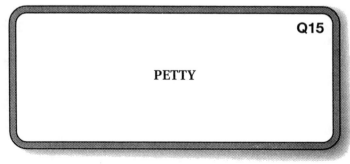

**Q15**

**PETTY**

*Your Own Answer*_____

# Correct Answers

**A13**

v.—to comply with; to consent to
With defeat imminent, the rebel army **acceded** to hash out a peace treaty.

**A14**

v.—to take place; to come about
With all that's **transpired** today, I'm exhausted.

**A15**

adj.—unimportant; of subordinate standing
With all of the crime in the world, stealing bubble gum is considered **petty** theft.

# *Questions*

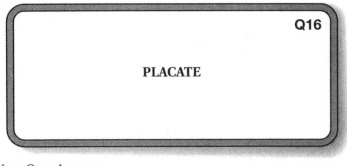

Q16

**PLACATE**

*Your Own Answer*_____

_____

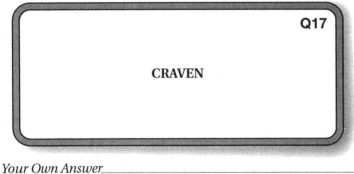

Q17

**CRAVEN**

*Your Own Answer*_____

_____

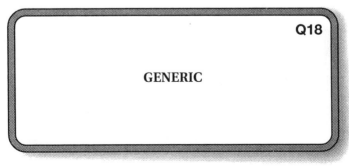

Q18

**GENERIC**

*Your Own Answer*_____

_____

# Correct Answers

**A16**

v.—to appease or pacify

With a soothing voice and the promise of a juicy steak, the trainer **placated** the escaped lion so that it wouldn't hurt anyone.

**A17**

n.—coward; abject person

While many fought for their rights, the **craven** sat shaking, off in a corner somewhere.

**A18**

adj.—common; general; universal

While **generic** drugs are often a better value, it is always a good idea to consult your doctor before purchasing them.

# *Questions*

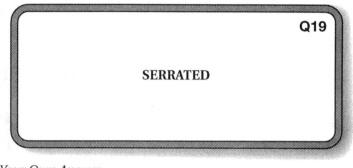

**Q19**

**SERRATED**

*Your Own Answer*_____

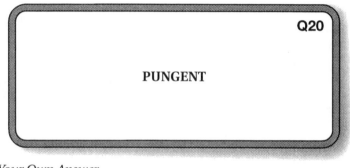

**Q20**

**PUNGENT**

*Your Own Answer*_____

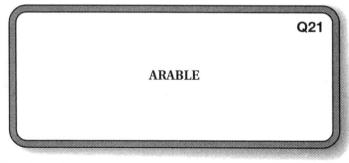

**Q21**

**ARABLE**

*Your Own Answer*_____

# Correct Answers

**A19**

adj.—having a saw-toothed edge
While camping, the family used a **serrated** band saw to cut firewood.

**A20**

adj.—sharp; stinging
When the refrigerator door opened, the smell of lemons was **pungent**.

**A21**

adj.—suitable (as land) for plowing
When the land was deemed **arable**, the farmer decided to plow.

# *Questions*

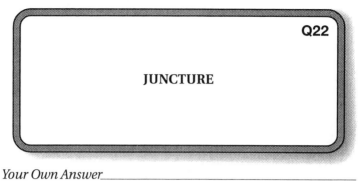

**Q22**

**JUNCTURE**

*Your Own Answer*_____

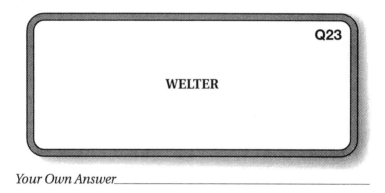

**Q23**

**WELTER**

*Your Own Answer*_____

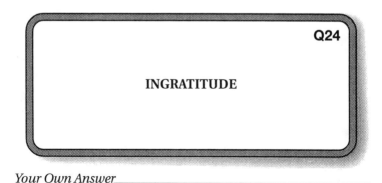

**Q24**

**INGRATITUDE**

*Your Own Answer*_____

# Correct Answers

**A22**

n.—critical point; meeting

When the gas changed into a liquid, they sensed that they'd come to a critical **juncture** in their experimentation.

**A23**

n.—a confused mass; turmoil

When the emergency alarm sounded, a **welter** of shivering office workers formed in the street as people evacuated the site.

**A24**

n.—ungratefulness

When she failed to send a thank-you card, her friend took it as a sign of **ingratitude**.

# Questions

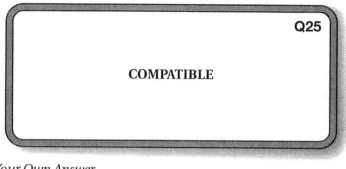

Q25

**COMPATIBLE**

*Your Own Answer*_____

---

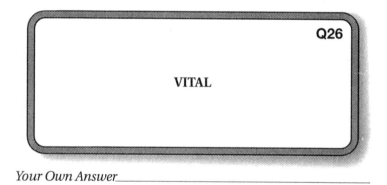

Q26

**VITAL**

*Your Own Answer*_____

---

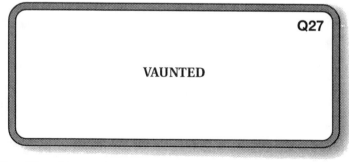

Q27

**VAUNTED**

*Your Own Answer*_____

# Correct Answers

**A25**

adj.—in agreement with; harmonious

When repairing an automobile, it is necessary to use parts **compatible** with its make and model.

**A26**

adj.—important; spirited

When in a foreign country, a passport is a **vital** piece of paperwork to have at all times.

**A27**

v.—to boast

When her son was accepted to college, she **vaunted** his success to everyone.

# *Questions*

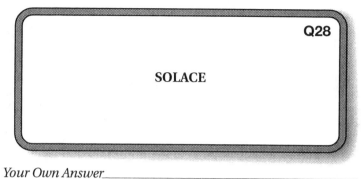

**Q28**

**SOLACE**

*Your Own Answer*_____

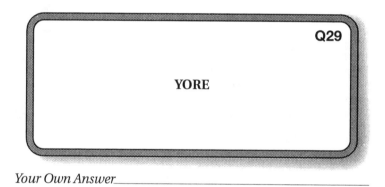

**Q29**

**YORE**

*Your Own Answer*_____

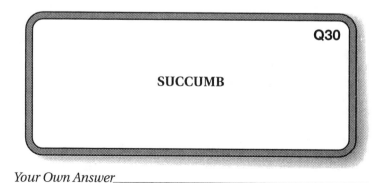

**Q30**

**SUCCUMB**

*Your Own Answer*_____

# *Correct Answers*

**A28**

n.—hope; comfort during a time of grief

When her father passed away, she found **solace** amongst her friends and family.

**A29**

n.—former period of time

When he sees his childhood friends, they speak about the days of **yore**.

**A30**

v.—to give in; to yield; to collapse

When dieting, it is difficult not to **succumb** to temptation.

# Questions

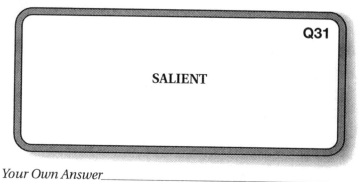

**Q31**

**SALIENT**

*Your Own Answer*_____

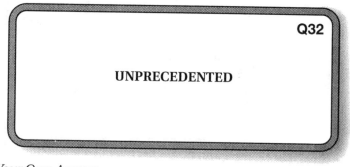

**Q32**

**UNPRECEDENTED**

*Your Own Answer*_____

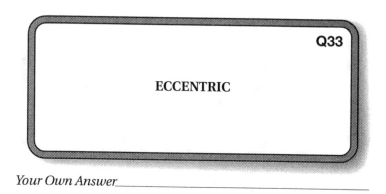

**Q33**

**ECCENTRIC**

*Your Own Answer*_____

# Correct Answers

**A31**

adj.—noticeable; prominent

What's **salient** about the report is its documentation of utter despair in the heartland of the richest nation on Earth.

**A32**

adj.—unheard of; exceptional

Weeks of intense heat created **unprecedented** power demands, which the utilities were hard pressed to meet.

**A33**

adj.—odd; peculiar; strange

Wearing polka dot pants and a necklace made of recycled bottle tops is considered **eccentric**.

# Questions

Q34

**DOCILE**

*Your Own Answer*_____

Q35

**DISENTANGLE**

*Your Own Answer*_____

Q36

**PEDESTRIAN**

*Your Own Answer*_____

# *Correct Answers*

adj.—manageable; obedient; gentle

We needed to choose a **docile** pet because we hadn't the patience for a lot of training.

v.—to free from confusion

We need to **disentangle** ourselves from the dizzying variety of choices.

adj.—mediocre; ordinary

We expected the meal to be exceptional, but it was just **pedestrian**.

# Questions

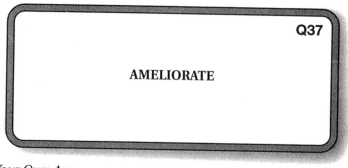

Q37

**AMELIORATE**

*Your Own Answer*_____

_____

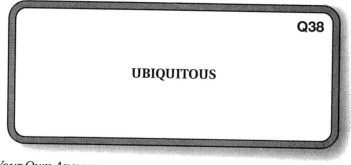

Q38

**UBIQUITOUS**

*Your Own Answer*_____

_____

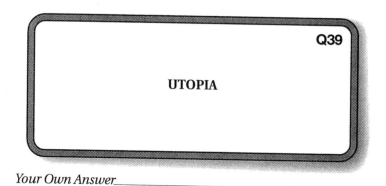

Q39

**UTOPIA**

*Your Own Answer*_____

_____

# *Correct Answers*

**A37**

v.—to improve or make better
We can **ameliorate** the flooding problem by changing the grading.

**A38**

adj.—omnipresent; present everywhere
Water may seem **ubiquitous**, until a drought comes along.

**A39**

n.—imaginary land with perfect social and political systems
Voltaire wrote of a **utopia** where the streets were paved with gold.

# *Questions*

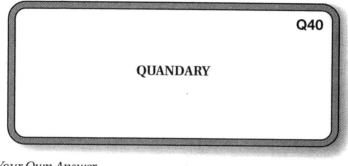

Q40

**QUANDARY**

*Your Own Answer* _____

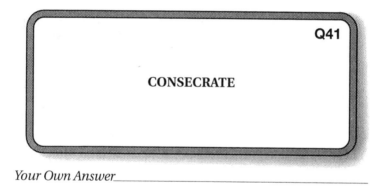

Q41

**CONSECRATE**

*Your Own Answer* _____

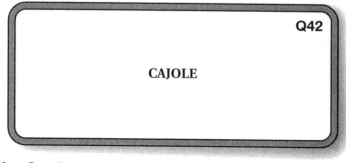

Q42

**CAJOLE**

*Your Own Answer* _____

# *Correct Answers*

n.—dilemma

Tristan and Elizabeth were caught in a **quandary**: Should they spend Thanksgiving with his parents or hers?

v.—to sanctify; to make sacred; to immortalize

To make the new statue worthy of worship, it had to be **consecrated** by the priest.

v.—to coax with insincere talk

To **cajole** the disgruntled employee, the manager coaxed him with lies and sweet talk.

# Questions

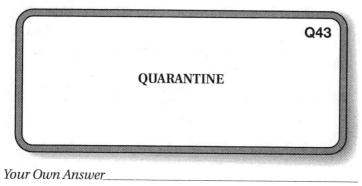

Q43

**QUARANTINE**

*Your Own Answer*_____

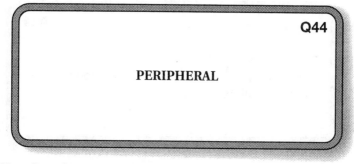

Q44

**PERIPHERAL**

*Your Own Answer*_____

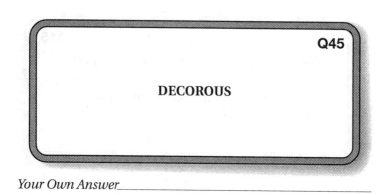

Q45

**DECOROUS**

*Your Own Answer*_____

# *Correct Answers*

**A43**

n.—isolation of a person or persons to prevent the spread of disease

To be sure they didn't bring any contagions back to Earth, the astronauts were put under **quarantine** when they returned.

**A44**

adj.—marginal; outer

Those are **peripheral** problems; let's look at the central challenge.

**A45**

adj.—showing decorum; propriety; good taste

This movie provides **decorous** refuge from the violence and mayhem that permeates the latest crop of Hollywood films.

# *Questions*

Q46

**MACERATE**

*Your Own Answer*_____

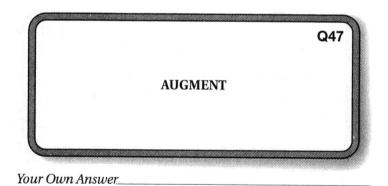

Q47

**AUGMENT**

*Your Own Answer*_____

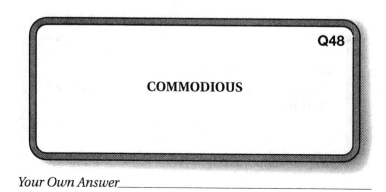

Q48

**COMMODIOUS**

*Your Own Answer*_____

# Correct Answers

**A46**

v.—to soften by steeping in liquid (including stomach juices)

They placed her foot in the solvent to **macerate** the cement she had stepped in.

**A47**

v.—to increase or add to; to make larger

They needed more soup so they **augmented** the recipe.

**A48**

adj.—spacious and convenient; roomy

They need a **commodious** apartment to fit all their furniture.

# *Questions*

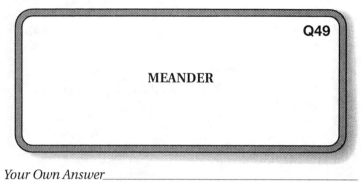

Q49

**MEANDER**

*Your Own Answer*_____

_____

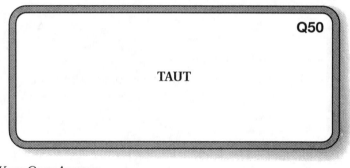

Q50

**TAUT**

*Your Own Answer*_____

_____

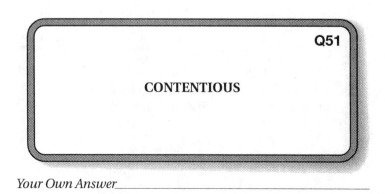

Q51

**CONTENTIOUS**

*Your Own Answer*_____

_____

# *Correct Answers*

**A49**

v.—to go aimlessly
They **meandered** through the woods for the afternoon.

**A50**

adj.—stretched tightly
They knew a fish was biting because the line suddenly became **taut**.

**A51**

adj.—quarrelsome
They hate his **contentious** behavior because every suggestion they give ends in a fight.

# Questions

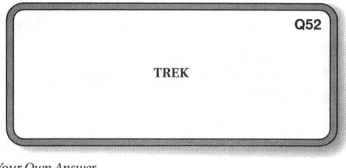

**Q52**

**TREK**

*Your Own Answer*_____

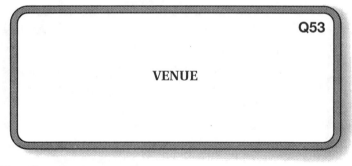

**Q53**

**VENUE**

*Your Own Answer*_____

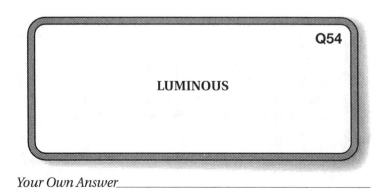

**Q54**

**LUMINOUS**

*Your Own Answer*_____

# Correct Answers

**A52**

v.—to make a journey

They had to **trek** through the dense forest to reach the nearest village.

**A53**

n.—location

They had always had their holiday party in the town hall; after ten years they were ready for a change of **venue**.

**A54**

adj.—emitting light; shining; also enlightened or intelligent

They found their way through the darkness by heading toward the **luminous** object in the distance.

# *Questions*

**Q55**

**GIBBER**

*Your Own Answer*_____

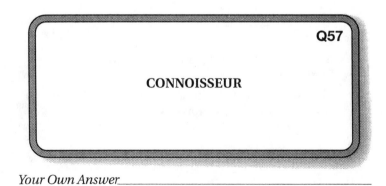

**Q56**

**VALANCE**

*Your Own Answer*_____

**Q57**

**CONNOISSEUR**

*Your Own Answer*_____

# *Correct Answers*

v.—to speak foolishly

They did not want him to represent their position in front of the committee since he was prone to **gibbering** when speaking in front of an audience.

n.—short drapery hanging over the window frame

They decided to hang a floral **valance** over the kitchen window.

n.—expert; authority (usually refers to a wine or food expert)

They allowed her to choose the wine for dinner since she was the **connoisseur**.

# *Questions*

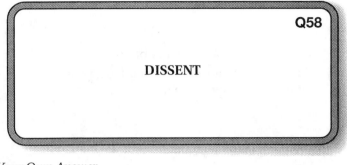

Q58

**DISSENT**

*Your Own Answer*_____

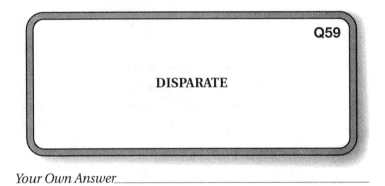

Q59

**DISPARATE**

*Your Own Answer*_____

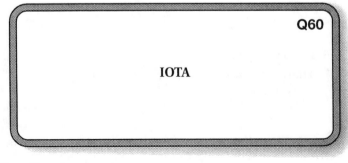

Q60

**IOTA**

*Your Own Answer*_____

# Correct Answers

v.—to disagree; to differ in opinion

They agreed that something had to be done, but **dissented** on how to do it.

adj.—unequal; dissimilar; different

They came from **disparate** backgrounds, one a real estate magnate, the other a custodian.

n.—a very small piece

There wasn't one **iota** of evidence to suggest a conspiracy.

# *Questions*

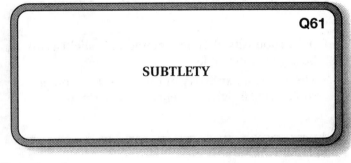

**Q61**

**SUBTLETY**

*Your Own Answer*_____

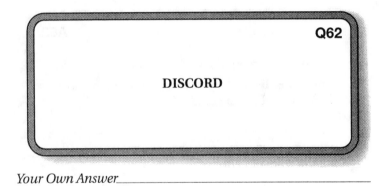

**Q62**

**DISCORD**

*Your Own Answer*_____

**Q63**

**PLETHORA**

*Your Own Answer*_____

# Correct Answers

**A61**

n.—propensity of understatement; so slight as to be barely noticeable

There was no **subtlety** in the protest; each person carried a sign and yelled for civil rights.

**A62**

n.—disagreement; lack of harmony

There was **discord** amidst the jury; therefore a decision could not be made.

**A63**

n.—a superabundance

There was a **plethora** of food at the royal feast.

# Questions

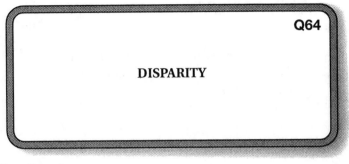

**Q64**

**DISPARITY**

*Your Own Answer*_____

_____

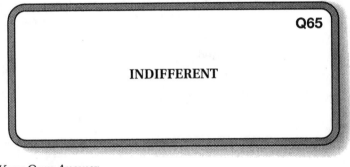

**Q65**

**INDIFFERENT**

*Your Own Answer*_____

_____

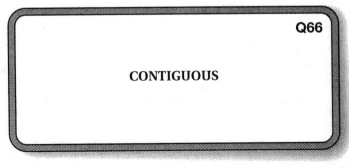

**Q66**

**CONTIGUOUS**

*Your Own Answer*_____

_____

# Correct Answers

**A64**

n.—difference in form, character, or degree

There is a great **disparity** between a light snack and a great feast.

**A65**

adj.—unconcerned

There he lay, **indifferent** to all the excitement around him.

**A66**

adj.—touching; adjoining and close, but may not be touching

There are many **contiguous** buildings in the city because there is no excess land to allow space between them.

# *Questions*

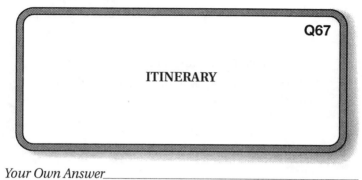

**Q67**

**ITINERARY**

*Your Own Answer*_____

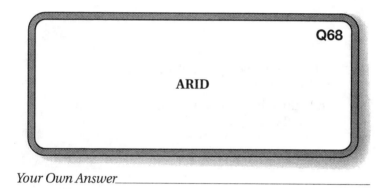

**Q68**

**ARID**

*Your Own Answer*_____

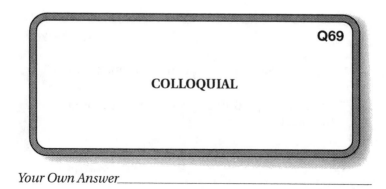

**Q69**

**COLLOQUIAL**

*Your Own Answer*_____

# Correct Answers

**A67**

n.—travel plan; schedule; course

Their trip **itinerary** was disrupted by an unexpected snow storm.

**A68**

adj.—extremely dry; parched; barren; unimaginative

Their thirst became worse due to the **arid** condition of the desert.

**A69**

adj.—casual; common; conversational; idiomatic

Their **colloquial** manner was not accepted in high society.

# *Questions*

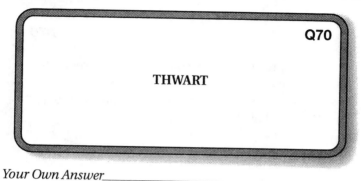

**Q70**

**THWART**

*Your Own Answer*_____

_____

**Q71**

**ZEALOT**

*Your Own Answer*_____

_____

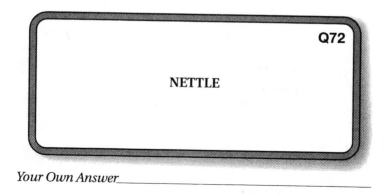

**Q72**

**NETTLE**

*Your Own Answer*_____

_____

# Correct Answers

**A70**

v.—to prevent from accomplishing a purpose; to frustrate

Their attempt to take over the country was **thwarted** by the palace guard.

**A71**

n.—believer; enthusiast; fan

The **zealot** followed whatever rules the cult leader set.

**A72**

v.—to annoy; to irritate

The younger brother **nettled** his older sister until she slapped him.

# *Questions*

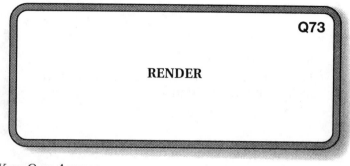

**Q73**

**RENDER**

*Your Own Answer*_____

_____

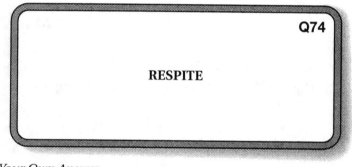

**Q74**

**RESPITE**

*Your Own Answer*_____

_____

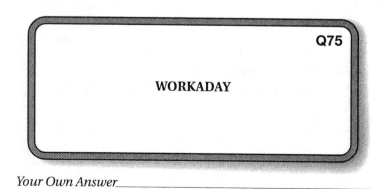

**Q75**

**WORKADAY**

*Your Own Answer*_____

_____

# Correct Answers

**A73**

v.—to deliver; to provide
The Yorkville First Aid Squad was first on the scene to **render** assistance.

**A74**

n.—recess; rest period
The workers talked and drank coffee during the **respite**.

**A75**

adj.—commonplace
The **workaday** meal was not exciting to the world-class chef.

# *Questions*

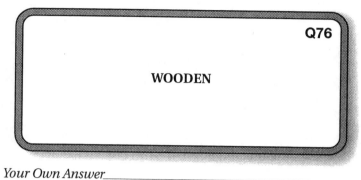

**Q76**

**WOODEN**

*Your Own Answer*_____

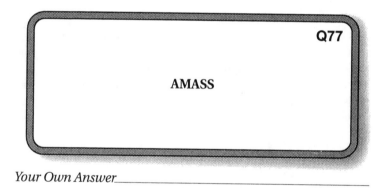

**Q77**

**AMASS**

*Your Own Answer*_____

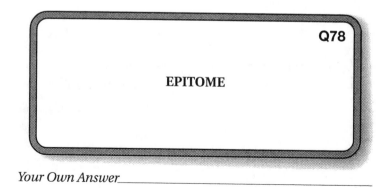

**Q78**

**EPITOME**

*Your Own Answer*_____

# Correct Answers

adj.—to be expressionless or dull
The **wooden** expression of the man made him look like a statue.

v.—to collect together; to accumulate
The women **amassed** a huge collection of priceless diamonds and pearls.

n.—model; typification; representation
The woman chosen to lead the dancers was the **epitome** of true grace.

# *Questions*

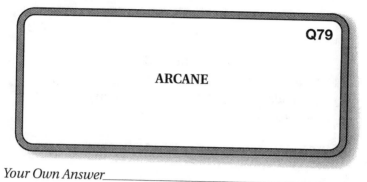

**Q79**

**ARCANE**

*Your Own Answer*_____

_____

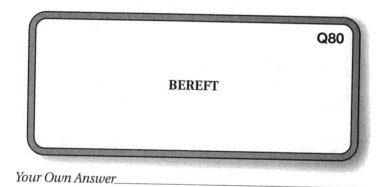

**Q80**

**BEREFT**

*Your Own Answer*_____

_____

**Q81**

**PROFUSION**

*Your Own Answer*_____

_____

# *Correct Answers*

**A79**

adj.—obscure; secret; mysterious

The wizard's description of his magic was purposefully **arcane** so that others would be unable to copy it.

**A80**

adj.—hurt by someone's death

The widower was **bereft** for many years after his wife's death.

**A81**

n.—great amount; abundance

The wet winter brought about a **profusion** of mosquitoes.

# Questions

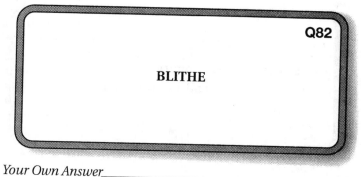

Q82

**BLITHE**

*Your Own Answer*_____

_____

Q83

**PAVILION**

*Your Own Answer*_____

_____

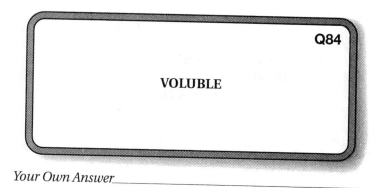

Q84

**VOLUBLE**

*Your Own Answer*_____

_____

# *Correct Answers*

**A82**

adj.—happy; cheery; merry
The wedding was a **blithe** celebration.

**A83**

n.—a large tent or covered area, usually used for entertainment
The wedding **pavilion** was not only beautifully decorated, but also served as welcome protection from a sudden downpour.

**A84**

adj.—fluent (characterized by a great flow of words, talkative)
The **voluble** host barely let his guests get a word in edgewise.

# Questions

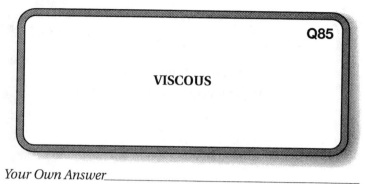

**Q85**

**VISCOUS**

*Your Own Answer*_____

---

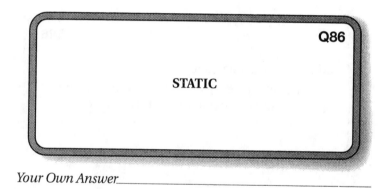

**Q86**

**STATIC**

*Your Own Answer*_____

---

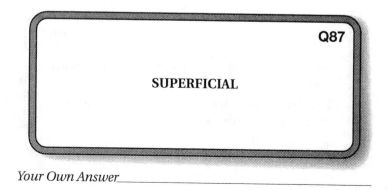

**Q87**

**SUPERFICIAL**

*Your Own Answer*_____

# Correct Answers

**A85**

adj.—thick and sticky (said of fluids)
The **viscous** honey poured slowly from the jar.

**A86**

adj.—inactive; changeless
The view while riding in the train across the end-less, flat landscape remained **static** for days.

**A87**

adj.—on the surface; narrow minded; lacking depth
The victim had two stab wounds, but luckily they were only **superficial**.

# Questions

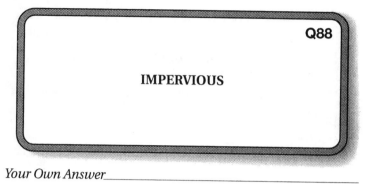

**Q88**

**IMPERVIOUS**

*Your Own Answer*_____

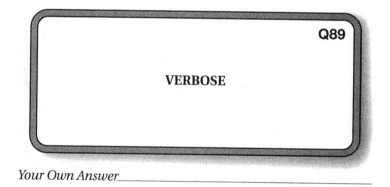

**Q89**

**VERBOSE**

*Your Own Answer*_____

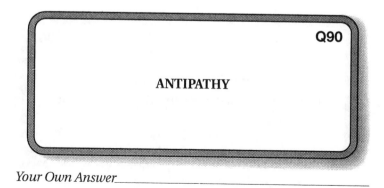

**Q90**

**ANTIPATHY**

*Your Own Answer*_____

# Correct Answers

**A88**

adj.—impenetrable; not allowing anything to pass through; unaffected

The vest that the policeman wears is **impervious** to bullets.

**A89**

adj.—wordy; talkative

The **verbose** speech was too long and difficult to follow.

**A90**

n.—a natural dislike or repugnance

The vegetarian had an **antipathy** toward meat.

# Questions

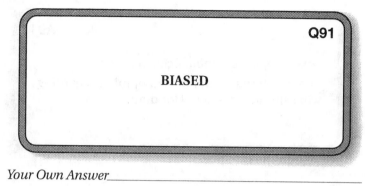

Q91

**BIASED**

*Your Own Answer*_____

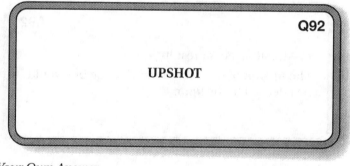

Q92

**UPSHOT**

*Your Own Answer*_____

Q93

**BLASPHEMOUS**

*Your Own Answer*_____

# Correct Answers

**A91**

adj.—prejudiced; influenced; not neutral

The vegetarian had a **biased** opinion regarding what should be ordered for dinner.

**A92**

n.—the final act or result

The **upshot** of the debate was that the bill would be released to the floor.

**A93**

adj.—irreligious; away from acceptable standards

The upper-class parents thought that it was **blasphemous** for their son to marry a waitress.

# *Questions*

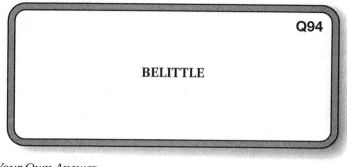

Q94

**BELITTLE**

*Your Own Answer*_____

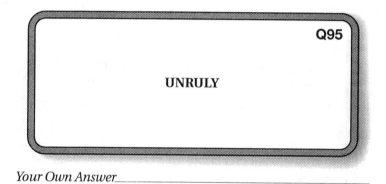

Q95

**UNRULY**

*Your Own Answer*_____

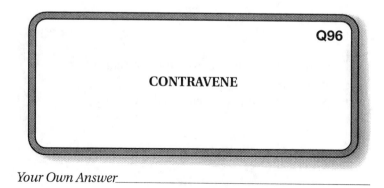

Q96

**CONTRAVENE**

*Your Own Answer*_____

# Correct Answers

**A94**

v.—to make small; to think lightly of

The unsympathetic friend **belittled** her friend's problems and spoke of her own as the most important.

**A95**

adj.—not submitting to discipline; disobedient

The **unruly** boys had to be removed from the concert hall.

**A96**

v.—to act contrary to; to oppose or contradict

The United Nations held that the Eastern European nation had **contravened** the treaty.

# *Questions*

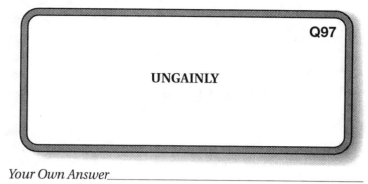

**Q97**

**UNGAINLY**

*Your Own Answer*_____

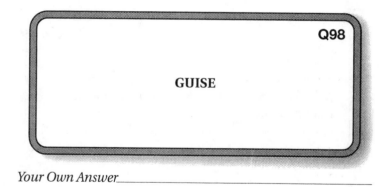

**Q98**

**GUISE**

*Your Own Answer*_____

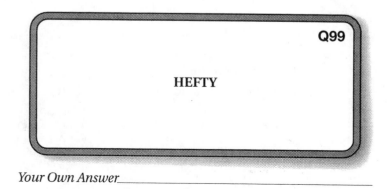

**Q99**

**HEFTY**

*Your Own Answer*_____

# Correct Answers

**A97**

adj.—clumsy and unattractive
The **ungainly** man knocked over the plant stand.

**A98**

n.—appearance
The undercover detective, under the **guise** of friendship, offered to help the drug runner make a connection.

**A99**

adj.—heavy or powerful
The unabridged dictionary makes for a **hefty** book.

# Questions

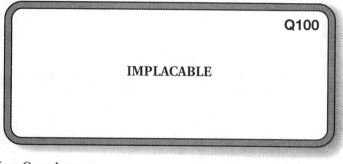

Q100

**IMPLACABLE**

*Your Own Answer*_____

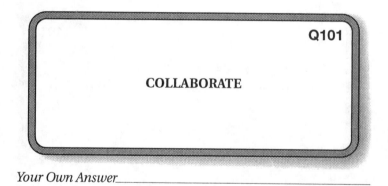

Q101

**COLLABORATE**

*Your Own Answer*_____

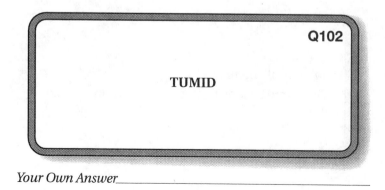

Q102

**TUMID**

*Your Own Answer*_____

# Correct Answers

**A100**

adj.—unwilling to be pacified or appeased

The two-year-old was an **implacable** child; he cried no matter what his parents did to comfort him.

**A101**

v.—to work together; to cooperate

The two builders **collaborated** to get the house finished.

**A102**

adj.—swollen; inflated

The **tumid** balloon floated, but the empty one did not.

# *Questions*

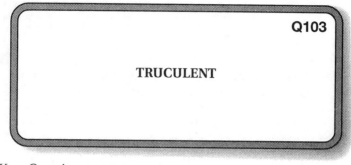

**Q103**

**TRUCULENT**

*Your Own Answer*_____

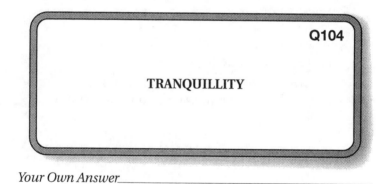

**Q104**

**TRANQUILLITY**

*Your Own Answer*_____

**Q105**

**TABLE**

*Your Own Answer*_____

# Correct Answers

**A103**

adj.—fierce; savage; cruel

The **truculent** beast approached the crowd with wild eyes and sharpened claws.

**A104**

n.—peace; stillness; harmony

The **tranquillity** of the tropical island was reflected in its calm blue waters and warm sunny climate.

**A105**

n.—a systematic list of details

The train schedule was set up as a **table**.

# *Questions*

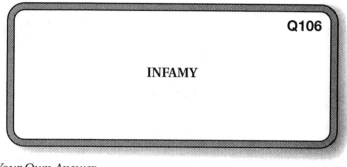

Q106

**INFAMY**

*Your Own Answer*_____

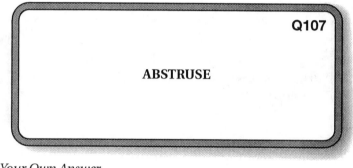

Q107

**ABSTRUSE**

*Your Own Answer*_____

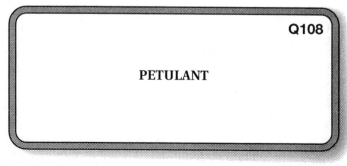

Q108

**PETULANT**

*Your Own Answer*_____

# Correct Answers

**A106**

n.—a bad reputation

The town had only 98 residents, so all it took was one bad apple to bring **infamy** on the whole place.

**A107**

adj.—hard to understand; deep; recondite

The topic was so **abstruse**, the student was forced to stop reading.

**A108**

adj.—peevish; cranky; rude

The tone of his voice and the things that he says become quite **petulant** when he has not gotten enough sleep.

# *Questions*

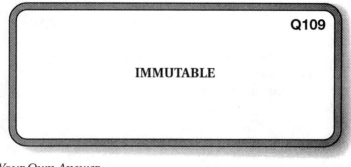

Q109

**IMMUTABLE**

*Your Own Answer*_____

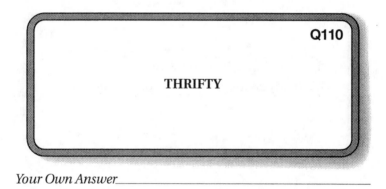

Q110

**THRIFTY**

*Your Own Answer*_____

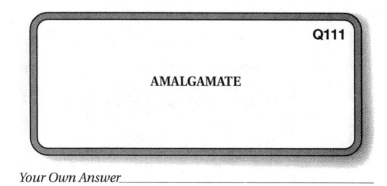

Q111

**AMALGAMATE**

*Your Own Answer*_____

# *Correct Answers*

A109

adj.—unchangeable; permanent
The ties that bind alumni to their university are **immutable**.

A110

adj.—economical; penny-wise
The **thrifty** couple saved money by taking the bus to work.

A111

v.—to mix; to merge; to combine
The three presidents decided to **amalgamate** their businesses to build one strong company.

# Questions

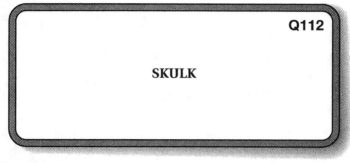

**Q112**

**SKULK**

*Your Own Answer*_____

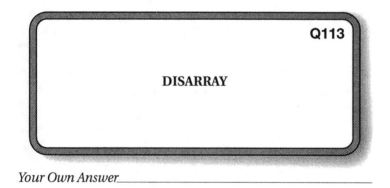

**Q113**

**DISARRAY**

*Your Own Answer*_____

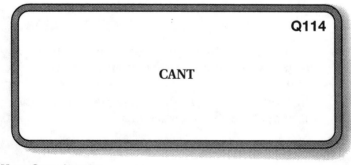

**Q114**

**CANT**

*Your Own Answer*_____

# *Correct Answers*

v.—to move secretly, implies sinister intent
The thief **skulked** around the neighborhood hoping to find his next target.

n.—state of disorder
The thief left the house in **disarray**.

n.—insincere or hypocritical statements of high ideals; the jargon of a particular group or occupation
The theater majors had difficulty understanding the **cant** of the computer scientists.

# *Questions*

**VENDETTA**

*Your Own Answer*_____

**FORTUITOUS**

*Your Own Answer*_____

**VILIFY**

*Your Own Answer*_____

# *Correct Answers*

**A115**

n.—feud

The families' **vendetta** kept them off speaking terms for 50 years.

**A116**

adj.—happening accidentally

Finding the money under the bush was **fortuitous**.

**A117**

v.—to speak abusively of

The workers too often **vilify** an employer when upset with working conditions.

# *Questions*

Q118

**TEPID**

*Your Own Answer*_____

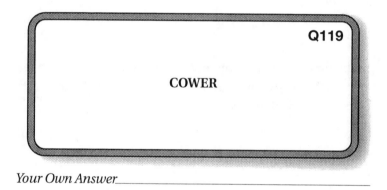

Q119

**COWER**

*Your Own Answer*_____

Q120

**INNOCUOUS**

*Your Own Answer*_____

# Correct Answers

**A118**

adj.—lacking warmth, interest, enthusiasm; luke-warm

The **tepid** bath water was perfect for relaxing after a long day.

**A119**

v.—to crouch down in fear or shame

The tellers **cowered** in the corner as the bandit ransacked the bank.

**A120**

adj.—harmless; innocent

The teens engaged in an **innocuous** game of touch football.

# *Questions*

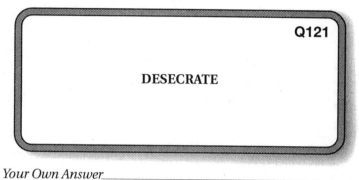

Q121

**DESECRATE**

*Your Own Answer*_____

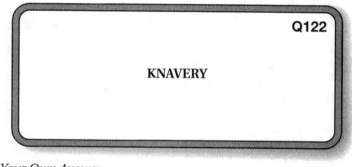

Q122

**KNAVERY**

*Your Own Answer*_____

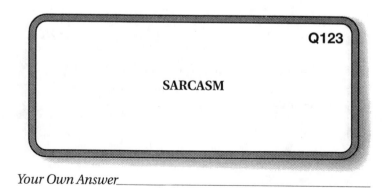

Q123

**SARCASM**

*Your Own Answer*_____

# Correct Answers

**A121**

v.—to profane; violate the sanctity of
The teenagers' attempt to **desecrate** the church roiled the community.

**A122**

n.—rascality; trickery
The teacher refused to have **knavery** in his classroom.

**A123**

n.—ironic; bitter humor designed to wound
The teacher did not appreciate the student's **sarcasm** and gave him detention.

# *Questions*

**Q124**

**CONVOKE**

*Your Own Answer*_____

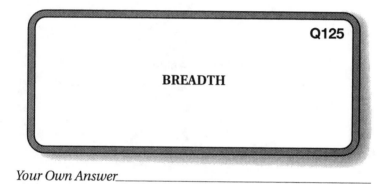

**Q125**

**BREADTH**

*Your Own Answer*_____

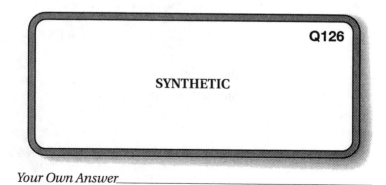

**Q126**

**SYNTHETIC**

*Your Own Answer*_____

# *Correct Answers*

**A124**

v.—to call to assemble

The teacher **convoked** her students in the auditorium to help prepare them for the play.

**A125**

n.—the distance from one side to another

The tablecloth was too small to cover the **breadth** of the table.

**A126**

adj.—not real, rather artificial

The **synthetic** skin was made of a thin rubber.

# *Questions*

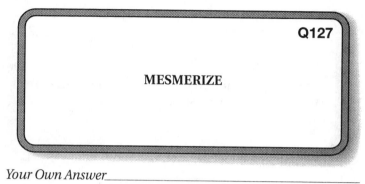

**Q127**

**MESMERIZE**

*Your Own Answer*_____

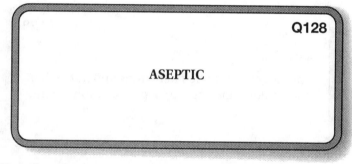

**Q128**

**ASEPTIC**

*Your Own Answer*_____

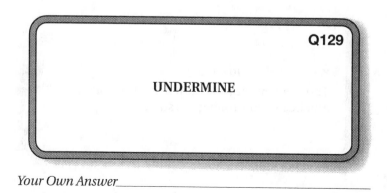

**Q129**

**UNDERMINE**

*Your Own Answer*_____

# *Correct Answers*

**A127**

v.—to hypnotize

The swaying motion of the swing **mesmerized** the baby into a deep sleep.

**A128**

adj.—germ free

The surgeon scrubbed her hands and put on her mask before entering the **aseptic** operating room.

**A129**

v.—to weaken; to ruin

The supervisor **undermined** the director's power and began controlling the staff.

# *Questions*

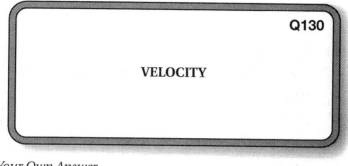

Q130

**VELOCITY**

*Your Own Answer*_____

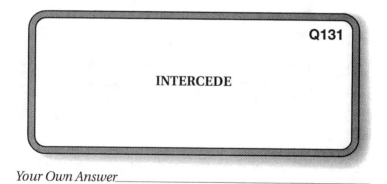

Q131

**INTERCEDE**

*Your Own Answer*_____

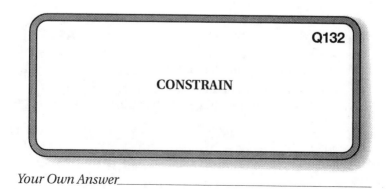

Q132

**CONSTRAIN**

*Your Own Answer*_____

# Correct Answers

**A130**

n.—speed

The supersonic transport travels at an amazing **velocity**.

---

**A131**

v.—to plead on behalf of another; to mediate

The superpowers were called on to **intercede** in the talks between the two warring nations.

---

**A132**

v.—to force, compel; to restrain

The student was **constrained** to remain in her seat until the teacher gave her permission to leave.

# *Questions*

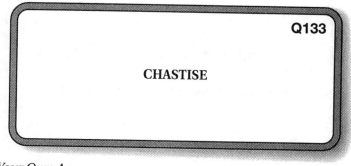

Q133

**CHASTISE**

*Your Own Answer*_____

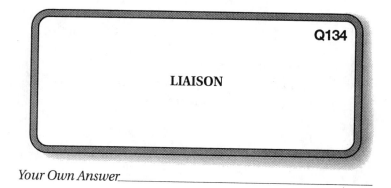

Q134

**LIAISON**

*Your Own Answer*_____

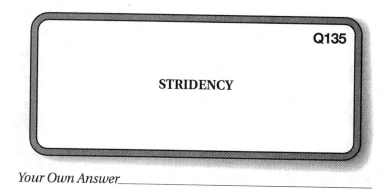

Q135

**STRIDENCY**

*Your Own Answer*_____

# Correct Answers

**A133**

v.—to punish; to discipline; to admonish; to re-buke

The student was **chastised** for being tardy so fre-quently.

**A134**

n.—connection; link

The student council served as a **liaison** between the faculty and the student body.

**A135**

n.—harshness or shrillness sound

The **stridency** of the whistle hurt the dog's ears.

# *Questions*

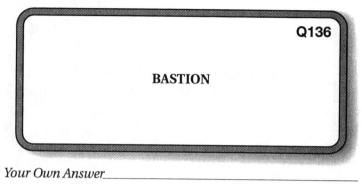

Q136

**BASTION**

*Your Own Answer*_____

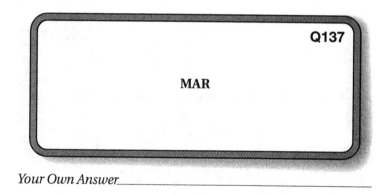

Q137

**MAR**

*Your Own Answer*_____

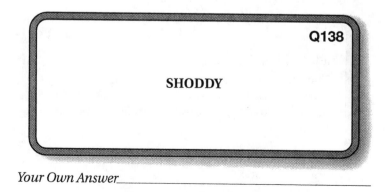

Q138

**SHODDY**

*Your Own Answer*_____

# *Correct Answers*

**A136**

n.—a fortified place or strong defense
The strength of the **bastion** saved the soldiers inside of it.

**A137**

v.—to damage
The statue was **marred** by the ravages of time.

**A138**

adj.—of inferior quality; cheap
The state's attorney said many homes, as they were built with **shoddy** materials, were bound to just blow apart even in winds of 60 or 70 miles per hour.

# *Questions*

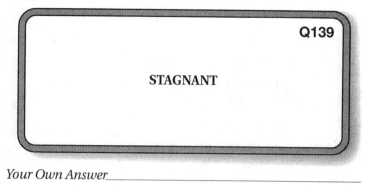

**Q139**

**STAGNANT**

*Your Own Answer*_____

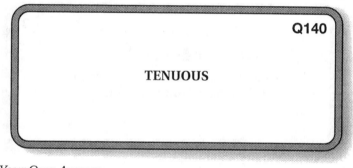

**Q140**

**TENUOUS**

*Your Own Answer*_____

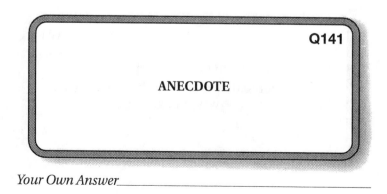

**Q141**

**ANECDOTE**

*Your Own Answer*_____

# Correct Answers

**A139**

adj.—motionless; uncirculating

The **stagnant** water in the puddle became infested with mosquitoes.

**A140**

adj.—thin; slim; delicate; weak

The spectators panicked as they watched the cement block dangle from one **tenuous** piece of twine.

**A141**

n.—a short account of happenings

The speaker told an **anecdote** about how he lost his shoes when he was young.

# *Questions*

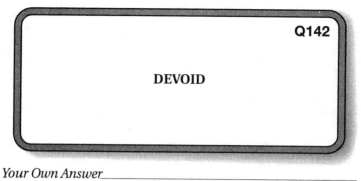

**Q142**

**DEVOID**

*Your Own Answer*_____

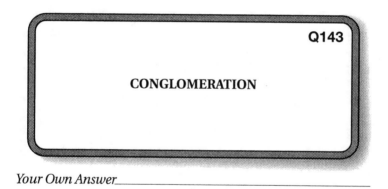

**Q143**

**CONGLOMERATION**

*Your Own Answer*_____

**Q144**

**SORDID**

*Your Own Answer*_____

# Correct Answers

**A142**

adj.—lacking; empty

The space probe indicated that the planet was **devoid** of any atmosphere.

**A143**

n.—mixture; collection

The soup was a **conglomeration** of meats and vegetables.

**A144**

adj.—filthy; base; vile

The **sordid** gutters needed to be cleaned after the long, rainy autumn.

# *Questions*

Q145

**SOPORIFIC**

*Your Own Answer*_____

Q146

**SOLUBILITY**

*Your Own Answer*_____

Q147

**SOLEMNITY**

*Your Own Answer*_____

# Correct Answers

**A145**

adj.—causing sleep

The **soporific** medication should not be taken when you need to drive.

**A146**

n.—the extent or quality of being soluble; capable of being dissolved

The **solubility** of sugar causes it to disappear when put in water.

**A147**

n.—seriousness

The **solemnity** of the funeral procession stood in stark contrast to the young children splashing with delight in a nearby pool.

# *Questions*

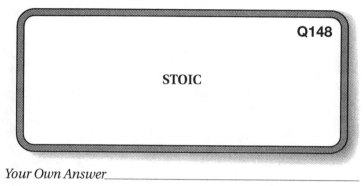

**Q148**

**STOIC**

*Your Own Answer*_____

_____

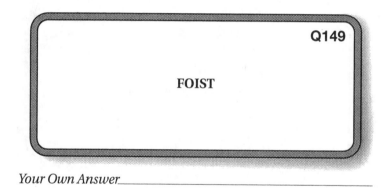

**Q149**

**FOIST**

*Your Own Answer*_____

_____

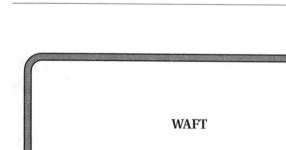

**Q150**

**WAFT**

*Your Own Answer*_____

_____

# Correct Answers

**A148**

adj.—detached; unruffled; calm; austere indifference to joy, grief, pleasure, or pain

The soldier had been in week after week of fierce battle; nonetheless, he remained **stoic**.

**A149**

v.—to falsely identify as real

The smuggler tried to **foist** the cut glass as a priceless gem.

**A150**

v.—move gently by wind or breeze

The smoke **wafted** out of the chimney.

# *Questions*

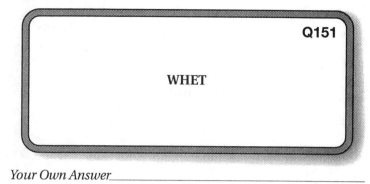

Q151

**WHET**

*Your Own Answer*_____

_____

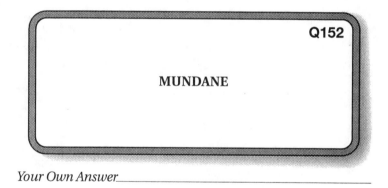

Q152

**MUNDANE**

*Your Own Answer*_____

_____

Q153

**SLOTHFUL**

*Your Own Answer*_____

_____

# *Correct Answers*

**A151**

v.—to sharpen
The smell of dinner cooking **whetted** her appetite.

**A152**

adj.—ordinary; commonplace
The small town was very **mundane**.

**A153**

adj.—lazy
The **slothful** actions of the player led to his benching.

# Questions

Q154

**COMPLIANT**

*Your Own Answer*_____

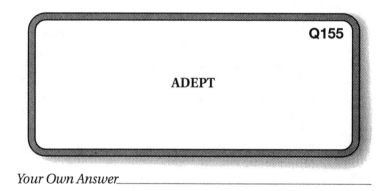

Q155

**ADEPT**

*Your Own Answer*_____

Q156

**INAUDIBLE**

*Your Own Answer*_____

# Correct Answers

**A154**

adj.—complying; obeying; yielding

The slave was **compliant** with every order to avoid being whipped.

**A155**

adj.—skilled; practiced

The skilled craftsman was quite **adept** at creating beautiful vases and candleholders.

**A156**

adj.—not able to be heard

The signals were **inaudible** when the fans began to cheer.

# *Questions*

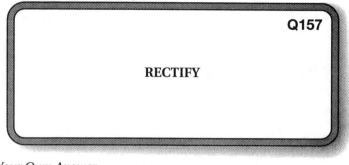

**Q157**

**RECTIFY**

*Your Own Answer*_____

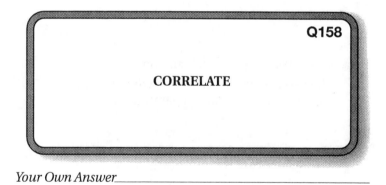

**Q158**

**CORRELATE**

*Your Own Answer*_____

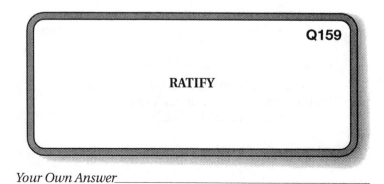

**Q159**

**RATIFY**

*Your Own Answer*_____

# Correct Answers

**A157**

v.—to correct

The service manager **rectified** the shipping mistake by refunding the customer's money.

**A158**

v.—to bring into mutual relation

The service man was asked to **correlate** the two computer demonstration pamphlets.

**A159**

v.—to make valid; confirm

The senate **ratified** the new law that would prohibit companies from discriminating according to race in their hiring practices.

# *Questions*

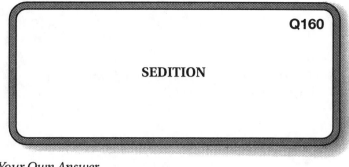

**Q160**

**SEDITION**

*Your Own Answer*_____

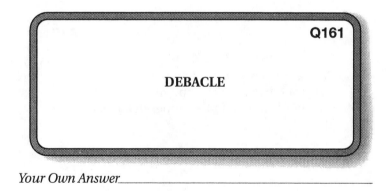

**Q161**

**DEBACLE**

*Your Own Answer*_____

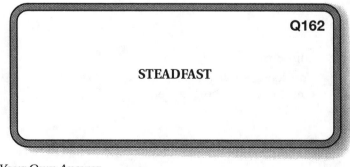

**Q162**

**STEADFAST**

*Your Own Answer*_____

# Correct Answers

n.—a revolt

The **sedition** by the guards ended with their being executed for treason.

n.—disaster; collapse; a rout

The Securities and Exchange Commission and the stock exchanges implemented numerous safeguards to head off another **debacle** on Wall Street.

adj.—loyal

The secret service agents are **steadfast** to their oath to protect the president.

# *Questions*

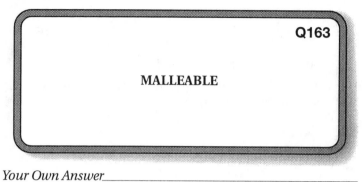

**Q163**

**MALLEABLE**

*Your Own Answer*_____

**Q164**

**INDECIPHERABLE**

*Your Own Answer*_____

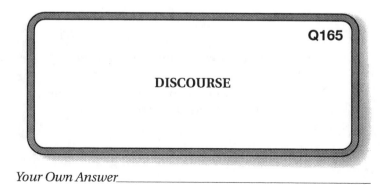

**Q165**

**DISCOURSE**

*Your Own Answer*_____

# *Correct Answers*

**A163**

adj.—easy to shape or bend

The sculptor uses **malleable** substances to create complex masterpieces.

**A164**

adj.—illegible

The scribbling on the paper is **indecipherable**.

**A165**

v.—to converse; to communicate in an orderly fashion

The scientists **discoursed** on a conference call for just five minutes but were able to solve three major problems.

# *Questions*

**Q166**

**ARCHETYPE**

*Your Own Answer*_____

**Q167**

**AMORPHOUS**

*Your Own Answer*_____

**Q168**

**SAGA**

*Your Own Answer*_____

# Correct Answers

**A166**

n.—the first model from which others are copied; prototype

The scientist was careful with the **archetype** of her invention so that once manufacturing began, it would be easy to reproduce.

**A167**

adj.—having no determinate form

The scientist could not determine the sex of the **amorphous** organism.

**A168**

n.—a legend; any long story of adventure or heroic deed

The **saga** of King Arthur and his court has been told for generations.

# *Questions*

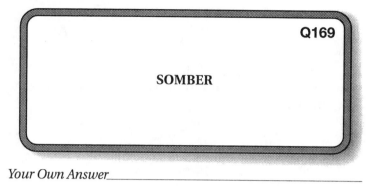

**Q169**

**SOMBER**

*Your Own Answer*_____

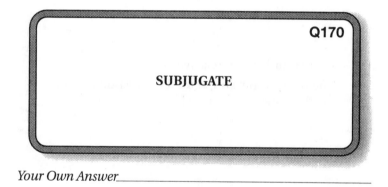

**Q170**

**SUBJUGATE**

*Your Own Answer*_____

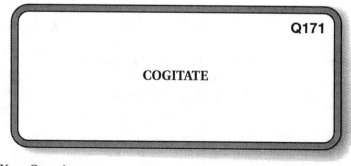

**Q171**

**COGITATE**

*Your Own Answer*_____

# Correct Answers

**A169**

adj.—dark and depressing; gloomy
The sad story had put everyone in a **somber** mood.

**A170**

v.—to dominate or enslave
The royal family **subjugated** the peasants, making them perform hard labor.

**A171**

v.—to think hard; to ponder; to meditate
The room was quiet while every student **cogitated** during the calculus exam.

# *Questions*

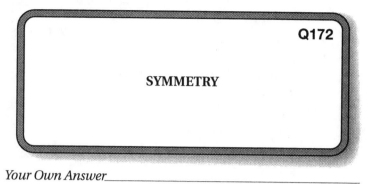

**Q172**

**SYMMETRY**

*Your Own Answer*_____

_____

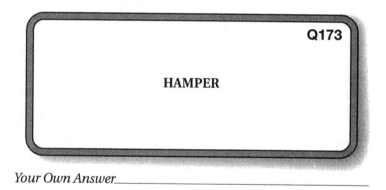

**Q173**

**HAMPER**

*Your Own Answer*_____

_____

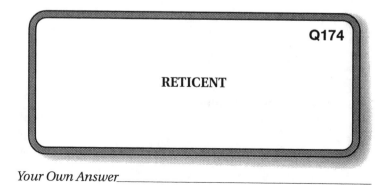

**Q174**

**RETICENT**

*Your Own Answer*_____

_____

# *Correct Answers*

n.—correspondence of parts; harmony

The Roman columns give the building a **symmetry**.

v.—to interfere with; to hinder

The roadblock **hampered** their progress, but they knew a shortcut.

adj.—silent; reserved; shy

The **reticent** girl played with her building blocks while the other children played tag.

# *Questions*

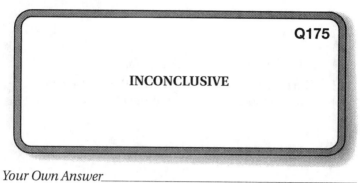

**Q175**

**INCONCLUSIVE**

*Your Own Answer*_____

**Q176**

**INCREDULOUS**

*Your Own Answer*_____

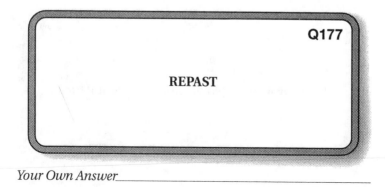

**Q177**

**REPAST**

*Your Own Answer*_____

# Correct Answers

**A175**

adj.—not final or of a definite result

The results being **inconclusive**, the doctors continued to look for a cause of the illness.

**A176**

adj.—skeptical; unbelieving

The reporter was **incredulous** on hearing the computer executive's UFO account.

**A177**

n.—food that is eaten

The **repast** consisted of cheese, wine, and bread.

# *Questions*

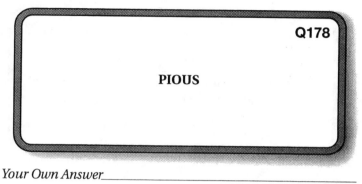

**Q178**

**PIOUS**

*Your Own Answer*_____

---

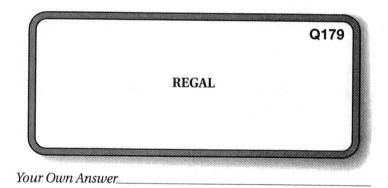

**Q179**

**REGAL**

*Your Own Answer*_____

---

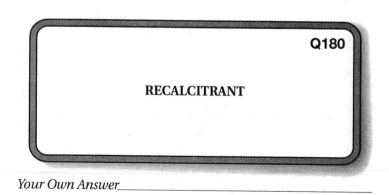

**Q180**

**RECALCITRANT**

*Your Own Answer*_____

# Correct Answers

**A178**

adj.—religious; devout; dedicated

The religious couple believed that their **pious** method of worship would bring them eternal life.

**A179**

adj.—royal; grand

The **regal** home was lavishly decorated and furnished with European antiques.

**A180**

adj.—stubbornly rebellious

The **recalcitrant** youth dyed her hair purple, dropped out of school, and generally worked hard at doing whatever others did not want her to do.

# Questions

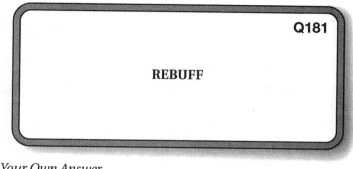

**Q181**

**REBUFF**

*Your Own Answer*_____

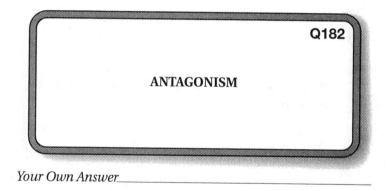

**Q182**

**ANTAGONISM**

*Your Own Answer*_____

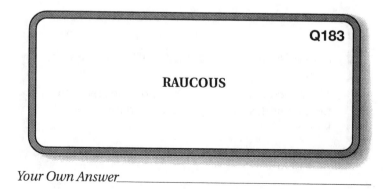

**Q183**

**RAUCOUS**

*Your Own Answer*_____

# Correct Answers

**A181**

n.—a blunt refusal to offered help
The **rebuff** of her aid plan came as a shock.

**A182**

n.—hostility; opposition
The rebellious clan captured a hostage to display
**antagonism** to the new peace treaty.

**A183**

adj.—disagreeable to the sense of hearing; harsh;
hoarse
The **raucous** protesters stayed on the street corner all night, shouting their disdain for the whale
killers.

# Questions

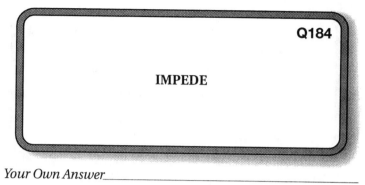

**Q184**

**IMPEDE**

*Your Own Answer*_____

_____

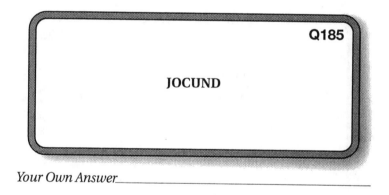

**Q185**

**JOCUND**

*Your Own Answer*_____

_____

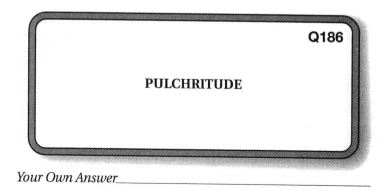

**Q186**

**PULCHRITUDE**

*Your Own Answer*_____

_____

# *Correct Answers*

**A184**

v.—to stop the progress of; to obstruct
The rain **impeded** the work on the building.

**A185**

adj.—happy; cheerful; genial; gay
The puppy kept a smile on the **jocund** boy's face.

**A186**

n.—beauty
The **pulchritude** of the girl is seen in her bright smile.

# Questions

Q187

**PREMISE**

*Your Own Answer*_____

_____

Q188

**REMORSE**

*Your Own Answer*_____

_____

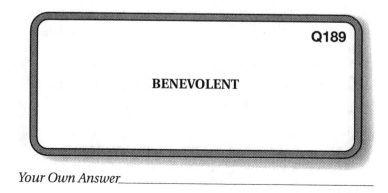

Q189

**BENEVOLENT**

*Your Own Answer*_____

_____

# Correct Answers

**A187**

n.—the basis for an argument

The prosecutor claimed that the defense lawyer's **premise** was shaky, and thus his whole argument was suspect.

**A188**

n.—guilt; sorrow

The prosecutor argued that the defendant had shown no **remorse** for his actions.

**A189**

adj.—kind; generous

The professor proved a tough questioner, but a **benevolent** grader.

# *Questions*

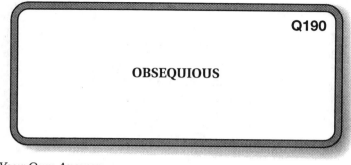

Q190

**OBSEQUIOUS**

*Your Own Answer*_____

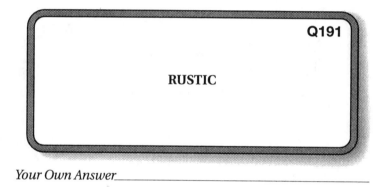

Q191

**RUSTIC**

*Your Own Answer*_____

Q192

**SOVEREIGN**

*Your Own Answer*_____

# Correct Answers

**A190**

adj.—servilely attentive; fawning

The princess only seemed to encourage the **obsequious** behavior of her court to enhance her own feeling of superiority.

**A191**

adj.—plain and unsophisticated; homely; of or living in the country

The couple enjoyed spending weekends at a **rustic** retreat in the woods.

**A192**

adj.—superior

The power was given to the **sovereign** warrior.

# *Questions*

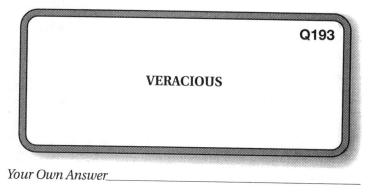

**Q193**

**VERACIOUS**

*Your Own Answer*_____

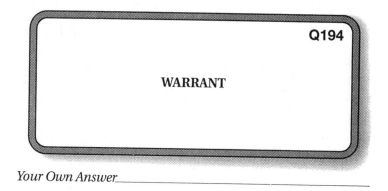

**Q194**

**WARRANT**

*Your Own Answer*_____

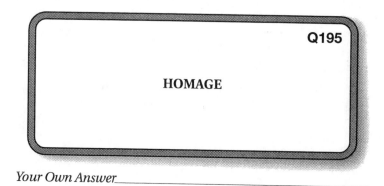

**Q195**

**HOMAGE**

*Your Own Answer*_____

# Correct Answers

**A193**

adj.—conforming to fact; accurate

The police were certain he had given a **veracious** account because the video confirmed everything.

**A194**

v.—to justify; to authorize

The police official **warranted** the arrest of the suspect once enough proof had been found.

**A195**

n.—honor; respect

The police officers paid **homage** to their fallen colleague with a ceremony that celebrated her life.

# *Questions*

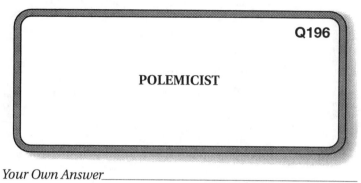

Q196

**POLEMICIST**

*Your Own Answer*_____

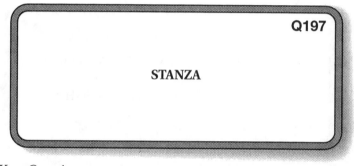

Q197

**STANZA**

*Your Own Answer*_____

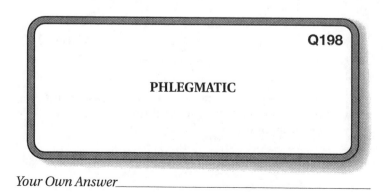

Q198

**PHLEGMATIC**

*Your Own Answer*_____

# Correct Answers

**A196**

n.—a person skilled in argument
The **polemicist** could debate any case skillfully.

**A197**

n.—group of lines in a poem having a definite pattern
The poet uses an odd simile in the second **stanza** of the poem.

**A198**

adj.—without emotion or interest
The playwright had hoped his story would take theatergoers on an emotional roller coaster, but on opening night they just sat there, stonefaced and **phlegmatic**.

# *Questions*

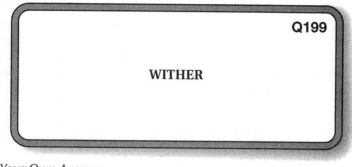

**Q199**

**WITHER**

*Your Own Answer*_____

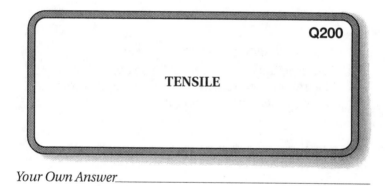

**Q200**

**TENSILE**

*Your Own Answer*_____

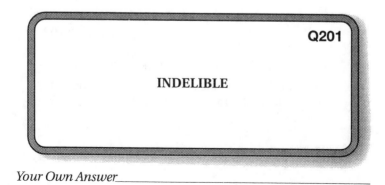

**Q201**

**INDELIBLE**

*Your Own Answer*_____

# *Correct Answers*

---

**A199**

v.—to wilt; to shrivel; to humiliate; to cut down

The plant **withered** slowly since it received little light and little water.

---

**A200**

adj.—undergoing or exerting tension

The pipeline was capable of flexing to withstand the tremendous **tensile** strain that might accompany any seismic movement.

---

**A201**

adj.—that which cannot be blotted out or erased

The photograph of Neil Armstrong setting foot on the moon made an **indelible** impression on all who saw it.

# *Questions*

Q202

**DEBILITATE**

*Your Own Answer*_____

Q203

**PERCEPTIVE**

*Your Own Answer*_____

Q204

**TYRANNY**

*Your Own Answer*_____

# Correct Answers

**A202**

v.—to enfeeble; to wear out

The phlebitis **debilitated** him to the point that he was unable even to walk.

**A203**

adj.—full of insight; aware

The **perceptive** detective discovered that the murder weapon was hidden in a safe under the floor.

**A204**

n.—absolute power; autocracy

The people were upset because they had no voice in the government that the king ran as a **tyranny**.

# *Questions*

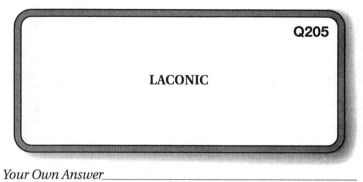

**Q205**

**LACONIC**

*Your Own Answer*_____

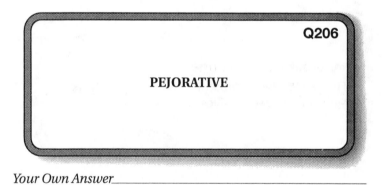

**Q206**

**PEJORATIVE**

*Your Own Answer*_____

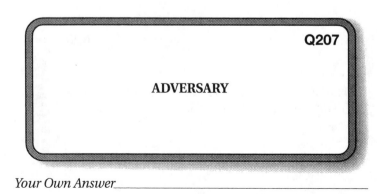

**Q207**

**ADVERSARY**

*Your Own Answer*_____

# Correct Answers

**A205**

adj.—sparing of words; terse, pithy

The people enjoyed the public addresses of the **laconic** queen.

**A206**

adj.—making things worse

The **pejorative** comment deepened the dislike between the two families.

**A207**

n.—an enemy; foe

The peace treaty united two countries that were historically great **adversaries**.

# *Questions*

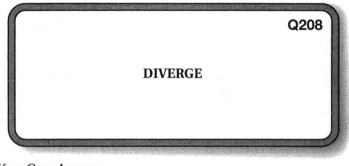

Q208

**DIVERGE**

*Your Own Answer*_____

---

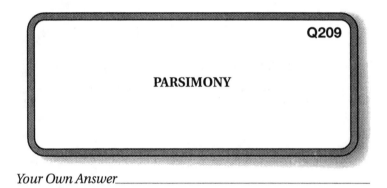

Q209

**PARSIMONY**

*Your Own Answer*_____

---

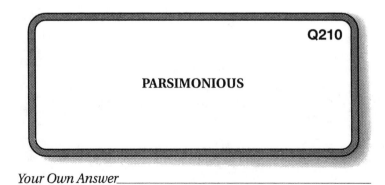

Q210

**PARSIMONIOUS**

*Your Own Answer*_____

# Correct Answers

**A208**

v.—to separate; to split

The path **diverges** at the old barn, one fork leading to the house, and the other leading to the pond.

**A209**

n.—a tendency to be over careful in spending

The **parsimony** of the wealthy woman was uncalled for.

**A210**

adj.—very frugal; unwilling to spend

The **parsimonious** individual argued that twenty-five cents was much too expensive for a pack of gum.

# *Questions*

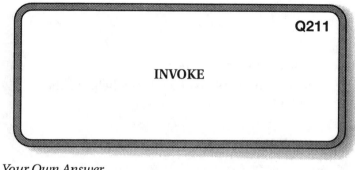

**Q211**

**INVOKE**

*Your Own Answer*_____

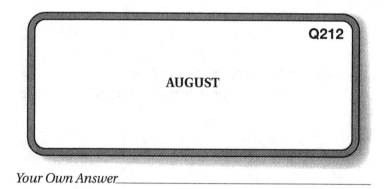

**Q212**

**AUGUST**

*Your Own Answer*_____

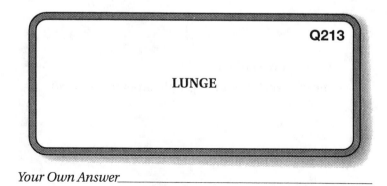

**Q213**

**LUNGE**

*Your Own Answer*_____

# Correct Answers

**A211**

v.—to ask for; to call upon

The parishioners **invoked** divine help for their troubles.

**A212**

adj.—to be imposing or magnificent

The palace was **august** in gold and crystal.

**A213**

v.—to move suddenly

The owl will **lunge** at its prey in order to take it off guard.

# Questions

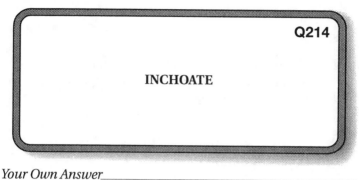

**Q214**

**INCHOATE**

*Your Own Answer*_____

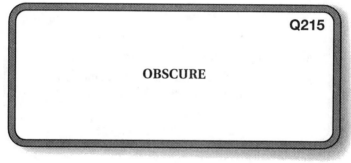

**Q215**

**OBSCURE**

*Your Own Answer*_____

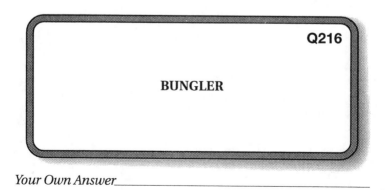

**Q216**

**BUNGLER**

*Your Own Answer*_____

# Correct Answers

**A214**

adj.—not yet fully formed; rudimentary
The outline of the thesis was the **inchoate** form of a very complex theory.

**A215**

adj.—not easily understood; dark
The orchestra enjoys performing **obscure** American works, hoping to bring them to a wider audience.

**A216**

n.—a clumsy person
The one who broke the crystal vase was a true **bungler**.

# *Questions*

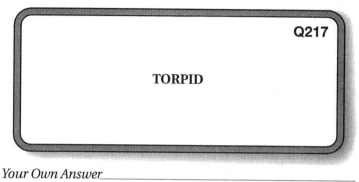

Q217

**TORPID**

*Your Own Answer*_____

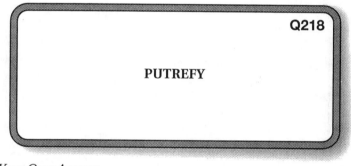

Q218

**PUTREFY**

*Your Own Answer*_____

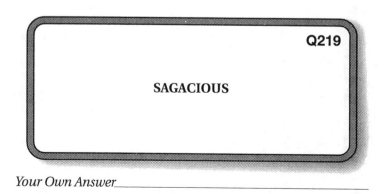

Q219

**SAGACIOUS**

*Your Own Answer*_____

# Correct Answers

**A217**

adj.—lacking alertness and activity; lethargic
The old, **torpid** dog spent most of his time sleeping.

**A218**

v.—to decompose; to rot
The old vegetables **putrefied** in the sun.

**A219**

adj.—wise
The old man gave **sagacious** advice.

# *Questions*

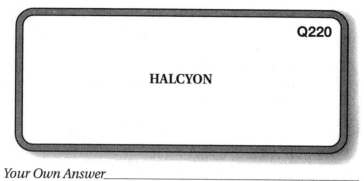

Q220

**HALCYON**

*Your Own Answer*_____

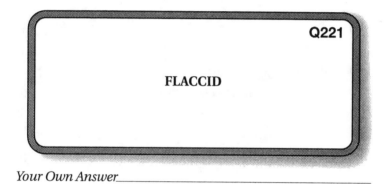

Q221

**FLACCID**

*Your Own Answer*_____

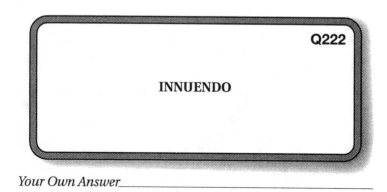

Q222

**INNUENDO**

*Your Own Answer*_____

# *Correct Answers*

A220

adj.—tranquil; happy
The old man fondly remembered his **halcyon** days growing up on the farm.

A221

adj.—lacking firmness
The old dog's **flaccid** tail refused to wag.

A222

n.—hint; insinuation
The office was rife with **innuendo** that a takeover was in the works.

# *Questions*

Q223

**REPUDIATE**

*Your Own Answer*_____

Q224

**OBDURATE**

*Your Own Answer*_____

Q225

**NOXIOUS**

*Your Own Answer*_____

# Correct Answers

v.—to reject; to cancel
The offer was **repudiated** because of its cost.

adj.—stubborn
The **obdurate** youngster refused to eat the Brussels sprouts.

adj.—harmful to one's health
The **noxious** fumes caused the person to become ill.

# Questions

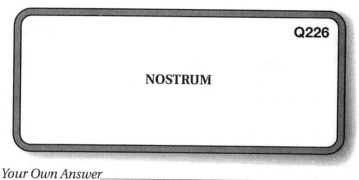

Q226

**NOSTRUM**

*Your Own Answer*_____

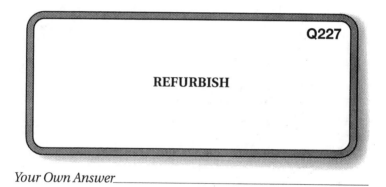

Q227

**REFURBISH**

*Your Own Answer*_____

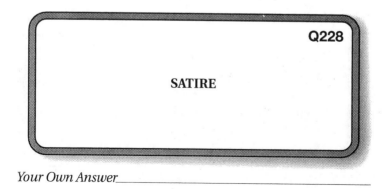

Q228

**SATIRE**

*Your Own Answer*_____

# *Correct Answers*

n.—a questionable remedy

The **nostrum** of pine leaves and water did not seem to cure the illness.

v.—to make new; to renovate

The Newsomes are **refurbishing** their old colonial home with the help of an interior designer.

n.—a novel or play that uses humor or irony to expose folly

The new play was a **satire** that exposed the president's inability to lead the country.

# *Questions*

**Q229**

**MANDATE**

*Your Own Answer*_____

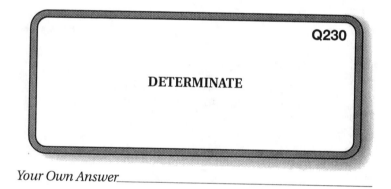

**Q230**

**DETERMINATE**

*Your Own Answer*_____

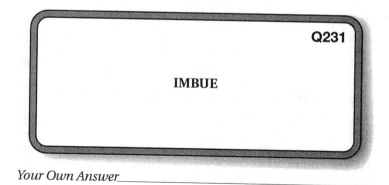

**Q231**

**IMBUE**

*Your Own Answer*_____

# *Correct Answers*

**A229**

n.—order; charge

The new manager wrote a **mandate** declaring that smoking was now prohibited in the office.

**A230**

adj.—distinct limits

The new laws were very **determinate** as far as what was allowed and what was not allowed.

**A231**

v.—to dye or to permeate

The new day **imbued** him with a sense of optimism.

# *Questions*

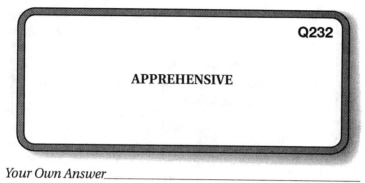

Q232

**APPREHENSIVE**

*Your Own Answer*_____

Q233

**NEFARIOUS**

*Your Own Answer*_____

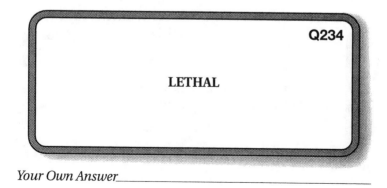

Q234

**LETHAL**

*Your Own Answer*_____

# Correct Answers

**A232**

adj.—fearful; aware; conscious
The nervous child was **apprehensive** about beginning a new school year.

**A233**

adj.—villainous or wicked
The **nefarious** ruler killed all the cattle and hoarded all of the food.

**A234**

adj.—deadly
The natural gas leak caused a **lethal** explosion that killed thousands of innocent people.

# *Questions*

Q235

**TACIT**

*Your Own Answer*_____

Q236

**MALEDICTION**

*Your Own Answer*_____

Q237

**NARCISSISTIC**

*Your Own Answer*_____

# Correct Answers

**A235**

adj.—not voiced or expressed

The National Security Agency aide argued, in effect, that he had received the president's **tacit** approval for the arms-for-hostages deal.

**A236**

n.—curse; evil spell

The nasty old man shouted **maledictions** at the children.

**A237**

adj.—egotistical; self-centered; self-love; excessive interest in one's appearance, comfort, abilities, etc.

The **narcissistic** actor was difficult to get along with.

# *Questions*

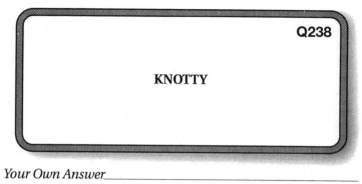

**Q238**

**KNOTTY**

*Your Own Answer*_____

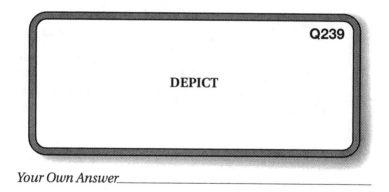

**Q239**

**DEPICT**

*Your Own Answer*_____

**Q240**

**MUNIFICENT**

*Your Own Answer*_____

# Correct Answers

**A238**

adj.—to be puzzling or hard to explain
The mystery was **knotty**.

**A239**

v.—to portray; to describe
The mural **depicts** the life of a typical urban dweller.

**A240**

adj.—very generous in giving; lavish
The **munificent** woman was well liked.

# Questions

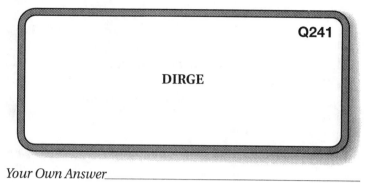

Q241

**DIRGE**

*Your Own Answer*_____

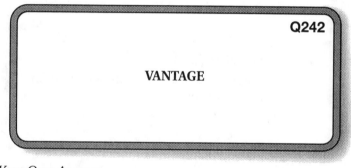

Q242

**VANTAGE**

*Your Own Answer*_____

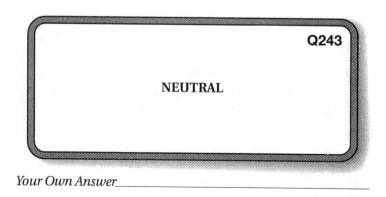

Q243

**NEUTRAL**

*Your Own Answer*_____

# *Correct Answers*

**A241**

n.—a hymn for a funeral; a song or poem expressing lament

The mourners sang a traditional Irish **dirge**.

**A242**

n.—position giving an advantage

The mountaintop was a great **vantage** point for seeing the meteor showers.

**A243**

adj.—impartial; unbiased

The mother remained **neutral** regarding the argument between her two children.

# *Questions*

Q244

**PALLOR**

*Your Own Answer*_____

Q245

**VENERATE**

*Your Own Answer*_____

Q246

**MISER**

*Your Own Answer*_____

# Correct Answers

**A244**

n.—lack of facial color

The more vivid the testimony grew, the more the witness seemed to take on a ghostly **pallor**.

**A245**

v.—to revere

The missionary was **venerated** for the help he had given the homeless.

**A246**

n.—penny-pincher; stingy person

The **miser** made no donations and loved counting his money every night.

# *Questions*

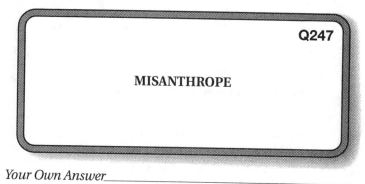

**Q247**

**MISANTHROPE**

*Your Own Answer*_____

_____

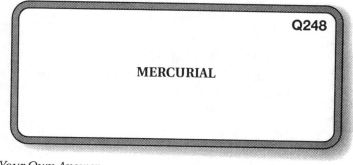

**Q248**

**MERCURIAL**

*Your Own Answer*_____

_____

**Q249**

**MELODIOUS**

*Your Own Answer*_____

_____

# *Correct Answers*

**A247**

n.—a hater of mankind

The **misanthrope** lived alone in the forest.

**A248**

adj.—quick; changeable; fickle

The **mercurial** actions of the boy kept his parents unsure of his state of mind.

**A249**

adj.—pleasing to hear

The **melodious** sounds of the band attracted many onlookers.

# *Questions*

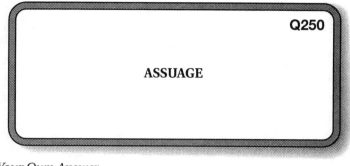

**Q250**

**ASSUAGE**

*Your Own Answer*_____

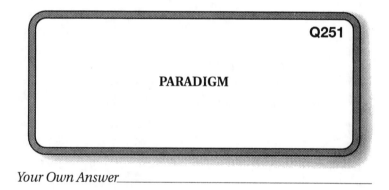

**Q251**

**PARADIGM**

*Your Own Answer*_____

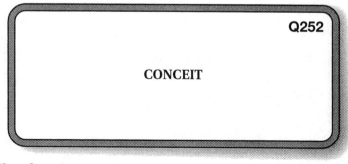

**Q252**

**CONCEIT**

*Your Own Answer*_____

# Correct Answers

**A250**

v.— to lessen or calm

The medication helped **assuage** the pain of the wound.

**A251**

n.—model; prototype; pattern

The Massachusetts gubernatorial race was considered a **paradigm** of campaign civility.

**A252**

n.—an exaggerated personal opinion

The man's belief that he was the best player on the team was pure **conceit**.

# *Questions*

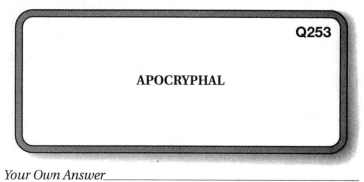

Q253

**APOCRYPHAL**

*Your Own Answer*_____

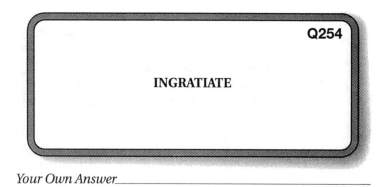

Q254

**INGRATIATE**

*Your Own Answer*_____

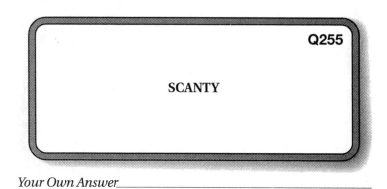

Q255

**SCANTY**

*Your Own Answer*_____

# Correct Answers

**A253**

adj.—counterfeit; of doubtful authorship or authenticity

The man who said he was a doctor was truly **apocryphal**.

**A254**

v.—to bring into one's good graces

The man was hoping to **ingratiate** himself with his wife by buying a bouquet of flowers and candy.

**A255**

adj.—inadequate; sparse

The malnutrition was caused by the **scanty** amount of healthy food eaten each day.

# *Questions*

Q256

**MALICIOUS**

*Your Own Answer*

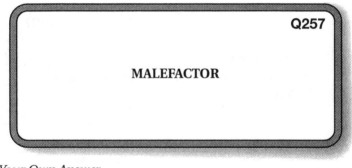

Q257

**MALEFACTOR**

*Your Own Answer*

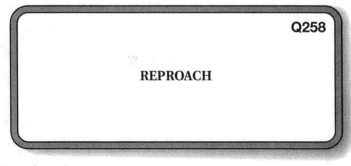

Q258

**REPROACH**

*Your Own Answer*

# Correct Answers

**A256**

adj.—spiteful; vindictive

The **malicious** employee slashed her tires for revenge.

**A257**

n.—an evil person

The **malefactor** ordered everyone to work over the holidays.

**A258**

v.—to blame and thus make feel ashamed; to rebuke

The major **reproached** his troops for not following orders.

# *Questions*

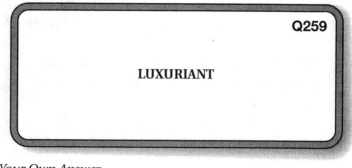

Q259

**LUXURIANT**

*Your Own Answer*_____

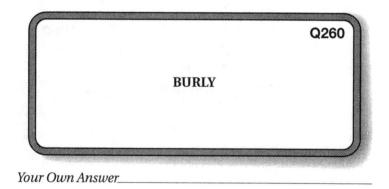

Q260

**BURLY**

*Your Own Answer*_____

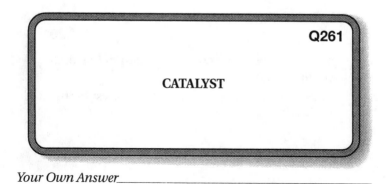

Q261

**CATALYST**

*Your Own Answer*_____

# Correct Answers

**A259**

adj.—grown with energy and in great abundance
The **luxuriant** flowers grew in every available space.

**A260**

adj.—strong; bulky; stocky
The lumberjack was a **burly** man.

**A261**

n.—anything which creates a situation in which change can occur
The low pressure system was the **catalyst** for the nor'easter.

# *Questions*

**SAUNTER**

*Your Own Answer*_____

**CONDONE**

*Your Own Answer*_____

**PERCUSSION**

*Your Own Answer*_____

# Correct Answers

v.—to walk at a leisurely pace; to stroll

The loving couple **sauntered** down the wooded path.

v.—to overlook; to forgive

The loving and forgiving mother **condoned** her son's life of crime.

n.—striking one object against another

The loud **percussion** of the hunter's gunshot startled the birds.

# *Questions*

**Q265**

**CONSTERNATION**

*Your Own Answer*_____

---

**Q266**

**PITTANCE**

*Your Own Answer*_____

---

**Q267**

**COAGULATE**

*Your Own Answer*_____

# *Correct Answers*

**A265**

n.—amazement or terror that causes confusion

The look of **consternation** on the child's face caused her father to panic.

**A266**

n.—small allowance

The little girl received a **pittance** every week for keeping her room clean.

**A267**

v.—to become a semisolid, soft mass; to clot

The liquid will **coagulate** and close the tube if left standing.

# *Questions*

**Q268**

**CONUNDRUM**

*Your Own Answer*_____

---

**Q269**

**LECHEROUS**

*Your Own Answer*_____

---

**Q270**

**REBUTTAL**

*Your Own Answer*_____

# Correct Answers

**A268**

n.—a puzzle or riddle

The legend says that to enter the secret passageway, one must answer the ancient **conundrum**.

**A269**

adj.—impure in thought and act

The **lecherous** Humbert Humbert is Nabokov's protagonist in *Lolita*, a novel that sparked great controversy because of Humbert's romantic attachment to a young girl.

**A270**

n.—refutation

The lawyer's **rebuttal** to the judge's sentencing was to present more evidence to the case.

# *Questions*

**DURESS**

*Your Own Answer*_____

**METICULOUS**

*Your Own Answer*_____

**IMPALE**

*Your Own Answer*_____

# *Correct Answers*

**A271**

n.—force; constraint

The Labor Department inspector needed to establish whether the plant workers had been held under **duress**.

**A272**

adj.—exacting; precise

The lab technicians must be **meticulous** in their measurements to obtain exact results.

**A273**

v.—to pierce through with, or stick on, something pointed

The knight was **impaled** by the sharp lance.

# *Questions*

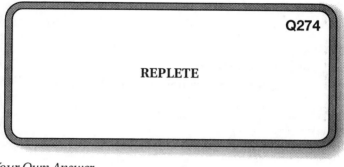

**Q274**

**REPLETE**

*Your Own Answer*_____

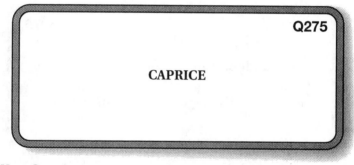

**Q275**

**CAPRICE**

*Your Own Answer*_____

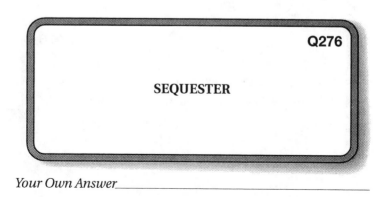

**Q276**

**SEQUESTER**

*Your Own Answer*_____

# Correct Answers

**A274**

adj.—well supplied
The kitchen came **replete** with food and utensils.

**A275**

n.—a sudden, unpredictable, or whimsical change
The king ruled by **caprice** as much as law.

**A276**

v.—to separate or segregate
The jury was **sequestered** at the local inn.

# *Questions*

Q277

**SPECIOUS**

*Your Own Answer*_____

Q278

**APPROBATORY**

*Your Own Answer*_____

Q279

**DESIST**

*Your Own Answer*_____

# Correct Answers

**A277**

adj.—plausible, but deceptive; apparently, but not actually true

The jury forewoman said the jury saw through the defense lawyer's **specious** argument and convicted his client on the weight of the evidence.

**A278**

adj.—approving or sanctioning

The judge showed his acceptance in his **approbatory** remark.

**A279**

v.—to stop or cease

The judge ordered the man to **desist** from calling his ex-wife in the middle of the night.

# *Questions*

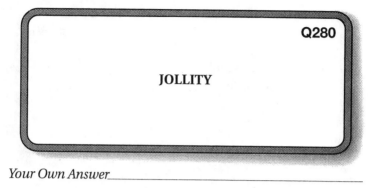

Q280

**JOLLITY**

*Your Own Answer*_____

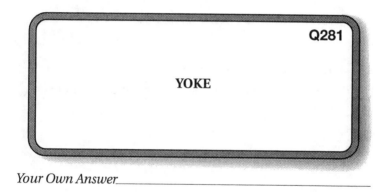

Q281

**YOKE**

*Your Own Answer*_____

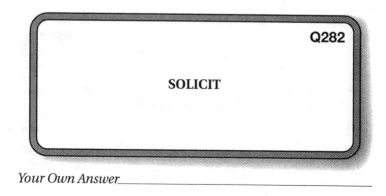

Q282

**SOLICIT**

*Your Own Answer*_____

# Correct Answers

**A280**

n.—being fun or jolly

The crowd's **jollity** was seen in the cheering and laughing.

**A281**

n.—harness; collar; bond

The jockey led her horse by the **yoke** around its neck and face.

**A282**

v.—to ask; to seek

The jobless man **solicited** employment from many factories before he was able to find work.

# *Questions*

**Q283**

**UNIQUE**

*Your Own Answer*_____

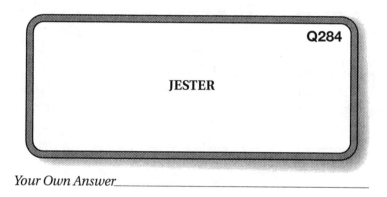

**Q284**

**JESTER**

*Your Own Answer*_____

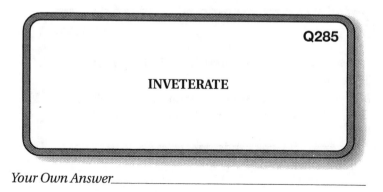

**Q285**

**INVETERATE**

*Your Own Answer*_____

# *Correct Answers*

**A283**

adj.—without equal; incomparable

The jeweler assured him that the dubloon was **unique**, as it was part of the long lost treasure of the Atocha.

**A284**

n.—a person employed to amuse

The **jester** tried all of his tricks to get the girl to laugh.

**A285**

adj.—a practice settled on over a long period of time

The **inveterate** induction ceremony bespoke one of the school's great traditions.

# *Questions*

**Q286**

**INTREPID**

*Your Own Answer*_____

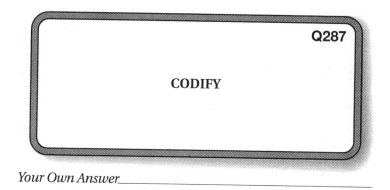

**Q287**

**CODIFY**

*Your Own Answer*_____

**Q288**

**GARBLED**

*Your Own Answer*_____

# Correct Answers

**A286**

adj.—fearless; bold

The **intrepid** photographer flew on some of the fiercest bombing raids of the war.

**A287**

v.—to organize laws or rules into a systematic collection (code)

The intern **codified** all the city's laws into a computerized filing system.

**A288**

adj.—mixed up; distorted or confused

The interference on the phone line caused the data to become **garbled** on the computer screen.

# *Questions*

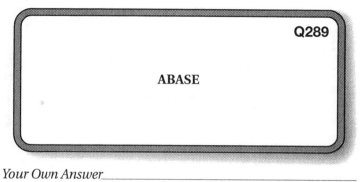

Q289

**ABASE**

*Your Own Answer*_____

Q290

**INGENUOUS**

*Your Own Answer*_____

Q291

**IMPERTURBABLE**

*Your Own Answer*_____

# Correct Answers

v.—to degrade; to humiliate; to disgrace

The insecure father, after failing to achieve his own lifelong goals, **abased** his children whenever they failed.

adj.—noble; honorable; candid; also naive, simple, artless, without guile

The **ingenuous** doctor had a great bedside manner, especially when it came to laying out the full implications of an illness.

adj.—calm; not easily excited

The **imperturbable** West Point graduate made a fine negotiator.

# *Questions*

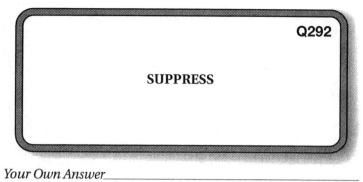

Q292

**SUPPRESS**

*Your Own Answer*_____

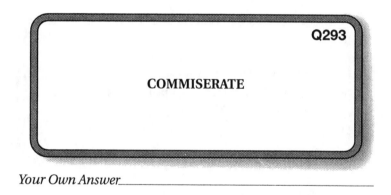

Q293

**COMMISERATE**

*Your Own Answer*_____

Q294

**IRREPROACHABLE**

*Your Own Answer*_____

# Correct Answers

v.—to bring to an end; to hold back

The illegal aliens were **suppressed** by the border patrol.

v.—to show sympathy for

The hurricane victims **commiserated** about the loss of their homes.

adj.—without blame or faults

The honesty of the priest made him **irreproachable**.

# *Questions*

**AFFILIATE**

*Your Own Answer*_____

**IRREPARABLE**

*Your Own Answer*_____

**HAUGHTY**

*Your Own Answer*_____

# *Correct Answers*

**A295**

v.—to connect or associate with; to accept as a member

The hiking club **affiliated** with the bird-watching club.

**A296**

adj.—not repairable

The head-on collision left the car **irreparable**.

**A297**

adj.—to have or show great pride in oneself

The **haughty** girl displayed her work as if she were the most prized artist.

# *Questions*

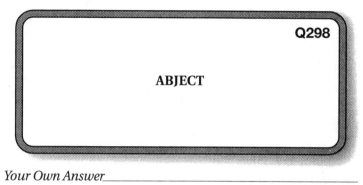

Q298

**ABJECT**

*Your Own Answer*_____

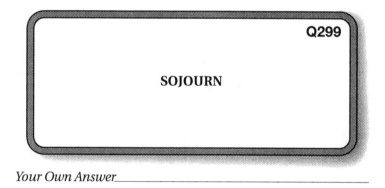

Q299

**SOJOURN**

*Your Own Answer*_____

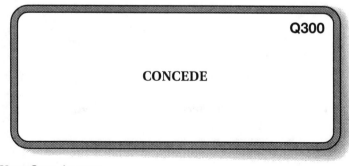

Q300

**CONCEDE**

*Your Own Answer*_____

# Correct Answers

**A298**

adj.—of the worst or lowest degree

The Haldemans lived in **abject** poverty, with barely a roof over their heads.

**A299**

n.—temporary stay; visit

The guest remained only for a **sojourn**; she was going to leave in the afternoon.

**A300**

v.—1. to acknowledge; to admit 2. to surrender; to abandon one's position

1. After much wrangling, he **conceded** that the minister had a point.
2. Satisfied with the recount, the mayor **conceded** graciously.

# *Questions*

**Q301**

**CONTEMPT**

*Your Own Answer*_____

**Q302**

**IMPECUNIOUS**

*Your Own Answer*_____

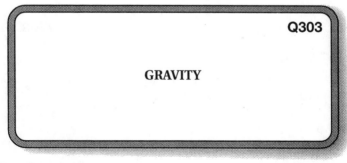

**Q303**

**GRAVITY**

*Your Own Answer*_____

# Correct Answers

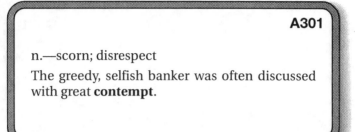

**A301**

n.—scorn; disrespect
The greedy, selfish banker was often discussed with great **contempt**.

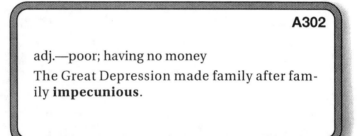

**A302**

adj.—poor; having no money
The Great Depression made family after family **impecunious**.

**A303**

n.—seriousness
The **gravity** of the incident was sufficient to involve the police and the FBI.

# *Questions*

**Q304**

**INDICT**

*Your Own Answer*_____

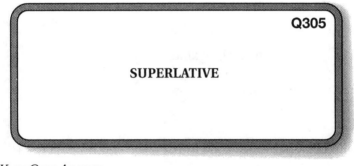

**Q305**

**SUPERLATIVE**

*Your Own Answer*_____

**Q306**

**GLUTTON**

*Your Own Answer*_____

# *Correct Answers*

**A304**

v.—to charge with a crime
The grand jury **indicted** her and her husband for
embezzlement and six other lesser counts.

**A305**

adj.—of the highest kind or degree
The Golden Gate Bridge is a **superlative** example
of civil engineering.

**A306**

n.—overeater
The **glutton** ate twelve hot dogs.

# *Questions*

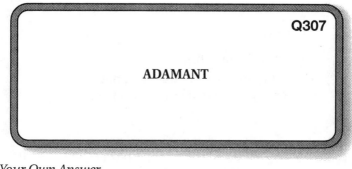

**Q307**

**ADAMANT**

*Your Own Answer*_____

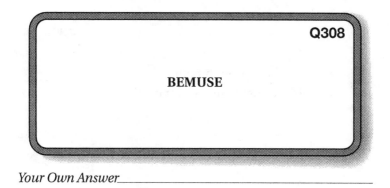

**Q308**

**BEMUSE**

*Your Own Answer*_____

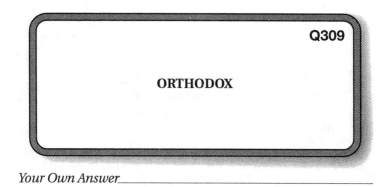

**Q309**

**ORTHODOX**

*Your Own Answer*_____

# Correct Answers

adj.—not yielding; firm

The girl's parents were **adamant** about not allowing her to go on a dangerous backpacking trip.

v.—to preoccupy in thought

The girl was **bemused** by her troubles.

adj.—traditional; accepted

The gifted child's parents concluded that **orthodox** methods of education would not do their son any good, so they decided to teach him at home.

# *Questions*

**EUPHONY**

*Your Own Answer*_____

**GAUNTLET**

*Your Own Answer*_____

**URBANE**

*Your Own Answer*_____

# *Correct Answers*

**A310**

n.—pleasant combination of sounds

The gently singing birds created a beautiful **euphony**.

---

**A311**

n.—a protective glove

The **gauntlet** saved the man's hand from being burned in the fire.

---

**A312**

adj.—cultured; suave

The gala concert and dinner dance was attended by the most **urbane** individuals.

# *Questions*

Q313

**MELANCHOLY**

*Your Own Answer*_____

Q314

**WANE**

*Your Own Answer*_____

Q315

**DEBASE**

*Your Own Answer*_____

# Correct Answers

A313

n.—depression; gloom
The funeral parlor was filled with the **melancholy** of mourning.

A314

v.—to grow gradually smaller
The full moon **waned** until it was nothing but a sliver in the sky.

A315

v.—to make lower in quality
The French are concerned that "Franglais," a blending of English and French, will **debase** their language.

# *Questions*

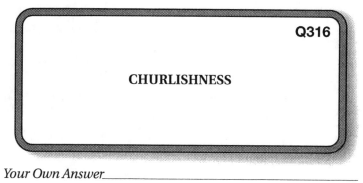

**Q316**

**CHURLISHNESS**

*Your Own Answer*_____

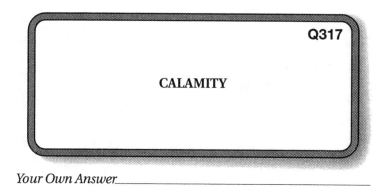

**Q317**

**CALAMITY**

*Your Own Answer*_____

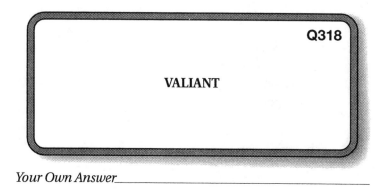

**Q318**

**VALIANT**

*Your Own Answer*_____

# *Correct Answers*

**A316**

n.—crude or surly behavior; behavior of a peasant

The fraternity's **churlishness** ran afoul of the dean's office.

**A317**

n.—disaster

The fire in the apartment building was a great **calamity**.

**A318**

adj.—full of courage or bravery

The firefighter made a **valiant** effort to save the trapped person.

# *Questions*

**ACRID**

*Your Own Answer*_____

**FINITE**

*Your Own Answer*_____

**INCOGNITO**

*Your Own Answer*_____

# Correct Answers

**A319**

adj.—sharp; bitter; foul-smelling
The fire at the plastics factory caused an **acrid** odor to be emitted throughout the surrounding neighborhood.

**A320**

adj.—measurable; limited; not everlasting
The **finite** amount of stored food will soon run out.

**A321**

adj.—unidentified; disguised; concealed
The federal Witness Protection Program makes its charges permanently **incognito**.

# *Questions*

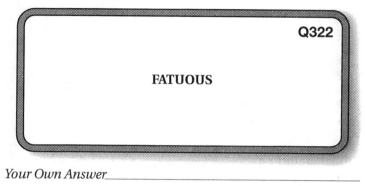

Q322

**FATUOUS**

*Your Own Answer*_____

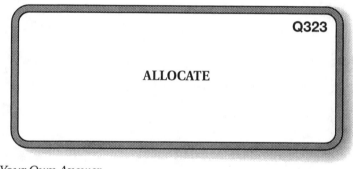

Q323

**ALLOCATE**

*Your Own Answer*_____

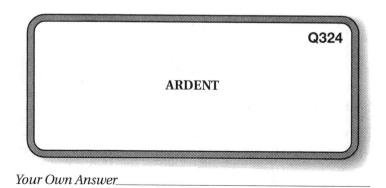

Q324

**ARDENT**

*Your Own Answer*_____

# Correct Answers

**A322**

adj.—lacking in seriousness
The **fatuous** prank was meant to add comedy to the situation.

**A323**

v.—to set aside; to designate; to assign
The farmer **allocated** three acres of his fields to corn.

**A324**

adj.—with passionate or intense feelings
The fans' **ardent** love of the game kept them re-turning to watch the terrible team.

# Questions

Q325

**INDIGENCE**

*Your Own Answer*_____

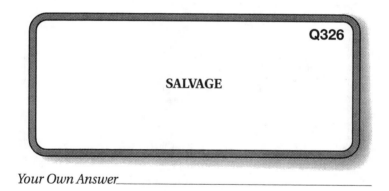

Q326

**SALVAGE**

*Your Own Answer*_____

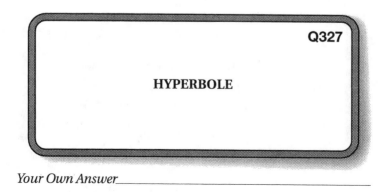

Q327

**HYPERBOLE**

*Your Own Answer*_____

# Correct Answers

n.—the condition of being poor

The family's **indigence** was evident by the run-down house they lived in.

v.—to rescue from loss

The family tried to **salvage** their belongings after their home was destroyed by a tornado.

n.—an exaggeration, not to be taken seriously

"The full moon was almost blinding in its brightness," he said with a measure of **hyperbole**.

# *Questions*

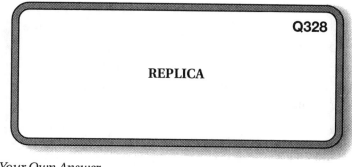

Q328

**REPLICA**

*Your Own Answer*_____

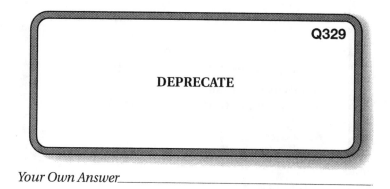

Q329

**DEPRECATE**

*Your Own Answer*_____

Q330

**PRODIGIOUS**

*Your Own Answer*_____

# Correct Answers

**A328**

n.—copy; representation; reproduction

The equine sculpture was a **replica** of a Remington.

**A329**

v.—to express disapproval of; to protest against

The environmentalists **deprecated** the paper companies for cutting down ancient forests.

**A330**

adj.—exceptional; tremendous

The Empire State Building required a **prodigious** amount of steel to erect.

# *Questions*

Q331

**RESILIENT**

*Your Own Answer*_____

Q332

**ABRIDGE**

*Your Own Answer*_____

Q333

**ADROIT**

*Your Own Answer*_____

# *Correct Answers*

**A331**

adj.—flexible; capable of withstanding stress

The elderly man attributed his **resilient** health to a good diet and frequent exercise.

**A332**

v.—to shorten; to limit

The editor **abridged** the story to make the book easier to digest.

**A333**

adj.—clever or expert

The driver's **adroit** driving avoided a serious accident.

# Questions

**Q334**

**DOGMA**

*Your Own Answer*_____

_____

**Q335**

**ABHOR**

*Your Own Answer*_____

_____

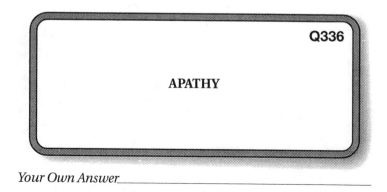

**Q336**

**APATHY**

*Your Own Answer*_____

_____

# *Correct Answers*

n.—a collection of beliefs

The **dogma** of the village was based on superstition.

v.—to hate

The dog **abhorred** cats, chasing and growling at them whenever it had the opportunity.

n.—lack of emotion or interest

The disheartened peasants expressed **apathy** toward the new law which promised new hope and prosperity for all.

# *Questions*

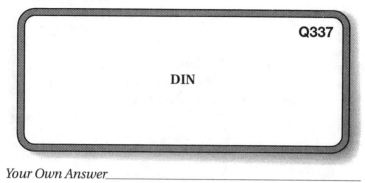

**Q337**

DIN

*Your Own Answer*_____

**Q338**

CONSPICUOUS

*Your Own Answer*_____

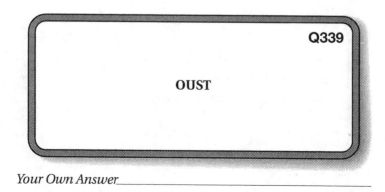

**Q339**

OUST

*Your Own Answer*_____

# Correct Answers

**A337**

n.—a noise which is loud and continuous

The **din** of the jackhammers reverberated throughout the concrete canyon.

**A338**

adj.—easy to see; noticeable

The diligent and hardworking editor thought the mistake was **conspicuous**.

**A339**

v.—to drive out; to eject

The dictator was **ousted** in a coup d'état.

# *Questions*

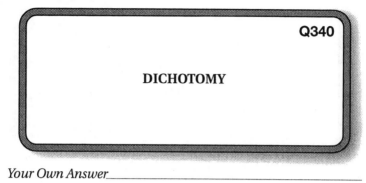

**Q340**

**DICHOTOMY**

*Your Own Answer*_____

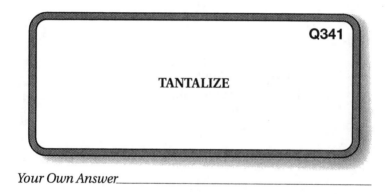

**Q341**

**TANTALIZE**

*Your Own Answer*_____

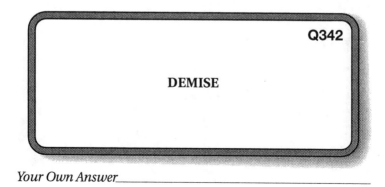

**Q342**

**DEMISE**

*Your Own Answer*_____

# *Correct Answers*

**A340**

n.—a division into two parts or kinds

The **dichotomy** within the party threatens to split it.

**A341**

v.—to tempt; to torment

The desserts were **tantalizing**, but he was on a diet.

**A342**

n.—ceasing to exist as in death

The **demise** of Gimbels followed years of decline.

# *Questions*

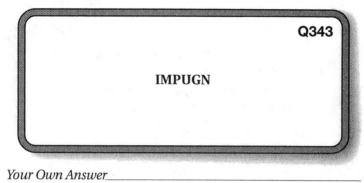

Q343

**IMPUGN**

*Your Own Answer*_____

Q344

**INCIDENTAL**

*Your Own Answer*_____

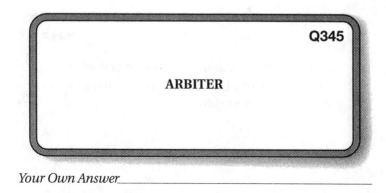

Q345

**ARBITER**

*Your Own Answer*_____

# Correct Answers

**A343**

v.—to attack with words; to question one's truthfulness or integrity

The defense lawyer **impugned** the witness's testimony, which set back the prosecution's case.

**A344**

adj.—extraneous; unexpected

The defense lawyer argued that the whereabouts of the defendant's sneakers were only **incidental** to the commission of the crime.

**A345**

n.—one who is authorized to judge or decide

The decision of who would represent the people was made by the **arbiter**.

# *Questions*

Q346

**LIMBER**

*Your Own Answer*_____

Q347

**CYNIC**

*Your Own Answer*_____

Q348

**FERVOR**

*Your Own Answer*_____

# Correct Answers

**A346**

adj.—flexible; pliant

The dancers must be **limber** to do their ballet steps.

**A347**

n.—one who believes that others are motivated entirely by selfishness.

The **cynic** felt that the hero saved the man to become famous.

**A348**

n.—passion; intensity of feeling

The crowd was full of **fervor** as the candidate entered the hall.

# *Questions*

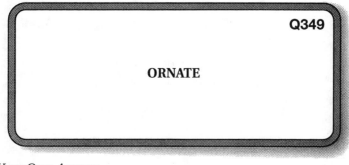

Q349

**ORNATE**

*Your Own Answer*_____

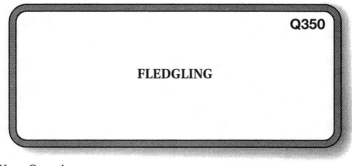

Q350

**FLEDGLING**

*Your Own Answer*_____

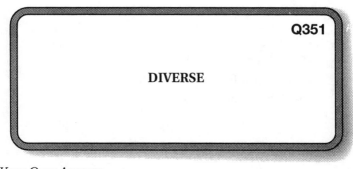

Q351

**DIVERSE**

*Your Own Answer*_____

# Correct Answers

**A349**

adj.—elaborate; lavish; decorated
The courthouse was framed by **ornate** friezes.

**A350**

adj.—inexperienced person; beginner
The course was not recommended for **fledgling** skiers.

**A351**

adj.—different; varied
The course offerings were so **diverse** I had a tough time choosing.

# *Questions*

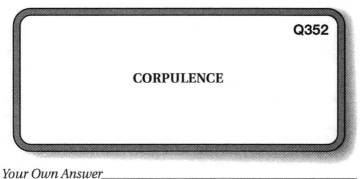

**Q352**

**CORPULENCE**

*Your Own Answer*_____

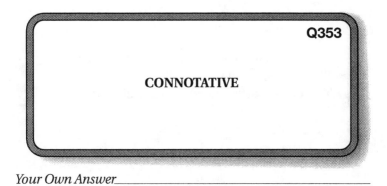

**Q353**

**CONNOTATIVE**

*Your Own Answer*_____

**Q354**

**REVERENT**

*Your Own Answer*_____

# Correct Answers

n.—obesity

The **corpulence** of the man kept him from fitting into the seat.

adj.—containing associated meanings in addition to the primary one

The **connotative** meaning of their music was spelled out in the video.

adj.—respectful; feeling or showing deep love, respect, or awe

The congregation was very **reverent** of its spiritual leader.

# *Questions*

**Q355**

**CONCISE**

*Your Own Answer*_____

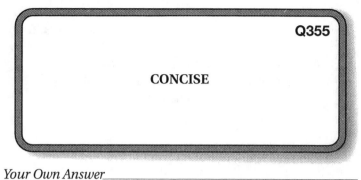

**Q356**

**COMPLAISANCE**

*Your Own Answer*_____

**Q357**

**COMMUNAL**

*Your Own Answer*_____

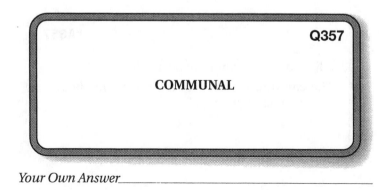

# Correct Answers

**A355**

adj.—in few words; brief; condensed

The **concise** instructions were printed on two pages rather than the customary five.

**A356**

n.—the quality of being agreeable or eager to please

The **complaisance** of the new assistant made it easy for the managers to give him a lot of work without worrying that he may complain.

**A357**

adj.—shared or common ownership

The **communal** nature of the project made everyone pitch in to help.

# *Questions*

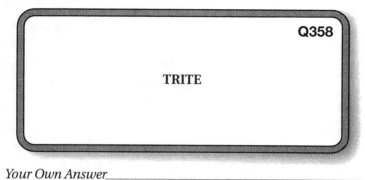

Q358

**TRITE**

*Your Own Answer*_____

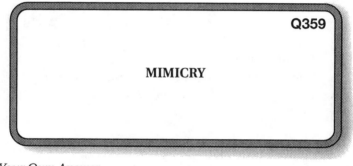

Q359

**MIMICRY**

*Your Own Answer*_____

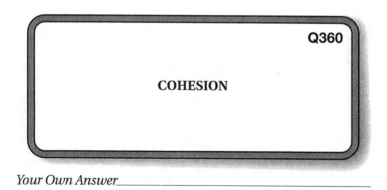

Q360

**COHESION**

*Your Own Answer*_____

# *Correct Answers*

**A358**

adj.—commonplace; overused

The committee was looking for something new, not the same **trite** ideas.

**A359**

n.—imitation

The comedian's **mimicry** of the president's gestures had the audience rolling in the aisles.

**A360**

n.—the act of holding together

The **cohesion** of different molecules forms different substances.

# *Questions*

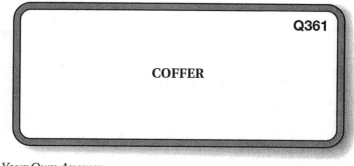

**Q361**

**COFFER**

*Your Own Answer*_____

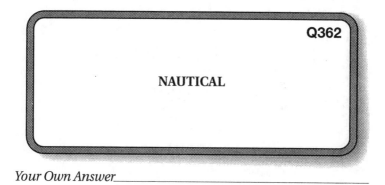

**Q362**

**NAUTICAL**

*Your Own Answer*_____

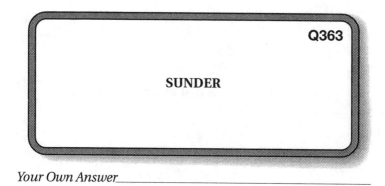

**Q363**

**SUNDER**

*Your Own Answer*_____

# Correct Answers

**A361**

n.—a chest where money or valuables are kept

The **coffer** that contained the jewels was stolen.

**A362**

adj.—of the sea; having to do with sailors, ships, or navigation

The coastal New England town had a charming **nautical** influence.

**A363**

v.—to break; to split in two

The Civil War threatened to **sunder** the United States.

# Questions

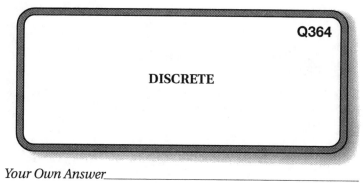

**Q364**

**DISCRETE**

*Your Own Answer*_____

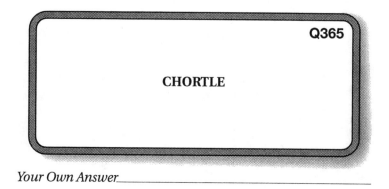

**Q365**

**CHORTLE**

*Your Own Answer*_____

**Q366**

**CENSOR**

*Your Own Answer*_____

# Correct Answers

**A364**

adj.—separate; individually distinct; composed of distinct parts

The citizens' committee maintained that road widening and drainage were hardly **discrete** issues.

**A365**

v.—to make a gleeful, chuckling sound

The audience **chortled**, indicating it wouldn't be as tough a crowd as the stand-up comic had expected.

**A366**

v.—to examine and delete objectionable material

The children were allowed to watch the adult movie only after it had been **censored**.

# *Questions*

**Q367**

**FLUENCY**

*Your Own Answer*_____

---

**Q368**

**BERATE**

*Your Own Answer*_____

---

**Q369**

**CIRCUMLOCUTION**

*Your Own Answer*_____

# *Correct Answers*

**A367**

n.—ability to write easily and expressively

The child's **fluency** in Spanish and English was remarkable.

**A368**

v.—to scold; to reprove; to reproach; to criticize

The child was **berated** by her parents for breaking the china.

**A369**

n.—a roundabout or indirect way of speaking; not to the point

The child made a long speech using **circumlocution** to avoid stating that it was she who had knocked over the lamp.

# *Questions*

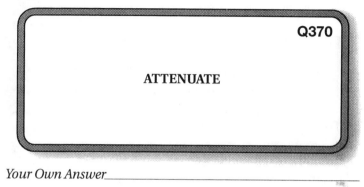

Q370

**ATTENUATE**

*Your Own Answer*_____

---

Q371

**UNWONTED**

*Your Own Answer*_____

---

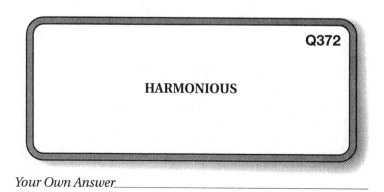

Q372

**HARMONIOUS**

*Your Own Answer*_____

# *Correct Answers*

**A370**

v.—to make thin or slender; to weaken or dilute

The chemist **attenuated** the solution by adding water.

**A371**

adj.—not ordinary; unusual

The changed migratory habits of the Canada geese, though **unwonted**, are undesired because of the mess they make.

**A372**

adj.—having proportionate and orderly parts

The challenge for the new conductor was to mold his musicians' talents into a **harmonious** orchestra.

# *Questions*

**Q373**

**COMPLACENT**

*Your Own Answer*_____

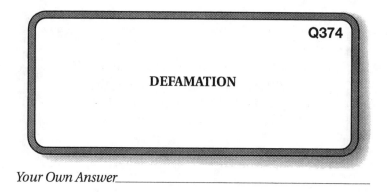

**Q374**

**DEFAMATION**

*Your Own Answer*_____

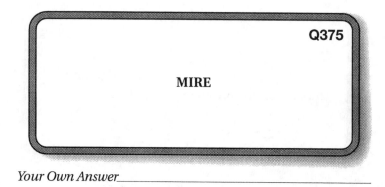

**Q375**

**MIRE**

*Your Own Answer*_____

# Correct Answers

**A373**

adj.—content; self-satisfied; smug
The CEO worries regularly that his firm's winning
ways will make it **complacent**.

**A374**

n.—to harm a name or reputation; to slander
The carpenter felt that the notoriousness of his
former partner brought **defamation** to his construction business.

**A375**

v.—to cause to get stuck in wet, soggy ground
The car became **mired** in the mud.

# *Questions*

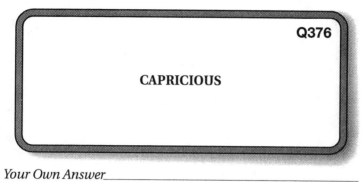

Q376

**CAPRICIOUS**

*Your Own Answer*_____

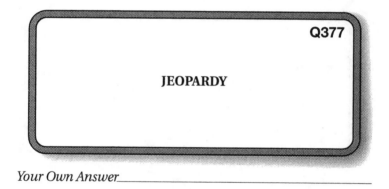

Q377

**JEOPARDY**

*Your Own Answer*_____

Q378

**ALOOF**

*Your Own Answer*_____

# *Correct Answers*

**A376**

adj.—changeable; fickle

The **capricious** bride-to-be has a different church in mind for her wedding every few days.

**A377**

n.—danger; peril

The campers realized they were in potential **jeopardy** when the bears surrounded their camp.

**A378**

adj.—distant in interest; reserved; cool

The calm defendant remained **aloof** when he was wrongly accused of fabricating his story.

# *Questions*

**CACOPHONOUS**

*Your Own Answer*_____

**TYCOON**

*Your Own Answer*_____

**PENITENT**

*Your Own Answer*_____

# Correct Answers

adj.—sounding jarring

The **cacophonous** sound from the bending metal sent shivers up our spines.

n.—wealthy leader

The business **tycoon** prepared to buy his fifteenth company.

adj.—feeling sorry for what one has done

The burglar expressed his **penitent** feelings during his confession.

# *Questions*

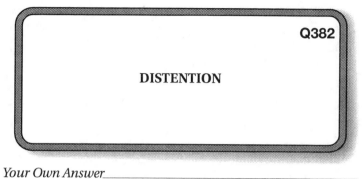

Q382

**DISTENTION**

*Your Own Answer*_____

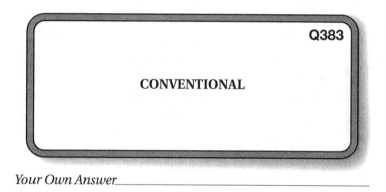

Q383

**CONVENTIONAL**

*Your Own Answer*_____

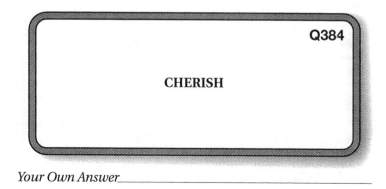

Q384

**CHERISH**

*Your Own Answer*_____

# Correct Answers

**A382**

n.—inflation or extension

The bulge in the carpet was caused by the **distention** of the wood underneath.

**A383**

adj.—traditional; common; routine

The bride wanted a **conventional** wedding ceremony, complete with a white wedding gown, a large bridal party, and a grand reception.

**A384**

v.—to feel love for

The bride vowed to **cherish** the groom for life.

# Questions

**Q385**

**INSUBORDINATE**

*Your Own Answer*________________________________________

**Q386**

**INANIMATE**

*Your Own Answer*________________________________________

**Q387**

**DIATRIBE**

*Your Own Answer*________________________________________

# Correct Answers

**A385**

adj.—disobedient to authority

The boy's **insubordinate** behavior was a constant source of tension between the school and his parents.

---

**A386**

adj.—to be dull or spiritless; not animated; not endowed with life

The boy nagged his father for a real puppy, not some **inanimate** stuffed animal.

---

**A387**

n.—an abusive criticism

The boss's **diatribe** had everyone scrambling to do a better job.

# *Questions*

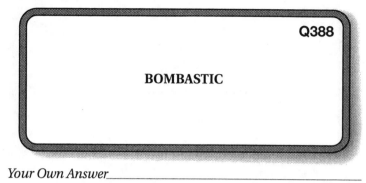

Q388

**BOMBASTIC**

*Your Own Answer*_____

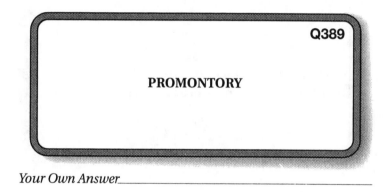

Q389

**PROMONTORY**

*Your Own Answer*_____

Q390

**CEREMONIOUS**

*Your Own Answer*_____

# *Correct Answers*

**A388**

adj.—pompous; wordy; turgid
The **bombastic** woman talks a lot about herself.

**A389**

n.—a piece of land jutting into a body of water
The boat hit the rocky **promontory**, splitting the bow.

**A390**

adj.—very formal or proper
The black-tie dinner was highly **ceremonious**.

# *Questions*

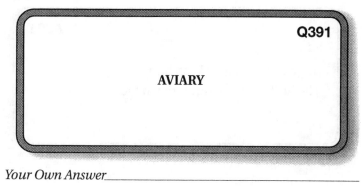

**Q391**

**AVIARY**

*Your Own Answer*_____

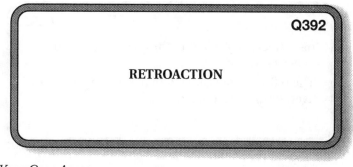

**Q392**

**RETROACTION**

*Your Own Answer*_____

**Q393**

**QUIESCENT**

*Your Own Answer*_____

# *Correct Answers*

---

**A391**

n.—a large place to keep birds

The birds were being stored in the **aviary**.

---

**A392**

n.—effect, as of a law, of things done prior to the enactment

The bill's **retroaction** stood to save taxpayers an average of $500 a head.

---

**A393**

adj.—inactive; at rest

The Bible says that the Lord created the Earth in six days, and, on the seventh, He was **quiescent**.

# *Questions*

**CACOPHONY**

*Your Own Answer*_____

**INTRANSIGENT**

*Your Own Answer*_____

**BAROQUE**

*Your Own Answer*_____

# *Correct Answers*

**A394**

n.—a harsh, inharmonious collection of sounds; dissonance

The beautiful harmony of the symphony was well enjoyed after the **cacophony** coming from the stage as the orchestra warmed up.

**A395**

adj.—uncompromising

The baseball owners and players remained **intransigent**, so a deal was never struck.

**A396**

adj.—extravagant; ornate

The **baroque** artwork was made up of intricate details, which kept the museum-goers enthralled.

# *Questions*

Q397

**FEALTY**

*Your Own Answer*_____

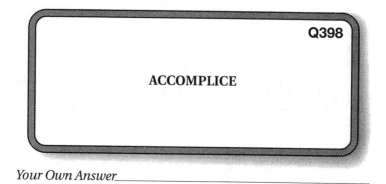

Q398

**ACCOMPLICE**

*Your Own Answer*_____

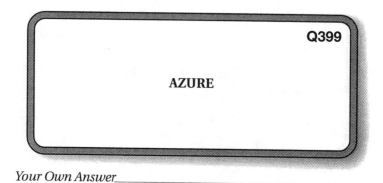

Q399

**AZURE**

*Your Own Answer*_____

# *Correct Answers*

**A397**

n.—loyalty
The baron was given land in exchange for his **fealty** to the king.

**A398**

n.—co-conspirator; partner; partner-in-crime
The bank robber's **accomplice** drove the getaway car.

**A399**

adj.—the clear blue color of the sky
The **azure** sky made the picnic day perfect.

# *Questions*

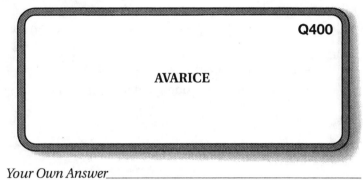

Q400

**AVARICE**

*Your Own Answer*_____

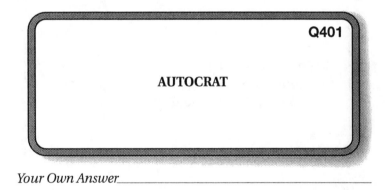

Q401

**AUTOCRAT**

*Your Own Answer*_____

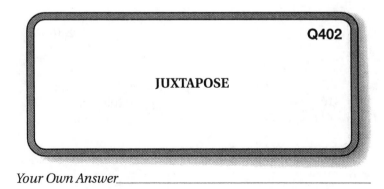

Q402

**JUXTAPOSE**

*Your Own Answer*_____

# *Correct Answers*

n.—a greed for wealth

The **avarice** of the president led to his downfall.

n.—an absolute ruler

The **autocrat** made every decision and divided the tasks among his subordinates.

v.—to place side-by-side

The author decided to **juxtapose** the two sentences since each one strengthened the meaning of the other.

# *Questions*

**Q403**

**AUSTERE**

*Your Own Answer*_____

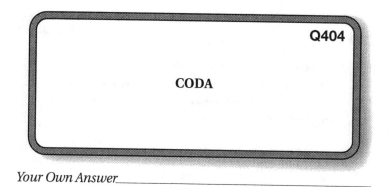

**Q404**

**CODA**

*Your Own Answer*_____

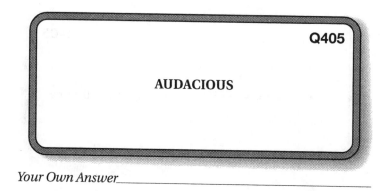

**Q405**

**AUDACIOUS**

*Your Own Answer*_____

# *Correct Answers*

**A403**

adj.—harsh; severe; strict; very plain, lacking ornament

The **austere** teacher assigned five pages of homework each day.

**A404**

n.—in music, a concluding passage

The audience knew that the concerto was about to end when they heard the orchestra begin playing the **coda**.

**A405**

adj.—fearless; bold

The **audacious** soldier went into battle without a shield.

# *Questions*

Q406

**ATYPICAL**

*Your Own Answer*_____

Q407

**CONCILIATION**

*Your Own Answer*_____

Q408

**ASTUTE**

*Your Own Answer*_____

# Correct Answers

**A406**

adj.—something that is abnormal

The **atypical** behavior of the wild animal alarmed the hunters.

**A407**

n.—an attempt to make friendly or placate

The attempt at **conciliation** between the two enemies was futile.

**A408**

adj.—cunning; sly; crafty

The **astute** lawyer's questioning convinced the jury of the defendant's guilt.

# *Questions*

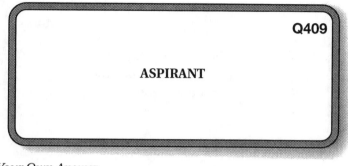

**Q409**

**ASPIRANT**

*Your Own Answer*_____

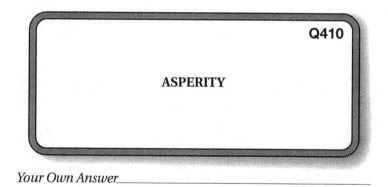

**Q410**

**ASPERITY**

*Your Own Answer*_____

**Q411**

**CONDESCEND**

*Your Own Answer*_____

# Correct Answers

**A409**

n.—a person who goes after high goals

The **aspirant** would not settle for assistant director—only the top job was good enough.

**A410**

n.—harshness

The **asperity** of the winter had almost everybody yearning for spring.

**A411**

v.—to come down from one's position or dignity

The arrogant, rich man was usually **condescending** toward his servants.

# *Questions*

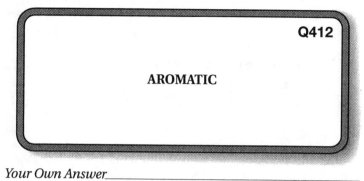

Q412

**AROMATIC**

*Your Own Answer*_____

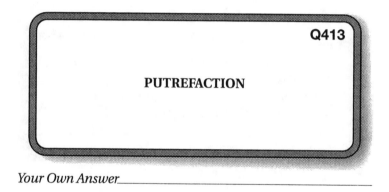

Q413

**PUTREFACTION**

*Your Own Answer*_____

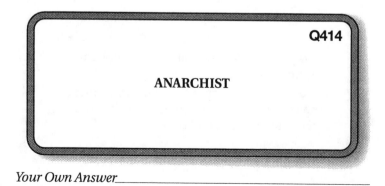

Q414

**ANARCHIST**

*Your Own Answer*_____

# *Correct Answers*

**A412**

adj.—having a smell which is sweet or spicy

The **aromatic** smell coming from the oven made the man's mouth water.

**A413**

n.—a smelly mass that is the decomposition of organic matter

The apple was nothing but a **putrefaction** after sitting on the windowsill for three weeks.

**A414**

n.—one who believes that a formal government is unnecessary

The **anarchist** attempted to overthrow the established democratic government of the new nation and reinstate chaos and disarray.

# Questions

Q415

**AMITY**

*Your Own Answer*_____

Q416

**AMIABLE**

*Your Own Answer*_____

Q417

**AMENDMENT**

*Your Own Answer*_____

# Correct Answers

**A415**

n.—friendly relations
The **amity** between the two bordering nations put the populations at ease.

**A416**

adj.—friendly
The **amiable** old man often entertained neighbors and friends with his banjo picking.

**A417**

n.—a positive change
The **amendment** in his ways showed there was still reason for hope.

# *Questions*

**AMBIVALENT**

*Your Own Answer*_____

**AMBIGUOUS**

*Your Own Answer*_____

**ALTRUISTIC**

*Your Own Answer*_____

# Correct Answers

**A418**

adj.—undecided

The **ambivalent** jury could not reach a unanimous verdict.

**A419**

adj.—not clear; uncertain; vague

The **ambiguous** law did not make a clear distinction between the new and old land boundary.

**A420**

adj.—unselfish

The **altruistic** volunteer donated much time and energy in an effort to raise funds for the children's hospital.

# *Questions*

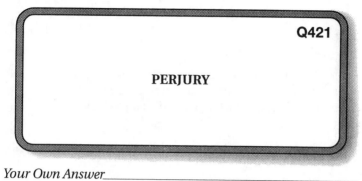

**Q421**

**PERJURY**

*Your Own Answer*_____

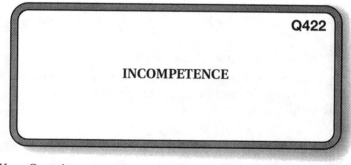

**Q422**

**INCOMPETENCE**

*Your Own Answer*_____

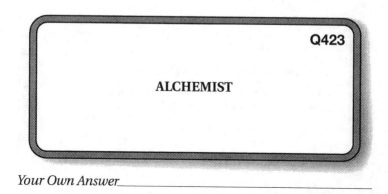

**Q423**

**ALCHEMIST**

*Your Own Answer*_____

# Correct Answers

**A421**

n.—the practice of lying

The already sensational  trial of a star athlete turned all the more so when it turned out that a police detective had committed **perjury**.

**A422**

n.—failing to meet necessary requirements

The alleged **incompetence** of the construction crew would later become the subject of a class-action suit.

**A423**

n.—a person who studies chemistry

The **alchemist**'s laboratory was full of bottles and tubes of strange looking liquids.

# *Questions*

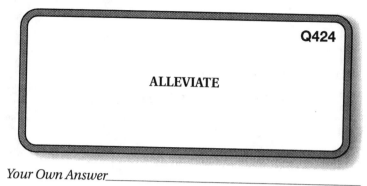

Q424

**ALLEVIATE**

*Your Own Answer*_____

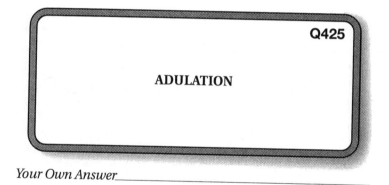

Q425

**ADULATION**

*Your Own Answer*_____

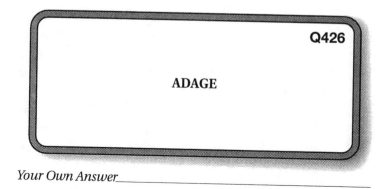

Q426

**ADAGE**

*Your Own Answer*_____

# Correct Answers

**A424**

v.—to lessen or make easier

The airport's monorail **alleviates** vehicular traffic.

**A425**

n.—high praise

The **adulation** given to the movie star was sickening.

**A426**

n.—an old saying now accepted as being truthful

The **adage** "Do unto others as you wish them to do unto you" has the very ring of logic and good sense.

# Questions

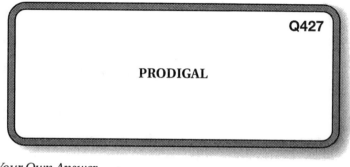

**Q427**

**PRODIGAL**

*Your Own Answer*_____

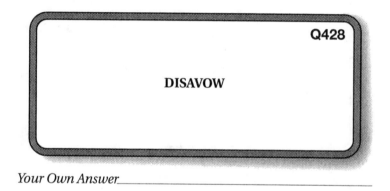

**Q428**

**DISAVOW**

*Your Own Answer*_____

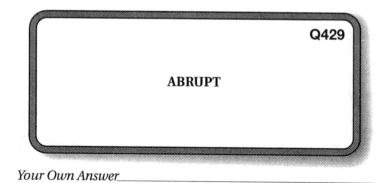

**Q429**

**ABRUPT**

*Your Own Answer*_____

# Correct Answers

**A427**

adj.—wasteful; lavish
The actor's **prodigal** lifestyle ultimately led to his undoing.

**A428**

v.—to deny; to refuse to acknowledge
The actor has **disavowed** the rumor.

**A429**

adj.—happening or ending unexpectedly
The **abrupt** end to their marriage was a shock to everyone.

# *Questions*

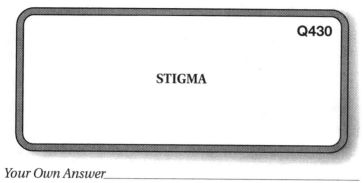

Q430

**STIGMA**

*Your Own Answer*_____

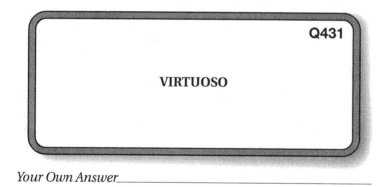

Q431

**VIRTUOSO**

*Your Own Answer*_____

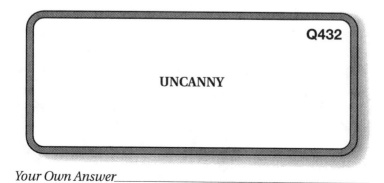

Q432

**UNCANNY**

*Your Own Answer*_____

# Correct Answers

n.—a mark of disgrace

The "F" on his transcript is a **stigma** on his record.

n.—highly skilled artist

The **virtuoso** performed with the best orchestras in the world.

adj.—of a strange nature; weird

That two people could be so alike was **uncanny**.

# *Questions*

Q433

**AMALGAM**

*Your Own Answer*_____

Q434

**LUSTROUS**

*Your Own Answer*_____

Q435

**RANCOR**

*Your Own Answer*_____

# Correct Answers

**A433**

n.—a mixture or combination (often of metals)

That ring is made from an **amalgam** of minerals; if it were pure gold, it would never hold its shape.

**A434**

adj.—bright; radiant; shining

Surrounded by rubies, the **lustrous** diamond looked magnificent.

**A435**

n.—strong ill will; enmity

Sure they had their disagreements, but there was no **rancor** between them.

# Questions

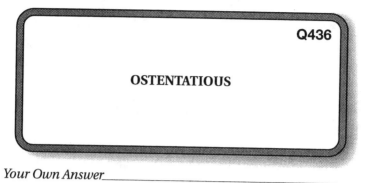

Q436

**OSTENTATIOUS**

*Your Own Answer*_____

_____

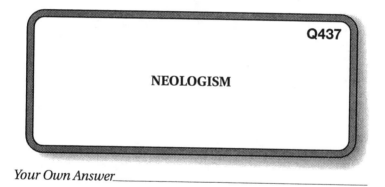

Q437

**NEOLOGISM**

*Your Own Answer*_____

_____

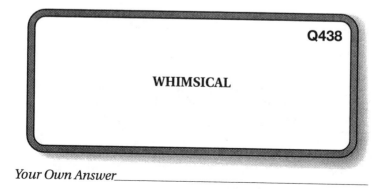

Q438

**WHIMSICAL**

*Your Own Answer*_____

_____

# Correct Answers

**A436**

adj.—being showy
Sure he'd won the lottery, but coming to work in a stretch limo seemed a bit **ostentatious**.

**A437**

n.—giving a new meaning to an old word
"Bad" is a **neologism** for good.

**A438**

adj.—fanciful; amusing
Strolling down Disney World's Main Street is bound to put child and adult alike in a **whimsical** mood.

# Questions

**Q439**

MOLTEN

*Your Own Answer*_____

_____

**Q440**

PERNICIOUS

*Your Own Answer*_____

_____

**Q441**

SPURIOUS

*Your Own Answer*_____

_____

# Correct Answers

**A439**

adj.—melted

Steel becomes **molten** after heating it to thousands of degrees.

**A440**

adj.—dangerous; harmful

Standing oil combined with a fresh rain on asphalt can have a **pernicious** impact on a driver's control of the road.

**A441**

adj.—not genuine; false; bogus

**Spurious** claims by the importer hid the fact that prison labor had been used in the garments' fabrication.

# *Questions*

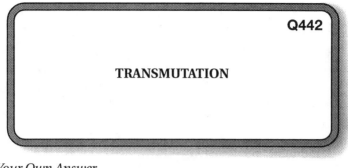

Q442

**TRANSMUTATION**

*Your Own Answer*_____

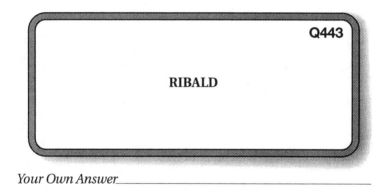

Q443

**RIBALD**

*Your Own Answer*_____

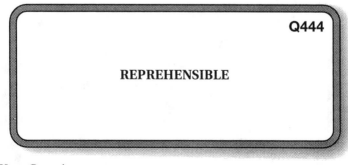

Q444

**REPREHENSIBLE**

*Your Own Answer*_____

# *Correct Answers*

**A442**

n.—a changed form

Somewhere in the network's entertainment division, the show underwent a **transmutation** from a half-hour sitcom into an hour-long drama.

**A443**

adj.—vulgar joking or mocking

Some people find the comedian's **ribald** act offensive.

**A444**

adj.—wicked; disgraceful

Slashing their tires was a **reprehensible** act.

# *Questions*

Q445

**SINUOUS**

*Your Own Answer*_____

Q446

**PRAGMATIC**

*Your Own Answer*_____

Q447

**INEPT**

*Your Own Answer*_____

# Correct Answers

**A445**

adj.—full of curves; twisting and turning

**Sinuous** mountain roads present extra danger at night when it's harder to see the road's edge.

**A446**

adj.—matter-of-fact; practical

Since they were saving money to buy a new home, the **pragmatic** married couple decided not to go on an expensive vacation.

**A447**

adj.—incompetent; clumsy

She would rather update the budget book herself since her assistant is so **inept**.

# Questions

Q448

**QUALIFIED**

*Your Own Answer*_____

_____

Q449

**ULTERIOR**

*Your Own Answer*_____

_____

Q450

**LAX**

*Your Own Answer*_____

_____

# *Correct Answers*

adj.—experienced; indefinite
She was well **qualified** for the job after working
the field for ten years.

adj.—buried; concealed; undisclosed
She was usually very selfish, so when she came
bearing gifts, he suspected that she had **ulterior**
motives.

adj.—careless; irresponsible
She was **lax** in everything she did and, therefore,
could not be trusted with important tasks.

# *Questions*

**Q451**

**PENSIVE**

*Your Own Answer*_____

---

**Q452**

**LOQUACIOUS**

*Your Own Answer*_____

---

**Q453**

**AUTOCRACY**

*Your Own Answer*_____

# *Correct Answers*

adj.—reflective; contemplative

She was in a **pensive** mood, just wanting to be alone to think.

adj.—very talkative; garrulous

She was having difficulty ending the conversation with her **loquacious** neighbor.

n.—an absolute monarchy; government where one person holds power

She was extremely power-hungry and, therefore, wanted her government to be an **autocracy**.

# *Questions*

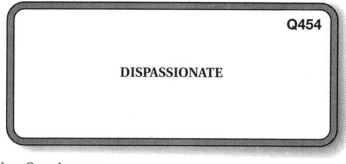

Q454

**DISPASSIONATE**

*Your Own Answer*_____

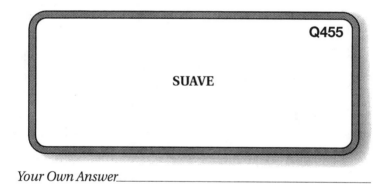

Q455

**SUAVE**

*Your Own Answer*_____

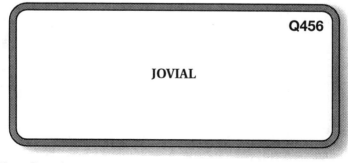

Q456

**JOVIAL**

*Your Own Answer*_____

# Correct Answers

**A454**

adj.—lack of feeling; impartial

She was a very emotional person and could not work with such a **dispassionate** employer.

**A455**

adj.—effortlessly gracious

She was a **suave** negotiator, always getting what she wanted without anyone feeling they'd lost anything.

**A456**

adj.—cheery; jolly; playful

She was a **jovial** person, always pleasant and fun to be with.

# Questions

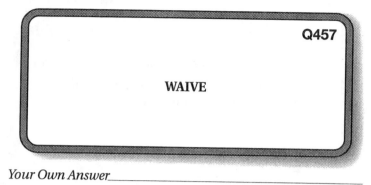

**Q457**

**WAIVE**

*Your Own Answer*_____

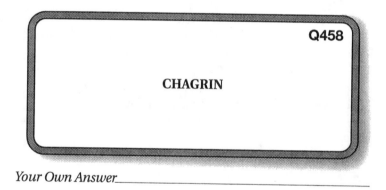

**Q458**

**CHAGRIN**

*Your Own Answer*_____

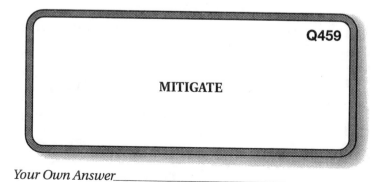

**Q459**

**MITIGATE**

*Your Own Answer*_____

# Correct Answers

**A457**

v.—to give up possession or right

She wanted to represent herself and, therefore, **waived** her right to an attorney.

**A458**

n.—distress; shame

She turned red-faced with **chagrin** when she learned that her son had been caught shoplifting.

**A459**

v.—to alleviate; to lessen; to soothe

She tried to **mitigate** the loss of his pet by buying him a kitten.

# *Questions*

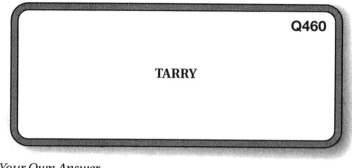

**Q460**

**TARRY**

*Your Own Answer*_____

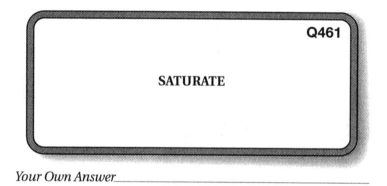

**Q461**

**SATURATE**

*Your Own Answer*_____

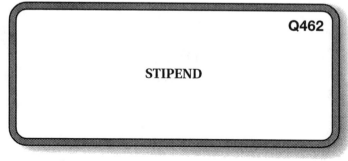

**Q462**

**STIPEND**

*Your Own Answer*_____

# Correct Answers

**A460**

v.—to go or move slowly; to delay
She **tarried** too long and missed her train.

**A461**

v.—to soak thoroughly; to drench
She **saturated** the sponge with soapy water before she began washing the car.

**A462**

n.—payment for work done
She receives a monthly **stipend** for her help with the project.

# Questions

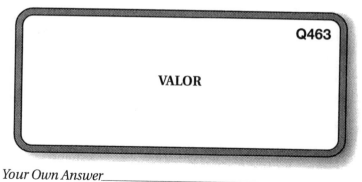

**Q463**

**VALOR**

*Your Own Answer*_____

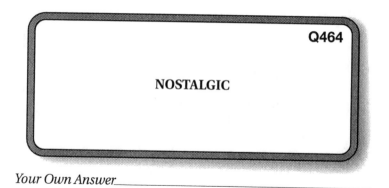

**Q464**

**NOSTALGIC**

*Your Own Answer*_____

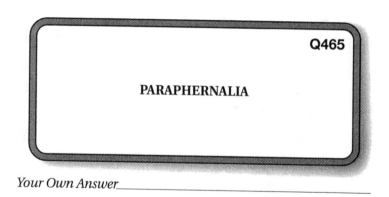

**Q465**

**PARAPHERNALIA**

*Your Own Answer*_____

# *Correct Answers*

**A463**

n.—bravery
She received a medal for her **valor** during the war.

**A464**

adj.—longing for the past; filled with bittersweet memories
She loved her new life, but became **nostalgic** when she met with her old friends.

**A465**

n.—equipment; accessories
She looked guilty since the drug **paraphernalia** was found in her apartment.

# Questions

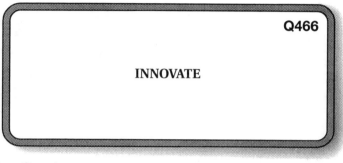

Q466

**INNOVATE**

*Your Own Answer*

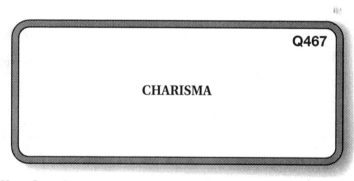

Q467

**CHARISMA**

*Your Own Answer*

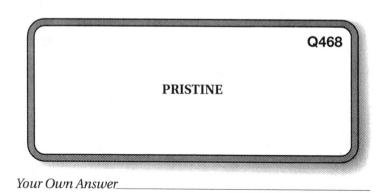

Q468

**PRISTINE**

*Your Own Answer*

# Correct Answers

**A466**

v.—to introduce a change; to depart from the old

She **innovated** a new product for the home construction market.

**A467**

n.—appeal; magnetism; presence

She has such **charisma** that everyone likes her the first time they meet her.

**A468**

adj.—primitive; pure; uncorrupted

She had such a **pristine** look about her, you would have thought she was an angel.

# *Questions*

Q469

**MALEVOLENT**

*Your Own Answer*_____

Q470

**QUIXOTIC**

*Your Own Answer*_____

Q471

**GLOAT**

*Your Own Answer*_____

# Correct Answers

adj.—wishing evil (opposite: benevolent)
She had **malevolent** feelings toward her sister.

adj.—foolishly idealistic
She had a **quixotic** view of the world, believing that humans need never suffer.

v.—brag; to glory over
She **gloated** over the fact that she received the highest score on the exam, annoying her class-mates to no end.

# Questions

**Q472**

**SUSCEPTIBLE**

*Your Own Answer*_____

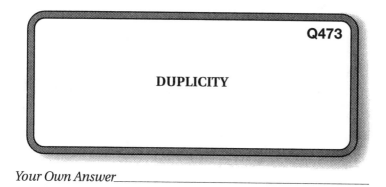

**Q473**

**DUPLICITY**

*Your Own Answer*_____

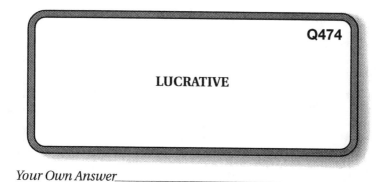

**Q474**

**LUCRATIVE**

*Your Own Answer*_____

# Correct Answers

**A472**

adj.—easily imposed; inclined
She gets an annual flu shot since she is
**susceptible** to becoming ill.

**A473**

n.—deception
She forgave his **duplicity** but divorced him anyway.

**A474**

adj.—profitable; gainful
She entered the pharmaceutical industry in the
belief that it would be **lucrative**.

# Questions

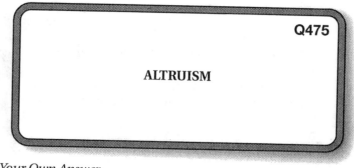

**Q475**

**ALTRUISM**

*Your Own Answer*_____

_____

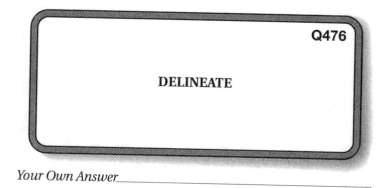

**Q476**

**DELINEATE**

*Your Own Answer*_____

_____

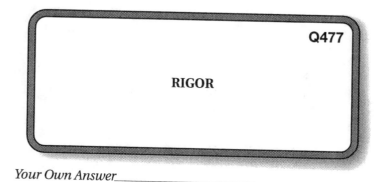

**Q477**

**RIGOR**

*Your Own Answer*_____

_____

# Correct Answers

**A475**

n.—unselfish devotion to the welfare of others rather than self

She displayed such **altruism** by giving up all of her belongings and joining the Peace Corps in Africa.

**A476**

v.—to outline; to describe

She **delineated** her plan so that everyone would have a basic understanding of it.

**A477**

n.—severity

She criticized the planning board's vote with **rigor**.

# *Questions*

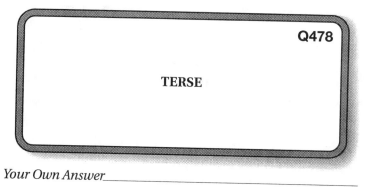

Q478

**TERSE**

*Your Own Answer*_____

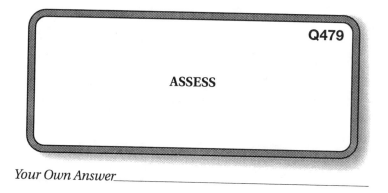

Q479

**ASSESS**

*Your Own Answer*_____

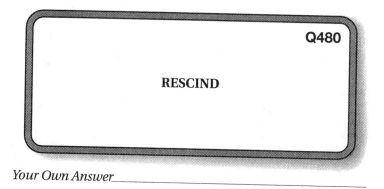

Q480

**RESCIND**

*Your Own Answer*_____

# *Correct Answers*

adj.—concise; abrupt
She believed in getting to the point, so she always gave **terse** answers.

v.—to estimate the value of
She **assessed** the possible rewards to see if the project was worth her time and effort.

v.—to retract; to discard; to revoke, repeal, or cancel
Sensing that the intent of the regulation had long ago been realized, the city agency **rescinded** the order.

# Questions

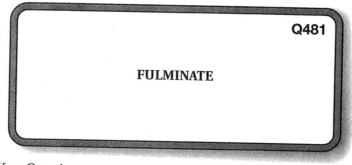

Q481

**FULMINATE**

*Your Own Answer*_____

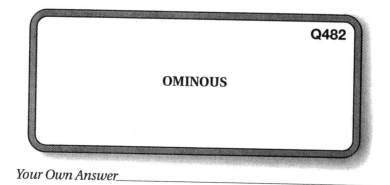

Q482

**OMINOUS**

*Your Own Answer*_____

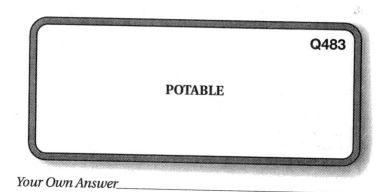

Q483

**POTABLE**

*Your Own Answer*_____

# Correct Answers

**A481**

v.—to issue a strong denunciation

Senator Shay **fulminated** against her opponent's double standard on campaign finance reform.

**A482**

adj.—threatening

Seeing **ominous** clouds on the horizon, the street fair organizers decided to fold up their tent and go home.

**A483**

n.—a beverage that is drinkable

Sea water isn't **potable**.

# *Questions*

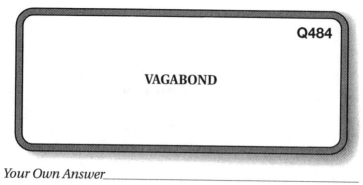

Q484

**VAGABOND**

*Your Own Answer*_____

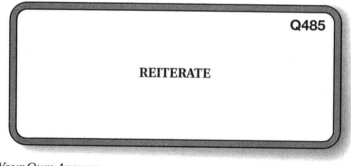

Q485

**REITERATE**

*Your Own Answer*_____

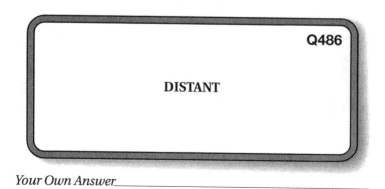

Q486

**DISTANT**

*Your Own Answer*_____

# Correct Answers

**A484**

n.—wanderer; one without a fixed place

Sam was the kind of **vagabond** who enjoyed hitching a ride on a freight train just to see where it would take him.

**A485**

v.—to repeat

Rose found that she had to **reiterate** almost everything, leading her to fear her husband was going deaf.

**A486**

adj.—having separations or being reserved

Rolonda's friends have become more **distant** in recent years.

# Questions

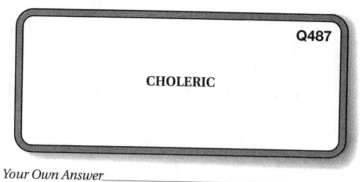

Q487

**CHOLERIC**

*Your Own Answer*_____

_____

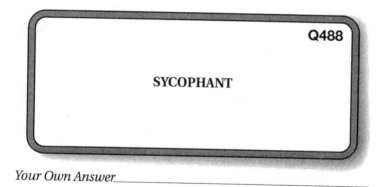

Q488

**SYCOPHANT**

*Your Own Answer*_____

_____

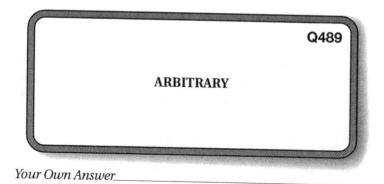

Q489

**ARBITRARY**

*Your Own Answer*_____

_____

# *Correct Answers*

**A487**

adj.—cranky; cantankerous; easily angered
Rolly becomes **choleric** when his views are challenged.

**A488**

n.—flatterer
Rodolfo honed his skills as a **sycophant**, hoping it would get him into Sylvia's good graces.

**A489**

adj.—based on one's preference or judgment
Rick admitted his decision had been **arbitrary**, as he claimed no expertise in the matter.

# Questions

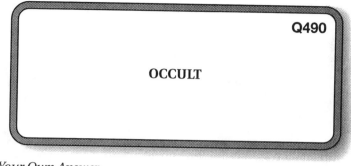

Q490

**OCCULT**

*Your Own Answer*_____

_____

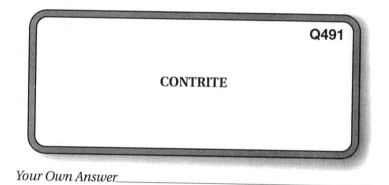

Q491

**CONTRITE**

*Your Own Answer*_____

_____

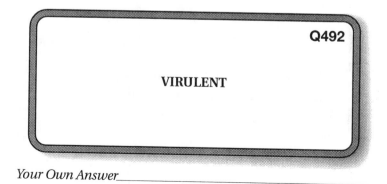

Q492

**VIRULENT**

*Your Own Answer*_____

_____

# Correct Answers

**A490**

adj.—mystical; mysterious

Relating to the **occult** world means entering a new realm.

**A491**

adj.—regretful; sorrowful

Regretting his decision not to attend college, the **contrite** man did not lead a very happy life.

**A492**

adj.—deadly; harmful; malicious

Rattlesnakes use a **virulent** substance to kill their prey.

# *Questions*

Q493

**ABOMINATE**

*Your Own Answer*_____

Q494

**FACILITATE**

*Your Own Answer*_____

Q495

**PREVALENT**

*Your Own Answer*_____

# *Correct Answers*

**A493**

v.—to loathe; to hate

Randall **abominated** all the traffic he encountered on every morning commute.

**A494**

v.—to make easier; to simplify

Ramps **facilitate** the entrance to buildings for many people.

**A495**

adj.—generally occurring

Rain is usually more **prevalent** than snow during April.

# *Questions*

Q496

**PEDANTIC**

*Your Own Answer*_____

Q497

**UNIVERSAL**

*Your Own Answer*_____

Q498

**OBLITERATE**

*Your Own Answer*_____

# Correct Answers

**A496**

adj.—emphasizing minutiae or form in scholarship or teaching

Professor Jones's lectures were so **pedantic** that his students sometimes had a tough time understanding the big picture.

**A497**

adj.—concerning everyone; existing everywhere

Pollution does not affect just one country or state—it's a **universal** problem.

**A498**

v.—destroy completely

Poaching nearly **obliterated** the world's whale population.

# *Questions*

Q499

**INDIGENOUS**

*Your Own Answer*_____

Q500

**PERPETUAL**

*Your Own Answer*_____

Q501

**CHIMERA**

*Your Own Answer*_____

# *Correct Answers*

**A499**

adj.—native to a region; inborn or innate
Piranha are **indigenous** to the tropics.

**A500**

adj.—never ceasing; continuous
**Perpetual** pain keeps the woman from walking.

**A501**

n.—an impossible fancy
Perhaps he saw a flying saucer, but perhaps it was
only a **chimera**.

# Questions

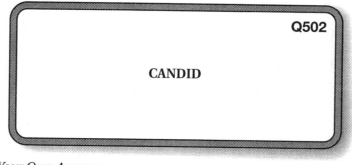

**Q502**

**CANDID**

*Your Own Answer*_____

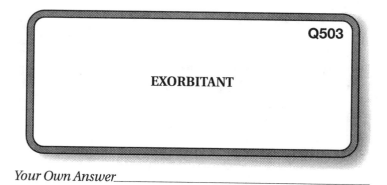

**Q503**

**EXORBITANT**

*Your Own Answer*_____

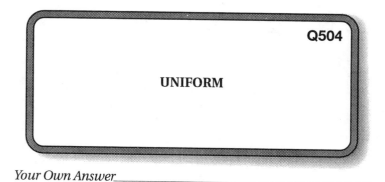

**Q504**

**UNIFORM**

*Your Own Answer*_____

# *Correct Answers*

**A502**

adj.—honest; truthful; sincere
People trust her because she's so **candid**.

**A503**

adj.—going beyond what is reasonable; excessive
Paying hundreds of dollars for the dress is an
**exorbitant** amount.

**A504**

adj.—consistent; unvaried; unchanging
Patrons of fast-food chains say they like the idea
of a **uniform** menu wherever they go.

# Questions

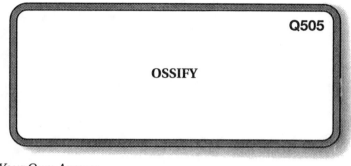

Q505

**OSSIFY**

*Your Own Answer*_____

Q506

**SLANDER**

*Your Own Answer*_____

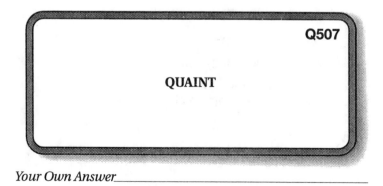

Q507

**QUAINT**

*Your Own Answer*_____

# Correct Answers

**A505**

v.—to turn to bone; to harden

Over time, the plant matter has **ossified**.

**A506**

v.—to defame; to maliciously misrepresent

Orville said he'd been **slandered**, and he asked the court who would—or could—give him his name back.

**A507**

adj.—old-fashioned; unusual; odd

One of the attractions of the bed-and-breakfast is its **quaint** setting in a charming New England village.

# *Questions*

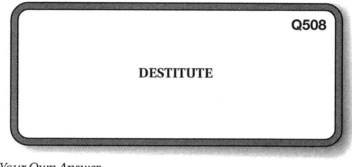

**Q508**

**DESTITUTE**

*Your Own Answer*_____

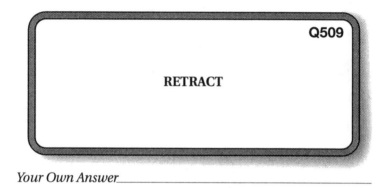

**Q509**

**RETRACT**

*Your Own Answer*_____

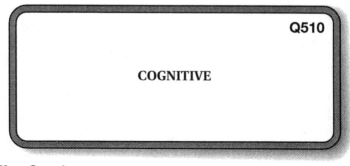

**Q510**

**COGNITIVE**

*Your Own Answer*_____

# *Correct Answers*

**A508**

adj.—poor; poverty-stricken

One Bangladeshi bank makes loans to **destitute** citizens so that they may overcome their poverty.

**A509**

v.—to draw or take back

Once you say something, it's hard to **retract**.

**A510**

adj.—possessing the power to think or meditate; meditative; capable of perception

Once the toddler was able to solve puzzles, it was obvious that her **cognitive** abilities were developing.

# *Questions*

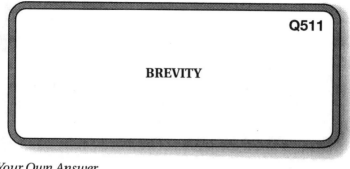

**Q511**

**BREVITY**

*Your Own Answer*_____

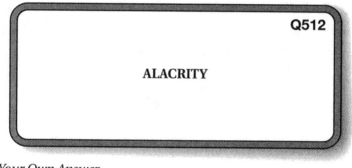

**Q512**

**ALACRITY**

*Your Own Answer*_____

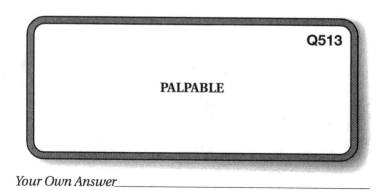

**Q513**

**PALPABLE**

*Your Own Answer*_____

# *Correct Answers*

**A511**

n.—briefness; shortness

On Top 40 AM radio, **brevity** was the coin of the realm.

**A512**

n.—cheerful promptness or speed

On the first day of her new job, the recent college graduate was able to leave early after completing all of her tasks with **alacrity**.

**A513**

adj.—touchable; clear; obvious

On a flight that had included a sudden 5,000-foot drop, the passengers' relief upon landing was **palpable**.

# Questions

Q514

**ANONYMOUS**

*Your Own Answer*_____

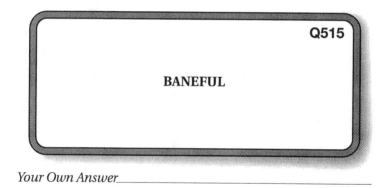

Q515

**BANEFUL**

*Your Own Answer*_____

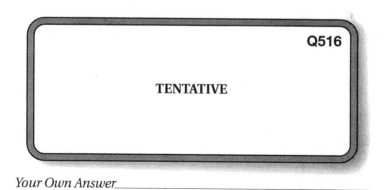

Q516

**TENTATIVE**

*Your Own Answer*_____

# Correct Answers

**A514**

adj.—nameless; unidentified

Not wishing to be identified by the police, he remained **anonymous** by returning the money he had stolen by sending it through the mail.

**A515**

adj.—deadly or causing distress, death

Not wearing a seat belt could be **baneful**.

**A516**

adj.—not confirmed; indefinite

Not knowing if he'd be able to get the days off, Al went ahead anyway and made **tentative** vacation plans with his pal.

# *Questions*

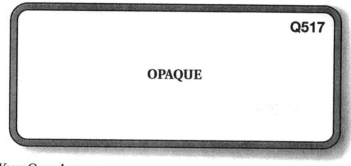

**Q517**

**OPAQUE**

*Your Own Answer*_____

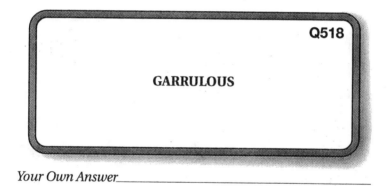

**Q518**

**GARRULOUS**

*Your Own Answer*_____

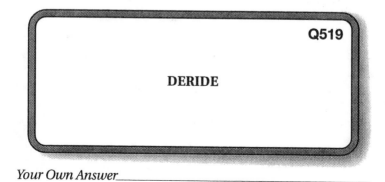

**Q519**

**DERIDE**

*Your Own Answer*_____

# Correct Answers

**A517**

adj.—dull; cloudy; non-transparent

Not having been washed for years, the once beautiful windows of the Victorian home became **opaque**.

**A518**

adj.—extremely talkative or wordy

No one wanted to speak with the **garrulous** man for fear of being stuck in a long, one-sided conversation.

**A519**

v.—to laugh at with contempt; to mock

No matter what he said, he was **derided**.

# *Questions*

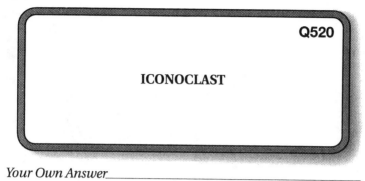

Q520

**ICONOCLAST**

*Your Own Answer*_____

Q521

**NEGLIGENCE**

*Your Own Answer*_____

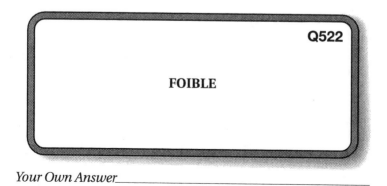

Q522

**FOIBLE**

*Your Own Answer*_____

# *Correct Answers*

**A520**

n.—one who smashes revered images; an attacker of cherished beliefs

Nietzche's attacks on government, religion, and custom made him an **iconoclast** of grand dimension.

**A521**

n.—carelessness

**Negligence** contributed to the accident: she was traveling too fast for the icy conditions.

**A522**

n.—a minor weakness of character

My major **foible** is an inability to resist chocolate.

# *Questions*

**DISSONANCE**

*Your Own Answer*_____

_____

**HYPOCRITICAL**

*Your Own Answer*_____

_____

**PAGAN**

*Your Own Answer*_____

_____

# *Correct Answers*

**A523**

n.—musical discord; a mingling of inharmonious sounds; nonmusical; disagreement; lack of harmony

Much twentieth-century music is not liked by classical music lovers because of the **dissonance** it holds and the harmonies it lacks.

**A524**

adj.—two-faced; deceptive

Most of his constituents believed the governor was **hypocritical** for calling his opponent a "mud-slinging hack" when his own campaign had slung more than its share of dirt.

**A525**

adj.—polytheistic

Moses, distraught over some of his people's continuing **pagan** ways, smashed the stone tablets bearing the Ten Commandments.

# *Questions*

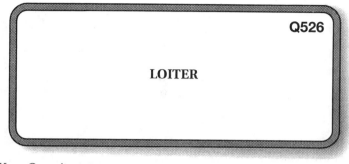

Q526

**LOITER**

*Your Own Answer*_____

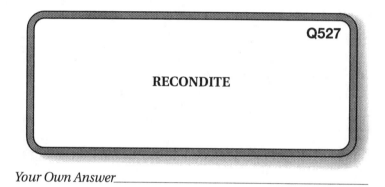

Q527

**RECONDITE**

*Your Own Answer*_____

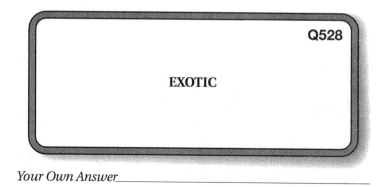

Q528

**EXOTIC**

*Your Own Answer*_____

# *Correct Answers*

**A526**

v.—to spend time aimlessly

Many teenagers **loiter** around the mall when there is nothing else to do.

**A527**

adj.—hard to understand; concealed; characterized by profound scholarship

Many scientific theories are **recondite**, and therefore not known at all by the general public.

**A528**

adj.—unusual; striking; foreign

Many people asked the name of her **exotic** perfume.

# *Questions*

Q529

**DUBIOUS**

*Your Own Answer*_____

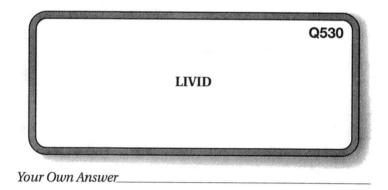

Q530

**LIVID**

*Your Own Answer*_____

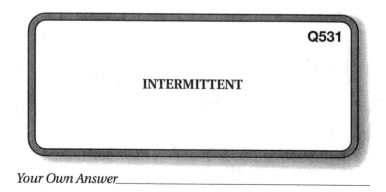

Q531

**INTERMITTENT**

*Your Own Answer*_____

# Correct Answers

**A529**

adj.—doubtful; uncertain; skeptical; suspicious

Many people are **dubious** about the possibility of intelligent life on other planets.

**A530**

adj.—1. black-and-blue; discolored  2. enraged; irate

1. After the accident, her leg was **livid**.
2. When she found out she had been robbed, the woman was **livid**.

**A531**

adj.—periodic; occasional

Luckily, the snow was only **intermittent**, so the accumulation was slight.

# *Questions*

**USURY**

*Your Own Answer*_____

**KINSHIP**

*Your Own Answer*_____

**MENAGERIE**

*Your Own Answer*_____

# *Correct Answers*

**A532**

n.—the art of lending money at illegal rates of interest

Loan sharks frequently practice **usury**, but their debtors usually have little choice but to keep quiet and pay up.

**A533**

n.—family relationship; affinity

Living in close proximity increased the **kinship** of the family.

**A534**

n.—a place to keep or a collection of wild or strange animals

Little Ryan couldn't wait to visit the zoo to see the **menagerie** of wild boars.

# *Questions*

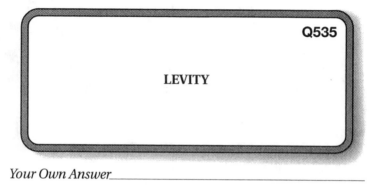

Q535

**LEVITY**

*Your Own Answer*_____

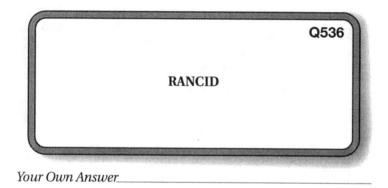

Q536

**RANCID**

*Your Own Answer*_____

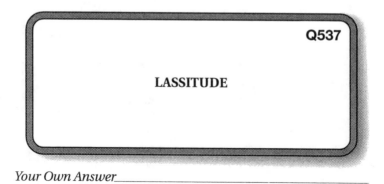

Q537

**LASSITUDE**

*Your Own Answer*_____

# Correct Answers

**A535**

n.—silliness; lack of seriousness
**Levity** is a necessary trait for a comedian.

**A536**

adj.—having a bad odor
Left out too long, the meat turned **rancid**.

**A537**

n.—a state of being tired or listless
**Lassitude** was evident in the nurses who had been working for 24 hours straight.

# *Questions*

**Q538**

**COMPROMISE**

*Your Own Answer*_____

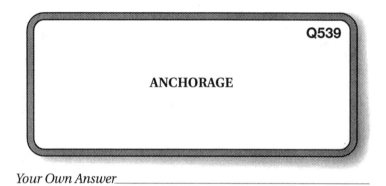

**Q539**

**ANCHORAGE**

*Your Own Answer*_____

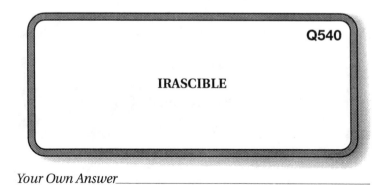

**Q540**

**IRASCIBLE**

*Your Own Answer*_____

# *Correct Answers*

**A538**

v.—to settle by mutual adjustment

Labor leaders and the automakers **compromised** by agreeing to a starting wage of $16 an hour in exchange for concessions on health-care premiums.

**A539**

n.—something that can be relied on

Knowing the neighbors were right next door was an **anchorage** for the elderly woman.

**A540**

adj.—prone to anger

Knowing that the king was **irascible**, the servants decided not to tell him about the broken crystal.

# *Questions*

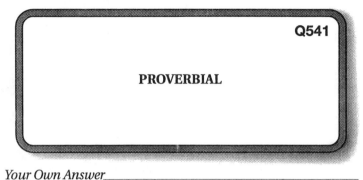

**Q541**

**PROVERBIAL**

*Your Own Answer*_____

**Q542**

**HACKNEYED**

*Your Own Answer*_____

**Q543**

**HAGGARD**

*Your Own Answer*_____

# Correct Answers

## A541

adj.—well-known because it is commonly referred to

King Solomon's **proverbial** wisdom has been admired through the ages.

## A542

adj.—commonplace; trite

Just when you thought neckties were becoming a **hackneyed** gift item, along comes the Grateful Dead collection.

## A543

adj.—tired-looking; fatigued

Just by looking at her **haggard** features, you can tell she has not slept for many hours.

# *Questions*

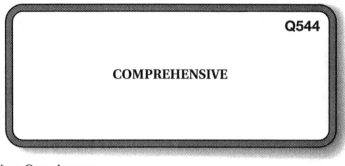

**Q544**

**COMPREHENSIVE**

*Your Own Answer*_____

**Q545**

**TOXIC**

*Your Own Answer*_____

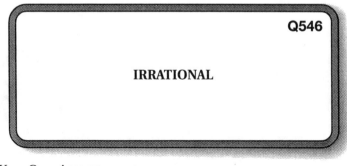

**Q546**

**IRRATIONAL**

*Your Own Answer*_____

# Correct Answers

**A544**

adj.—all-inclusive; complete; thorough
It's the only health facility around to offer **comprehensive** care.

**A545**

adj.—poisonous
It's best to store cleansing solutions out of children's reach because of their **toxic** contents.

**A546**

adj.—not logical
It would be **irrational** to climb Mt. Everest without some very warm clothing.

# *Questions*

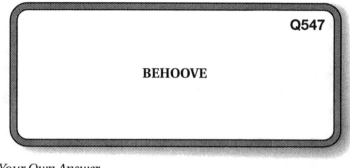

Q547

**BEHOOVE**

*Your Own Answer*_____

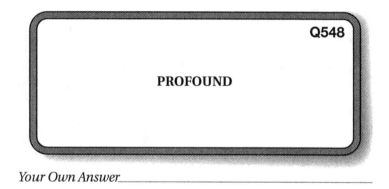

Q548

**PROFOUND**

*Your Own Answer*_____

Q549

**INSTIGATE**

*Your Own Answer*_____

# Correct Answers

**A547**

v.—to be advantageous; to be necessary

It will **behoove** the students to buy their textbooks early.

**A548**

adj.—deep; knowledgeable; thorough

It was with **profound** regret and sorrow that the family had to leave their homeland for a more prosperous country.

**A549**

v.—to start; to provoke

It was uncertain to the police as to which party **instigated** the riot.

# *Questions*

Q550

**CONVERGE**

*Your Own Answer*_____

Q551

**IGNOBLE**

*Your Own Answer*_____

Q552

**CHARLATAN**

*Your Own Answer*_____

# *Correct Answers*

**A550**

v.—to move toward one point (opposite: diverge)

It was obvious that an accident was going to occur as the onlookers watched the two cars **converge.**

**A551**

adj.—shameful; dishonorable

It was **ignoble** to disgrace the family in front of all of the townspeople.

**A552**

n.—an impostor; fake

It was finally discovered that the **charlatan** sitting on the throne was not the real king.

# *Questions*

Q553

**UNOBTRUSIVE**

*Your Own Answer*_____

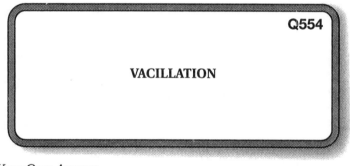

Q554

**VACILLATION**

*Your Own Answer*_____

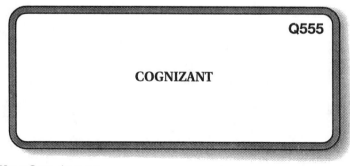

Q555

**COGNIZANT**

*Your Own Answer*_____

# *Correct Answers*

**A553**

adj.—inconspicuous; reserved
It was easy to miss the **unobtrusive** plaque above the fireplace.

**A554**

n.—fluctuation
It was difficult to draw a conclusion from the experiments since there was so much **vacillation** in the results.

**A555**

adj.—aware of; perceptive
It was critical to establish whether the defendant was **cognizant** of his rights.

# Questions

Q556

**INADVERTENT**

*Your Own Answer*_____

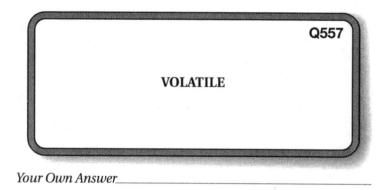

Q557

**VOLATILE**

*Your Own Answer*_____

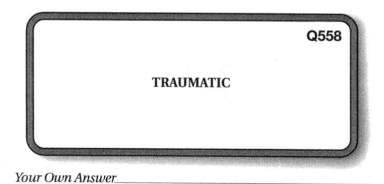

Q558

**TRAUMATIC**

*Your Own Answer*_____

# *Correct Answers*

**A556**

adj.—not on purpose; unintentional

It was an **inadvertent** error, to be sure, but nonetheless a mistake that required correction.

**A557**

adj.—changeable; undependable; unstable

It was a **volatile** situation; no one was willing to bet how things would turn out.

**A558**

adj.—causing a violent injury

It was a **traumatic** accident, leaving the driver with a broken vertebra, a smashed wrist, and a concussion.

# Questions

Q559

**NOVEL**

*Your Own Answer*_____

_____

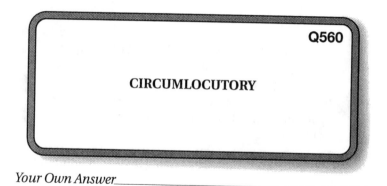

Q560

**CIRCUMLOCUTORY**

*Your Own Answer*_____

_____

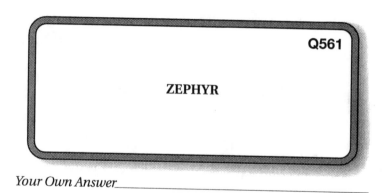

Q561

**ZEPHYR**

*Your Own Answer*_____

_____

# Correct Answers

**A559**

adj.—new

It was a **novel** idea for the rock group to play classical music.

**A560**

adj.—being too long, as in a description or expression; a roundabout, indirect, or ungainly way of expressing something

It was a **circumlocutory** documentary that could have been cut to half its running time to say twice as much.

**A561**

n.—a gentle wind; breeze

It was a beautiful day, with a **zephyr** blowing in from the sea.

# *Questions*

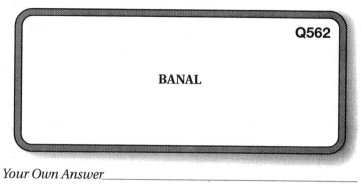

Q562

**BANAL**

*Your Own Answer*_____

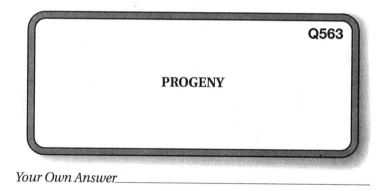

Q563

**PROGENY**

*Your Own Answer*_____

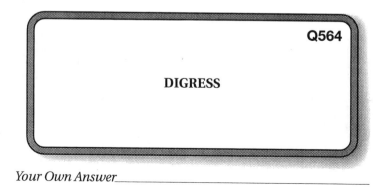

Q564

**DIGRESS**

*Your Own Answer*_____

# Correct Answers

**A562**

adj.—trite, without freshness or originality

It was a **banal** suggestion to have the annual picnic in the park since that was where it had been for the past five years.

**A563**

n.—children; offspring

It is through his **progeny** that his name shall live on.

**A564**

v.—to stray from the subject; to wander from the topic

It is important to not **digress** from the plan of action.

# Questions

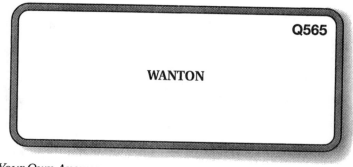

**Q565**

**WANTON**

*Your Own Answer*_____

_____

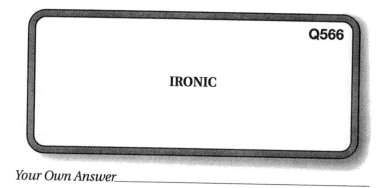

**Q566**

**IRONIC**

*Your Own Answer*_____

_____

**Q567**

**INTANGIBLE**

*Your Own Answer*_____

_____

# Correct Answers

**A565**

adj.—unruly; excessive

It is hard to lose weight when one has a **wanton** desire for sweets.

**A566**

adj.—contradictory; inconsistent; sarcastic

Is it not **ironic** that Americans will toss out left-over French fries while people around the globe continue to starve?

**A567**

adj.—incapable of being touched; immaterial

**Intangible** though it may be, sometimes just knowing that the work you do helps others is reward enough.

# *Questions*

**Q568**

INERT

*Your Own Answer*_____

---

**Q569**

FEASIBLE

*Your Own Answer*_____

---

**Q570**

INCESSANT

*Your Own Answer*_____

# Correct Answers

**A568**

adj.—not reacting chemically; inactive
**Inert** gases like krypton and argon can enhance window insulation.

**A569**

adj.—reasonable; practical
Increased exercise is a **feasible** means of weight loss.

**A570**

adj.—constant; continual
**Incessant** rain caused the river to flood over its banks.

# *Questions*

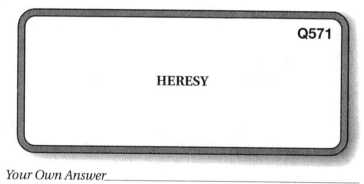

**Q571**

**HERESY**

Your Own Answer_____

**Q572**

**REALM**

Your Own Answer_____

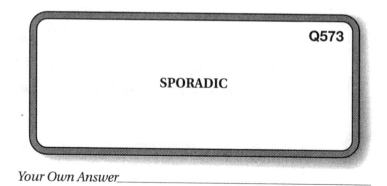

**Q573**

**SPORADIC**

Your Own Answer_____

# Correct Answers

**A571**

n.—opinion contrary to popular belief
In this town it is considered **heresy** to want parking spaces to have meters.

**A572**

n.—an area; sphere of activity
In the **realm** of health care, the issue of who pays and how is never far from the surface.

**A573**

adj.—rarely occurring or appearing; intermittent
In the desert, there is usually only **sporadic** rainfall.

# *Questions*

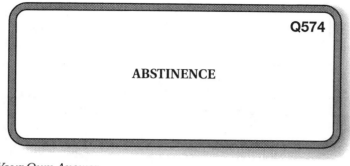

Q574

**ABSTINENCE**

*Your Own Answer*_____

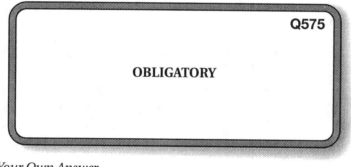

Q575

**OBLIGATORY**

*Your Own Answer*_____

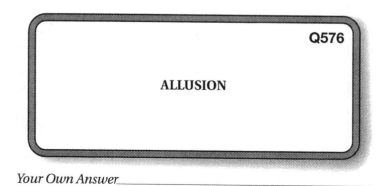

Q576

**ALLUSION**

*Your Own Answer*_____

# Correct Answers

**A574**

n.—the act or process of voluntarily refraining from any action or practice; self-control; chastity

In preparation for the Olympic games, the athletes practiced **abstinence** from red meat and junk food, adhering instead to a menu of pasta and produce.

**A575**

adj.—mandatory; necessary; legally or morally binding

In order to provide a reliable source of revenue for the government, it is **obligatory** for each citizen to pay taxes.

**A576**

n.—an indirect reference (often literary); a hint

In modern plays, **allusions** are often made to ancient drama.

# *Questions*

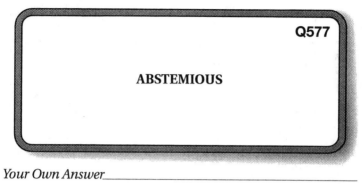

**Q577**

**ABSTEMIOUS**

*Your Own Answer*_____

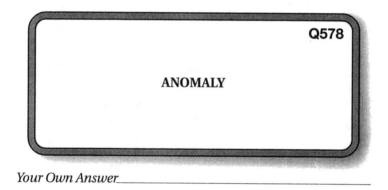

**Q578**

**ANOMALY**

*Your Own Answer*_____

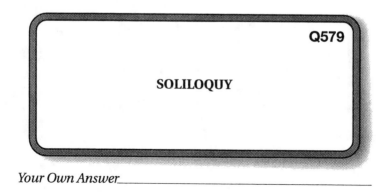

**Q579**

**SOLILOQUY**

*Your Own Answer*_____

# Correct Answers

**A577**

adj.—sparing in use of food or drink

In many **abstemious** cultures, the people are so thin because of their belief that too much taken into the body leads to contamination of the soul.

**A578**

n.—an oddity; inconsistency; a deviation from the norm

In a parking lot full of Buicks, Chevys, and Plymouths, the Jaguar was an **anomaly**.

**A579**

n.—a talk one has with oneself (esp. on stage)

Imagine T. S. Eliot's poem "The Waste Land" performed on stage as a kind of **soliloquy**!

# Questions

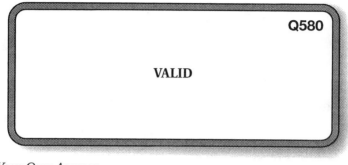

**Q580**

**VALID**

*Your Own Answer*_____

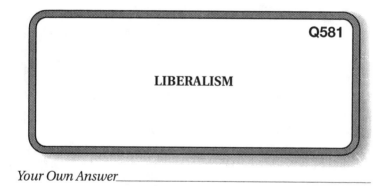

**Q581**

**LIBERALISM**

*Your Own Answer*_____

**Q582**

**INDOLENT**

*Your Own Answer*_____

# *Correct Answers*

**A580**

adj.—acceptable; legal
Illness is a **valid** reason for missing school.

**A581**

n.—believing in personal freedom (favoring reform or progress)
If you believe in **liberalism**, the First Amendment
is sacrosanct.

**A582**

adj.—lazy; inactive
If we find him goofing off one more time, we won't
be able to escape the fact that he's **indolent**.

# *Questions*

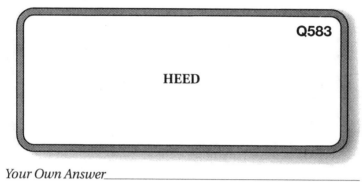

**Q583**

**HEED**

*Your Own Answer*_____

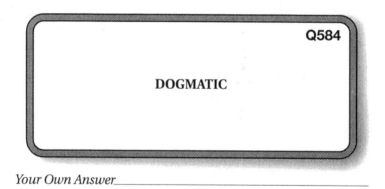

**Q584**

**DOGMATIC**

*Your Own Answer*_____

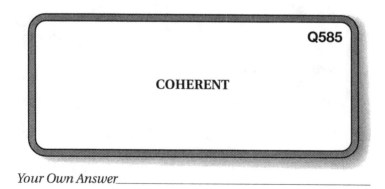

**Q585**

**COHERENT**

*Your Own Answer*_____

# *Correct Answers*

v.—to obey; to yield to

If the peasant **heeds** the king's commands, she will be able to keep her land.

adj.—stubborn; biased; opinionated

If I say he's **dogmatic**, he'll say he sticks to his guns.

adj.—sticking together; connected; logical; consistent

If he couldn't make a **coherent** speech, how could he run for office?

# *Questions*

Q586

**CONTEST**

*Your Own Answer*_____

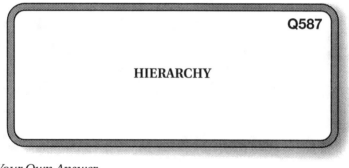

Q587

**HIERARCHY**

*Your Own Answer*_____

Q588

**MUSE**

*Your Own Answer*_____

# Correct Answers

**A586**

v.—to attempt to disprove or invalidate

I will attempt to **contest** the criminal charges against me.

**A587**

n.—a system of persons or things arranged according to rank

I was put at the bottom of the **hierarchy**, while Jane was put at the top.

**A588**

v.—to think or speak meditatively

I expect I'll have to **muse** on that question for a while.

# *Questions*

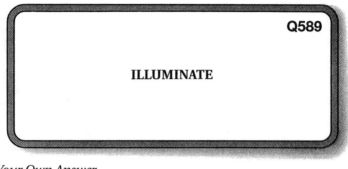

Q589

**ILLUMINATE**

*Your Own Answer*_____

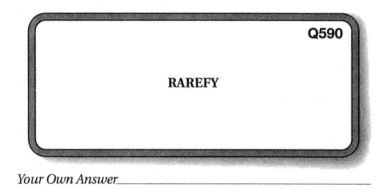

Q590

**RAREFY**

*Your Own Answer*_____

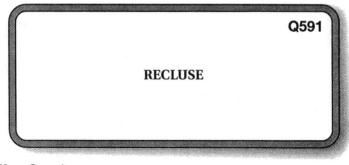

Q591

**RECLUSE**

*Your Own Answer*_____

# *Correct Answers*

**A589**

v.—to make understandable

I asked a classmate to **illuminate** the professor's far-ranging lecture for me.

**A590**

v.—to make less dense or refined

Hunters were called in to **rarefy** the deer population.

**A591**

n.—solitary and shut off from society

Howard Hughes, among the most famous and enigmatic figures of the twentieth century, ultimately retreated to a life as a **recluse**.

# *Questions*

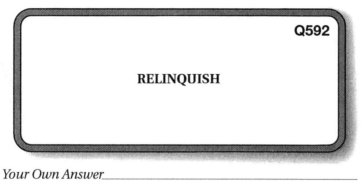

**Q592**

**RELINQUISH**

*Your Own Answer*_____

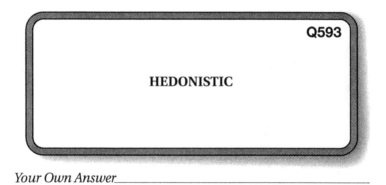

**Q593**

**HEDONISTIC**

*Your Own Answer*_____

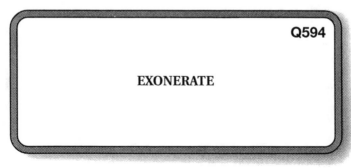

**Q594**

**EXONERATE**

*Your Own Answer*_____

# *Correct Answers*

**A592**

v.—to let go; to abandon

House Speaker Jim Wright had to **relinquish** his position after an ethics investigation undermined his authority.

**A593**

adj.—pleasure-seeking

Hot tubs, good food, and a plethora of leisure time were hallmarks of this **hedonistic** society.

**A594**

v.—to declare or prove blameless

Hopefully, the judge will **exonerate** you of any wrongdoing.

# Questions

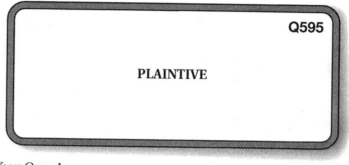

Q595

**PLAINTIVE**

*Your Own Answer*_____

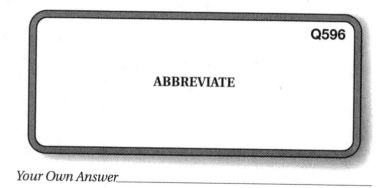

Q596

**ABBREVIATE**

*Your Own Answer*_____

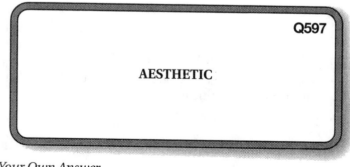

Q597

**AESTHETIC**

*Your Own Answer*_____

# Correct Answers

A595

adj.—being mournful or sad
His wife's death made Sam **plaintive**.

A596

v.—to shorten; to compress; to diminish
His vacation to Japan was **abbreviated** when he acquired an illness treatable only in the United States.

A597

adj.—artistic; of beauty; sensitive to beauty
His review made one wonder what kind of **aesthetic** taste the critic had.

# Questions

Q598

**UNEQUIVOCAL**

*Your Own Answer*_____

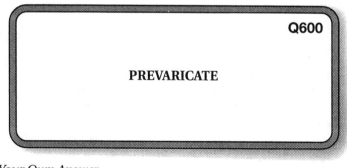

Q599

**PANEGYRIC**

*Your Own Answer*_____

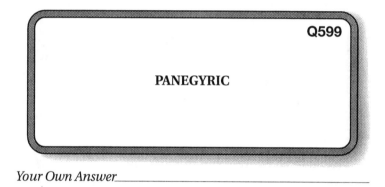

Q600

**PREVARICATE**

*Your Own Answer*_____

# *Correct Answers*

**A598**

adj.—clear; definite

His response was **unequivocal**, which seemed unusual for a politician.

---

**A599**

n.—high praise

His **panegyric** to his opponent stood in sharp contrast to the harsh tenor of the campaign.

---

**A600**

v.—to speak equivocally or evasively; to lie

His mother knew no one else could have done it, but the child foolishly **prevaricated** about the stain on the rug.

# Questions

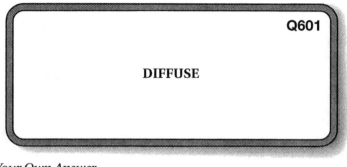

Q601

**DIFFUSE**

*Your Own Answer*_____

Q602

**INCISIVE**

*Your Own Answer*_____

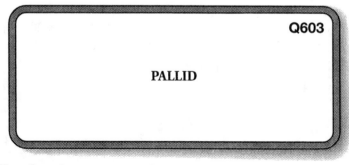

Q603

**PALLID**

*Your Own Answer*_____

# *Correct Answers*

**A601**

adj.—spread out; verbose (wordy); not focused

His monologue was so **diffuse** that all his points were lost.

**A602**

adj.—to be acute or penetrating

His **incisive** questioning helped settle the matter.

**A603**

adj.—sallow; colorless

His illness made him **pallid**.

# *Questions*

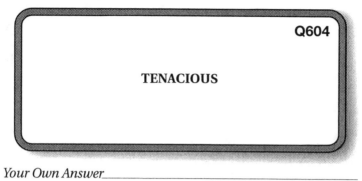

**Q604**

**TENACIOUS**

*Your Own Answer*_____

**Q605**

**GRANDIOSE**

*Your Own Answer*_____

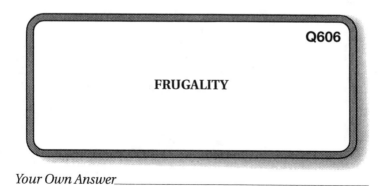

**Q606**

**FRUGALITY**

*Your Own Answer*_____

# *Correct Answers*

**A604**

adj.—persistently holding to something
His hold on his dreams is as **tenacious** as anyone's
I know.

**A605**

adj.—magnificent; flamboyant
His **grandiose** idea was to rent a plane to fly to
Las Vegas for the night.

**A606**

n.—thrift; economical use or expenditure
His **frugality** limited him to purchasing the item
for which he had a coupon.

# Questions

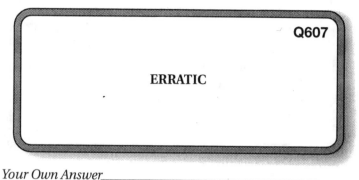

Q607

**ERRATIC**

*Your Own Answer*_____

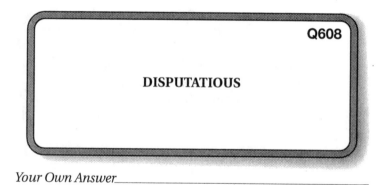

Q608

**DISPUTATIOUS**

*Your Own Answer*_____

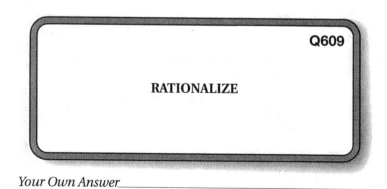

Q609

**RATIONALIZE**

*Your Own Answer*_____

# *Correct Answers*

**A607**

adj.—unpredictable; irregular

His **erratic** behavior was attributed to the shocking news he had received.

**A608**

adj.—argumentative; inclined to disputes

His **disputatious** streak eventually wore down his fellow Parliament members.

**A609**

v.—to offer reasons for; to account for on rational grounds

His daughter attempted to **rationalize** why she had dropped out of college, but she could not give any good reasons.

# Questions

**Q610**

**COPIOUS**

*Your Own Answer*_____

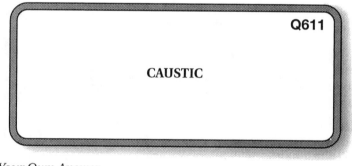

**Q611**

**CAUSTIC**

*Your Own Answer*_____

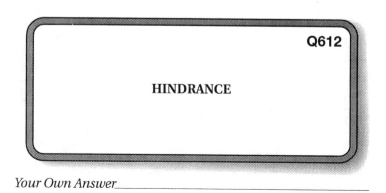

**Q612**

**HINDRANCE**

*Your Own Answer*_____

# *Correct Answers*

---

**A610**

adj.—full of information

His **copious** notes gave the reporter all of the information needed.

---

**A611**

adj.—burning; sarcastic; harsh

His **caustic** sense of humor doesn't go over so well when people don't know what they're in for.

---

**A612**

n.—blockage; obstacle

His assistance often seems to be more of a **hindrance** than a help.

# *Questions*

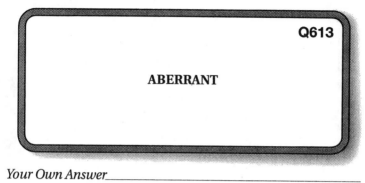

Q613

**ABERRANT**

*Your Own Answer*_____

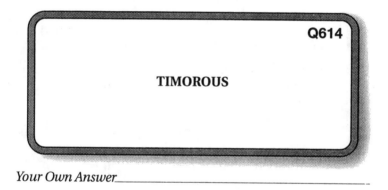

Q614

**TIMOROUS**

*Your Own Answer*_____

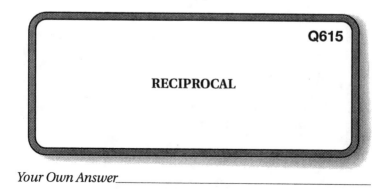

Q615

**RECIPROCAL**

*Your Own Answer*_____

# *Correct Answers*

**A613**

adj.— abnormal; straying from the normal or usual path

His **aberrant** behavior led his friends to worry the divorce had taken its toll.

**A614**

adj.— fearful

Hillary came to accept him as a **timorous** soul who needed succor.

**A615**

adj.— mutual; having the same relationship to each other

Hernando's membership in the Picture of Health Fitness Center gives him **reciprocal** privileges at 245 health clubs around the U.S.

# *Questions*

**Q616**

**INNATE**

*Your Own Answer*_____

---

**Q617**

**PRUDENT**

*Your Own Answer*_____

---

**Q618**

**PERVADE**

*Your Own Answer*_____

# Correct Answers

**A616**

adj.—natural; inborn
Her talent is wondrous: it hardly matters whether
it's **innate** or acquired.

**A617**

adj.—wise; careful; prepared
Her **prudent** ways saved her money, time, and
trouble.

**A618**

v.—to occupy the whole of
Her perfume was so strong that it **pervaded** the
whole room.

# *Questions*

Q619

**TRIBUTE**

*Your Own Answer*_____

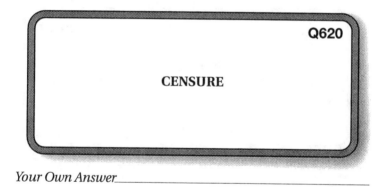

Q620

**CENSURE**

*Your Own Answer*_____

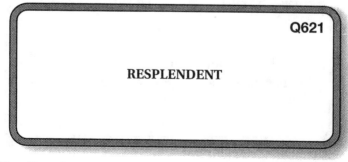

Q621

**RESPLENDENT**

*Your Own Answer*_____

# Correct Answers

A619

n.—expression of admiration

Her performance was a **tribute** to her retiring teacher.

A620

v.—to criticize or disapprove of

Her parents **censured** her idea of dropping out of school.

A621

adj.—dazzling and shining

Her new diamond was **resplendent** in the sunshine.

# *Questions*

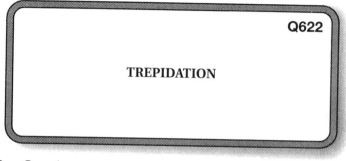

Q622

**TREPIDATION**

*Your Own Answer*_____

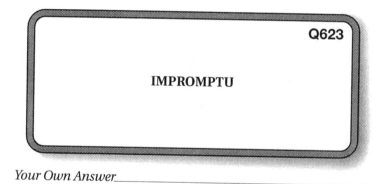

Q623

**IMPROMPTU**

*Your Own Answer*_____

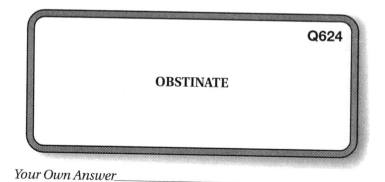

Q624

**OBSTINATE**

*Your Own Answer*_____

# *Correct Answers*

n.—apprehension; uneasiness
Her long absence caused more than a little **trepidation**.

adj.—without preparation
Her **impromptu** speech was well-received, giving her new confidence in her ability to speak-off-the-cuff.

adj.—stubborn
Her father would not allow her to stay out past midnight; she thought he was **obstinate** because he would not change his mind.

# Questions

**GERMANE**

*Your Own Answer*_____

_____

**DISAPPROBATION**

*Your Own Answer*_____

_____

**DIFFIDENT**

*Your Own Answer*_____

# *Correct Answers*

adj.—pertinent; related; to the point
Her essay contained **germane** information, relevant to the new Constitutional amendment.

n.—disapproval
Her **disapprobation** of her daughter's fiancé divided the family.

adj.—timid; lacking self-confidence
Her **diffident** sister couldn't work up the courage to ask for the sale.

# *Questions*

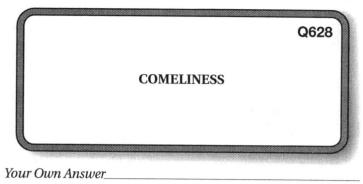

Q628

**COMELINESS**

*Your Own Answer*_____

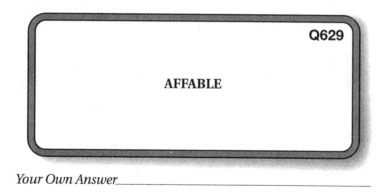

Q629

**AFFABLE**

*Your Own Answer*_____

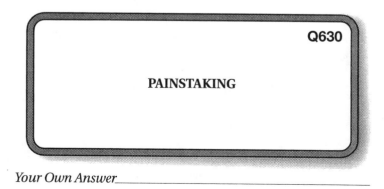

Q630

**PAINSTAKING**

*Your Own Answer*_____

# *Correct Answers*

**A628**

n.—beauty; attractiveness in appearance or behavior

Her **comeliness** attracted many suitors.

**A629**

adj.—friendly; amiable; good-natured

Her **affable** puppy loved to play with children.

**A630**

adj.—thorough; careful; precise

Helga's **painstaking** research paid off with a top grade on her essay.

# Questions

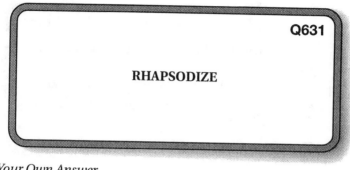

Q631

**RHAPSODIZE**

*Your Own Answer*_____

_____

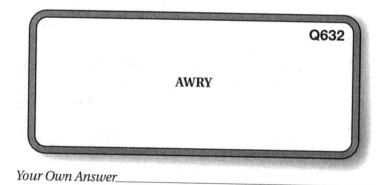

Q632

**AWRY**

*Your Own Answer*_____

_____

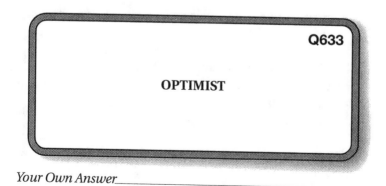

Q633

**OPTIMIST**

*Your Own Answer*_____

_____

# Correct Answers

**A631**

v.—to speak or write in a very enthusiastic manner

Hearing the general **rhapsodize** about his time as a plebe sent a wave of recognition through the academy grads.

**A632**

adv.—crooked(ly); uneven(ly); wrong; askew

Hearing the explosion in the laboratory, the scientist realized the experiment had gone **awry**.

**A633**

n.—person who hopes for the best, sees the good side

He's ever the **optimist**, always seeing the glass as half full.

# *Questions*

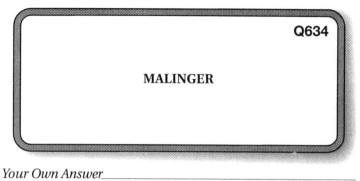

Q634

**MALINGER**

*Your Own Answer*_____

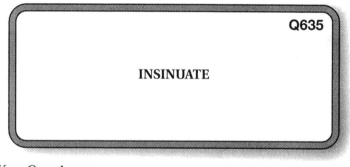

Q635

**INSINUATE**

*Your Own Answer*_____

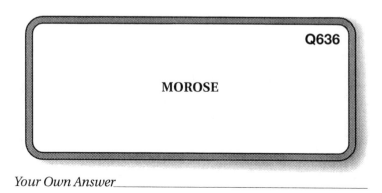

Q636

**MOROSE**

*Your Own Answer*_____

# Correct Answers

**A634**

v.—to pretend to be ill in order to escape work

He will **malinger** on Friday so he can go to the movies.

**A635**

v.—to work into gradually and indirectly

He will **insinuate** his need for a vacation by saying how tired he has been lately.

**A636**

adj.—moody, despondent

He was very **morose** over the death of his pet.

# *Questions*

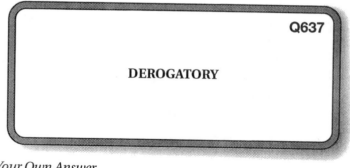

**Q637**

**DEROGATORY**

Your Own Answer_____

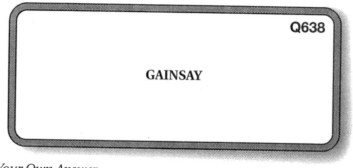

**Q638**

**GAINSAY**

Your Own Answer_____

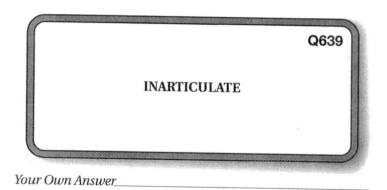

**Q639**

**INARTICULATE**

Your Own Answer_____

# Correct Answers

**A637**

adj.—belittling; uncomplimentary

He was upset because his annual review was full of **derogatory** comments.

**A638**

v.—to speak against; to contradict; to deny

He was the only one to **gainsay** the law, so it was passed.

**A639**

adj.—speechless; unable to speak clearly

He was so **inarticulate** that he had trouble making himself understood.

# *Questions*

Q640

**ILLUSORY**

*Your Own Answer*_____

---

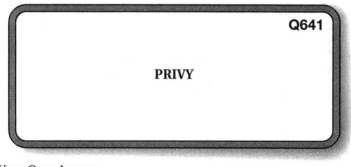

Q641

**PRIVY**

*Your Own Answer*_____

---

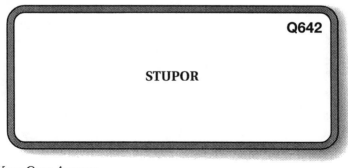

Q642

**STUPOR**

*Your Own Answer*_____

# Correct Answers

**A640**

adj.—unreal; false; deceptive
He was proven guilty when his alibi was found to be **illusory**.

**A641**

adj.—private; confidential
He was one of a handful of people **privy** to the news of the pending merger.

**A642**

n.—a stunned or bewildered condition
He was in a **stupor** after being hit on the head.

# *Questions*

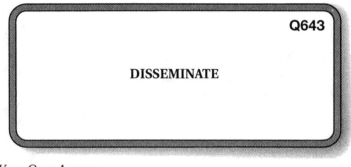

**Q643**

**DISSEMINATE**

*Your Own Answer*_____

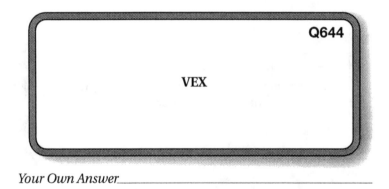

**Q644**

**VEX**

*Your Own Answer*_____

**Q645**

**UNPRETENTIOUS**

*Your Own Answer*_____

# *Correct Answers*

**A643**

v.—to circulate; to scatter

He was hired to **disseminate** newspapers to everyone in the town.

**A644**

v.—to trouble the nerves; to annoy

He was beginning to **vex** her by asking a question every time she passed his locker.

**A645**

adj.—simple; plain; modest

He was an **unpretentious** farmer: an old John Deere and a beat-up Ford pick-up were all he needed to get the job done.

# *Questions*

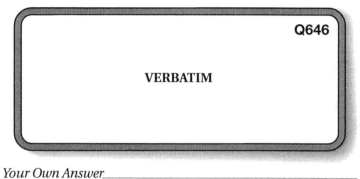

Q646

**VERBATIM**

*Your Own Answer*_____

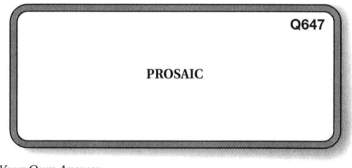

Q647

**PROSAIC**

*Your Own Answer*_____

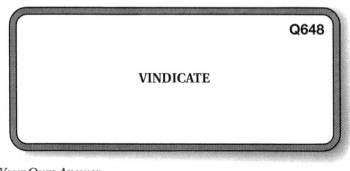

Q648

**VINDICATE**

*Your Own Answer*_____

# Correct Answers

adj.—employing the same words as another; literal

He was accused of plagiarism since he repeated **verbatim** what one of his professors had written many years before.

adj.—tiresome; ordinary

He wanted to do something new; he was tired of the **prosaic** activities his parents suggested each day.

v.—to free from charge; to clear

He **vindicated** the suspect by proving his alibi as truthful.

# *Questions*

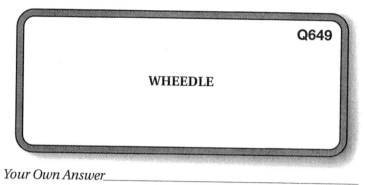

**Q649**

**WHEEDLE**

*Your Own Answer*_____

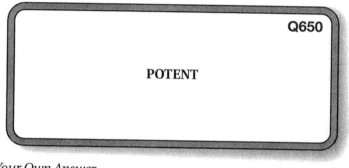

**Q650**

**POTENT**

*Your Own Answer*_____

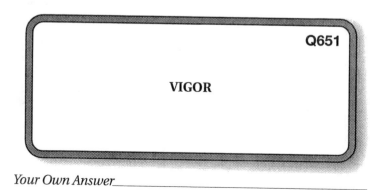

**Q651**

**VIGOR**

*Your Own Answer*_____

# Correct Answers

**A649**

v.—to try to persuade; to coax

He tried hard to **wheedle** his father into buying him a car.

**A650**

adj.—having great power or physical strength

He took very **potent** medication and felt better immediately.

**A651**

n.—energy; forcefulness

He took on the task with great **vigor**, proving his doubters wrong.

# *Questions*

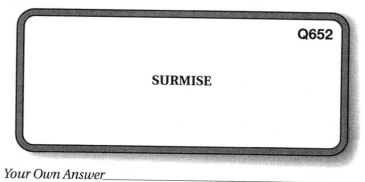

Q652

**SURMISE**

*Your Own Answer*_____

Q653

**SEETHE**

*Your Own Answer*_____

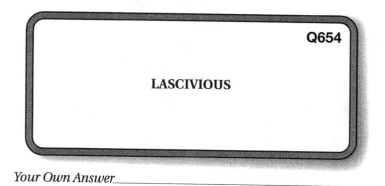

Q654

**LASCIVIOUS**

*Your Own Answer*_____

# Correct Answers

**A652**

v.—to draw an inference; to guess

He **surmised** how the play would end before the second act began.

**A653**

v.—to be in a state of emotional turmoil; to become angry

He **seethed** at the prospect of losing the business to his conniving uncle.

**A654**

adj.—indecent; immoral; involving lust

He said it was a harmless pin-up poster, but his mother called it **lascivious**.

# *Questions*

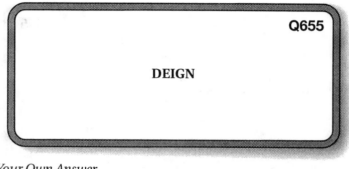

Q655

**DEIGN**

*Your Own Answer*_____

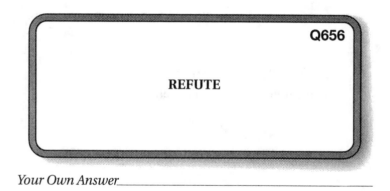

Q656

**REFUTE**

*Your Own Answer*_____

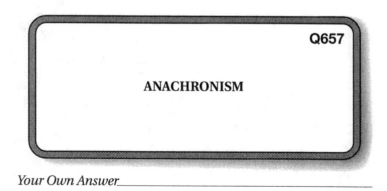

Q657

**ANACHRONISM**

*Your Own Answer*_____

# *Correct Answers*

v.—to condescend; to stoop

He said he wouldn't **deign** to dignify her statement with a response.

v.—to challenge; to disprove

He **refuted** the proposal, deeming it unfair.

n.—something out of place in time (e.g., an airplane in 1492)

He realized that the film about cavemen contained an **anachronism** when he saw a jet cut across the horizon during a hunting scene.

# *Questions*

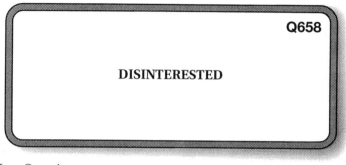

Q658

**DISINTERESTED**

*Your Own Answer*_____

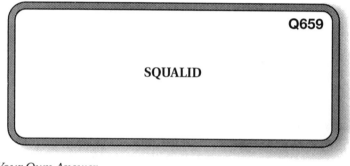

Q659

**SQUALID**

*Your Own Answer*_____

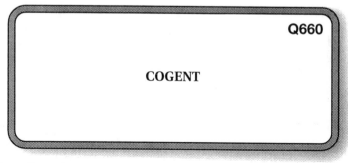

Q660

**COGENT**

*Your Own Answer*_____

# *Correct Answers*

**A658**

adj.—neutral; unbiased
He never takes sides; he's always **disinterested**.

**A659**

adj.—filthy; wretched (from squalor)
He makes good money, but I would never want
to work in those **squalid** crawl spaces.

**A660**

adj.—to the point; clear; convincing in its clarity
and presentation
He made a short, **cogent** speech which his audience easily understood.

# *Questions*

Q661

**LAUD**

*Your Own Answer*_____

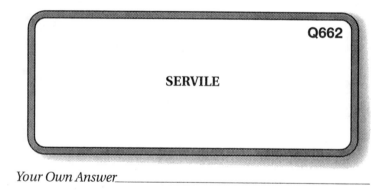

Q662

**SERVILE**

*Your Own Answer*_____

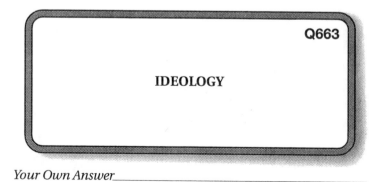

Q663

**IDEOLOGY**

*Your Own Answer*_____

# Correct Answers

v.—to praise
He **lauded** his daughter for winning the trophy.

adj.—slavish; groveling
He knew they both possessed equal abilities, and yet he was always treated as a **servile** underling.

n.—set of beliefs; principles
He joined the religious group because he agreed with its **ideology**.

# *Questions*

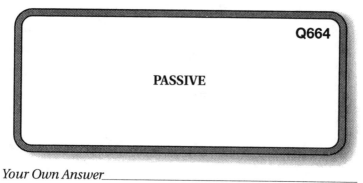

**Q664**

**PASSIVE**

*Your Own Answer*_____

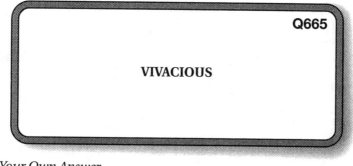

**Q665**

**VIVACIOUS**

*Your Own Answer*_____

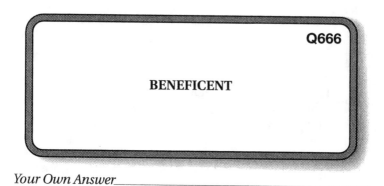

**Q666**

**BENEFICENT**

*Your Own Answer*_____

# *Correct Answers*

**A664**

adj.—submissive; unassertive
He is so **passive** that others walk all over him.

**A665**

adj.—animated; gay
He is a great storyteller; his **vivacious** manner
makes the tale come to life.

**A666**

adj.—conferring benefits; kindly; doing good
He is a **beneficent** person, always taking in stray
animals and talking to people who need someone to listen.

# *Questions*

Q667

**INDULGENT**

*Your Own Answer*_____

_____

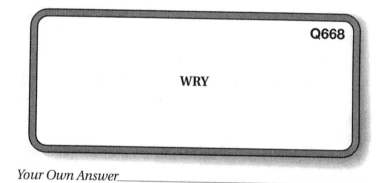

Q668

**WRY**

*Your Own Answer*_____

_____

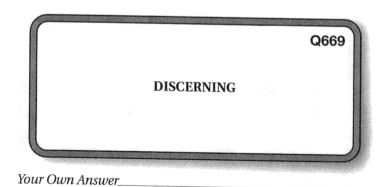

Q669

**DISCERNING**

*Your Own Answer*_____

_____

# Correct Answers

**A667**

adj.—-lenient; patient; permissive

He has **indulgent** tendencies to eat chocolate when he is happy.

**A668**

adj.—mocking; cynical

He has a **wry** sense of humor which sometimes hurts people's feelings.

**A669**

adj.—distinguishing one thing from another

He has a **discerning** eye for knowing the original from the copy.

# *Questions*

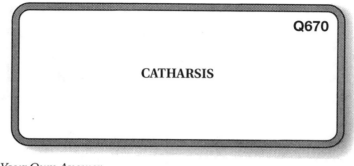

Q670

**CATHARSIS**

*Your Own Answer*_____

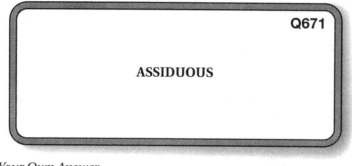

Q671

**ASSIDUOUS**

*Your Own Answer*_____

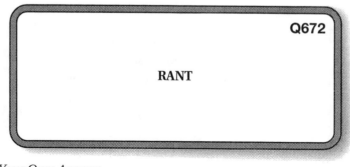

Q672

**RANT**

*Your Own Answer*_____

# Correct Answers

**A670**

n.—a purging or relieving of the body or soul

He experienced a total **catharsis** after the priest absolved his sins.

**A671**

adj.—carefully attentive; industrious

He enjoys having **assiduous** employees because he can explain a procedure once and have it performed correctly every time.

**A672**

v.—to speak in a loud, pompous manner; to rave

He disputed the bill with the shipper, **ranting** that he was dealing with thieves.

# *Questions*

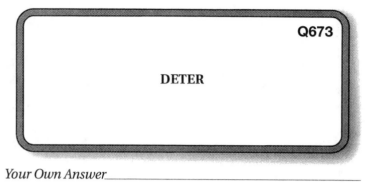

**Q673**

**DETER**

*Your Own Answer*_____

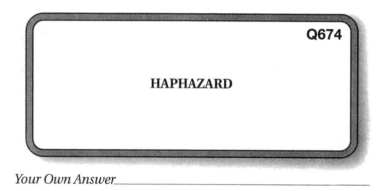

**Q674**

**HAPHAZARD**

*Your Own Answer*_____

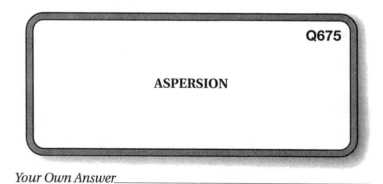

**Q675**

**ASPERSION**

*Your Own Answer*_____

# Correct Answers

**A673**

v.—to prevent; to discourage; to hinder

He **deterred** the rabbits by putting down garlic around the garden.

**A674**

adj.—disorganized; random

He constantly misplaced important documents because of his **haphazard** way of running his office.

**A675**

n.—slanderous statement; a damaging or derogatory criticism

He blamed the loss of his job on an **aspersion** stated by his coworker to his superior.

# *Questions*

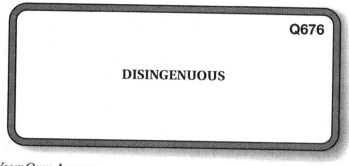

**Q676**

**DISINGENUOUS**

*Your Own Answer*_____

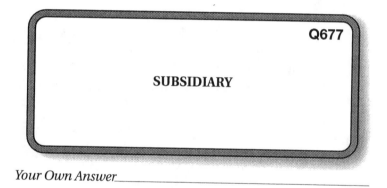

**Q677**

**SUBSIDIARY**

*Your Own Answer*_____

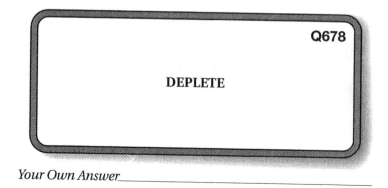

**Q678**

**DEPLETE**

*Your Own Answer*_____

# Correct Answers

**A676**

adj.—not frank or candid; deceivingly simple

He always gives a quick, **disingenuous** response; you never get a straight answer.

**A677**

adj.—subordinate

He acknowledged the importance of the issue, but called it **subsidiary** to a host of other concerns.

**A678**

v.—to reduce; to empty; to exhaust

Having to pay the entire bill will **deplete** the family's savings.

# *Questions*

**Q679**

**TRACTABLE**

*Your Own Answer*_____

**Q680**

**GULLIBLE**

*Your Own Answer*_____

**Q681**

**CONFLUENCE**

*Your Own Answer*_____

# Correct Answers

**A679**

adj.—easily managed (opposite: intractable)
Having a **tractable** staff made her job a lot easier.

**A680**

adj.—easily fooled
**Gullible** people are vulnerable to practical jokes.

**A681**

n.—a thing that is joined together
Great cities often lie at the **confluence** of great rivers.

# *Questions*

**Q682**

**MYRIAD**

*Your Own Answer_____*

**Q683**

**ABSTRACT**

*Your Own Answer_____*

**Q684**

**HUMILITY**

*Your Own Answer_____*

# *Correct Answers*

**A682**

adj.—innumerable; countless

Gazing up on the clear, dark midnight sky, the astronomer saw a **myriad** of stars.

**A683**

adj.—not easy to understand; theoretical

Gauss's law can seem very **abstract** unless you're a mathematician.

**A684**

n.—lack of pride; modesty

Full of **humility**, she accepted the award but gave all the credit to her mentor.

# *Questions*

Q685

**INFER**

*Your Own Answer*_____

Q686

**RESOLUTION**

*Your Own Answer*_____

Q687

**VEHEMENT**

*Your Own Answer*_____

# Correct Answers

**A685**

v.—to form an opinion; to conclude

From the broad outline he supplied, it was easy to **infer** that the applicant knew a great deal about trains.

**A686**

n.—proposal; promise; determination

Former U.S. Senator George Mitchell journeyed to Ireland to help bring about a peaceful **resolution** to years of strife.

**A687**

adj.—intense; excited; enthusiastic

Forced by news accounts to make a statement, the talk-show host issued a **vehement** denial of her involvement in the scheme.

# *Questions*

**Q688**

**REPROOF**

*Your Own Answer*_____

**Q689**

**VACUOUS**

*Your Own Answer*_____

**Q690**

**CONSUMMATION**

*Your Own Answer*_____

# *Correct Answers*

n.—a rebuke

For all his hard work, all he got was a **reproof** of his efforts.

adj.—dull; stupid; empty-headed

For a time, viewers of TV's *Murphy Brown* looked forward to the seemingly unending parade of **vacuous** secretaries that Murphy went through.

n.—the completion; finish

Following the **consummation** of final exams, most of the students graduated.

# *Questions*

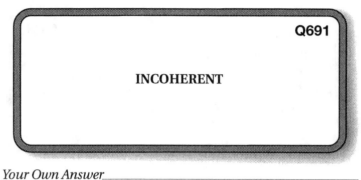

Q691

**INCOHERENT**

*Your Own Answer*

---

Q692

**LETHARGIC**

*Your Own Answer*

---

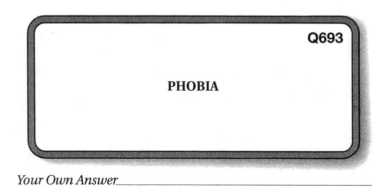

Q693

**PHOBIA**

*Your Own Answer*

---

# *Correct Answers*

**A691**

adj.—illogical; rambling; disjointed

Following the accident, the woman went into shock and became **incoherent** as medics struggled to understand her.

**A692**

adj.—lazy; passive

Feeling very **lethargic**, he watched television or slept the whole day.

**A693**

n.—morbid fear

Fear of heights is not an uncommon **phobia**.

# *Questions*

Q694

**DISHEARTENED**

*Your Own Answer*_____

Q695

**RUMINATE**

*Your Own Answer*_____

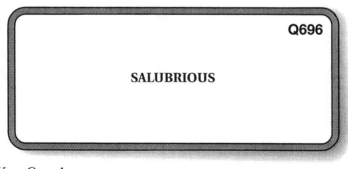

Q696

**SALUBRIOUS**

*Your Own Answer*_____

# *Correct Answers*

adj.—discouraged; depressed
Failing the exam left him **disheartened**.

v.—to think about through meditation
Facing a tough decision, he decided to **ruminate** before making his thoughts known.

adj.—promoting good health
Exercising frequently and eating healthy foods are **salubrious** habits.

# Questions

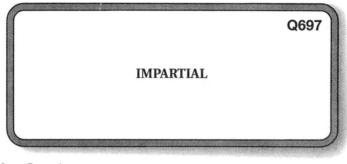

Q697

**IMPARTIAL**

*Your Own Answer*_____

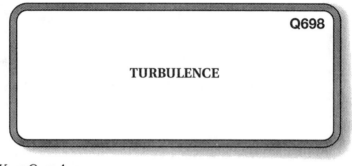

Q698

**TURBULENCE**

*Your Own Answer*_____

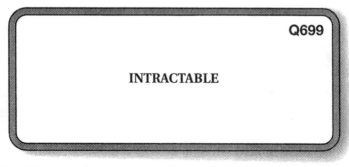

Q699

**INTRACTABLE**

*Your Own Answer*_____

# *Correct Answers*

**A697**

adj.—unbiased; fair

Exasperated by charges to the contrary, the judge reiterated that he had bent over backwards to be **impartial** in a case that crackled with emotion.

**A698**

n.—condition of being physically agitated; disturbance

Everyone on the plane had to fasten their seat belts as the plane entered an area of **turbulence**.

**A699**

adj.—stubborn; obstinate; not easily taught or disciplined

Every teacher in the school became frustrated with the **intractable** student and sent him to the principal's office.

# *Questions*

**Q700**

**COTERIE**

*Your Own Answer*_____

---

**Q701**

**IMPASSIVE**

*Your Own Answer*_____

---

**Q702**

**SKEPTIC**

*Your Own Answer*_____

# *Correct Answers*

**A700**

n.—a clique; a group who meets frequently, usually socially

Every day after school, she joins her **coterie** on the playground, and they go out for a soda.

**A701**

adj.—showing no emotion

Even when his father died, he gave an **impassive** response and walked out tearless.

**A702**

n.—doubter

Even after seeing evidence that his competitor's new engine worked, the engineer remained a **skeptic** that it was marketable.

# *Questions*

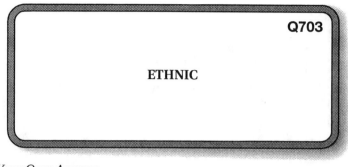

Q703

**ETHNIC**

*Your Own Answer*_____

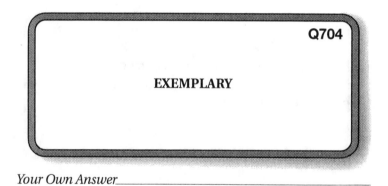

Q704

**EXEMPLARY**

*Your Own Answer*_____

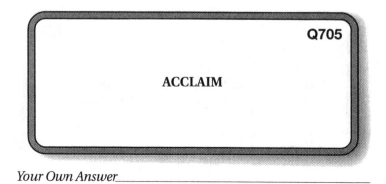

Q705

**ACCLAIM**

*Your Own Answer*_____

# Correct Answers

**A703**

adj.—pertaining to races or peoples and their origin classification or characteristics

**Ethnic** foods from five continents were set up on the table.

**A704**

adj.—serving as an example; outstanding

Employees of the month are chosen for their **exemplary** service to the firm.

**A705**

n.—loud approval; applause

Edward Albee's brilliantly written Broadway revival of *A Delicate Balance* received wide **acclaim**.

# *Questions*

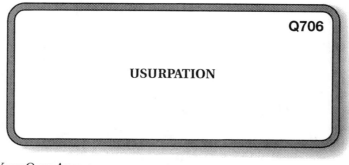

Q706

**USURPATION**

*Your Own Answer*_____

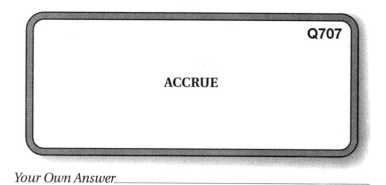

Q707

**ACCRUE**

*Your Own Answer*_____

Q708

**LANGUID**

*Your Own Answer*_____

# Correct Answers

**A706**

n.—the art of taking something for oneself; seizure

During the war, the **usurpation** of the country forced an entirely new culture on the natives.

**A707**

v.—to collect; to build up

During his many years of collecting stamps, he was able to **accrue** a large collection of valuable items.

**A708**

adj.—weak; fatigued

During her illness, she was so **languid** she could not leave her bed.

# Questions

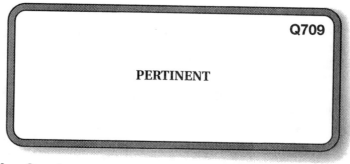

Q709

**PERTINENT**

*Your Own Answer*_____

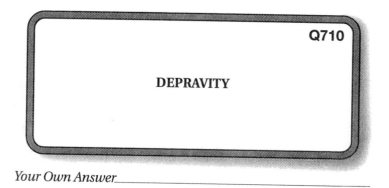

Q710

**DEPRAVITY**

*Your Own Answer*_____

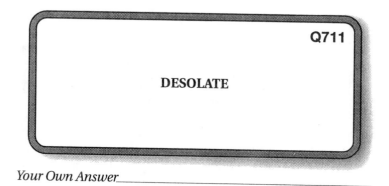

Q711

**DESOLATE**

*Your Own Answer*_____

# *Correct Answers*

**A709**

adj.—related to the matter at hand

During a trial, everyone should concentrate on the same subject, stating only **pertinent** information.

**A710**

n.—moral corruption; badness

Drugs and money caused **depravity** throughout the once decorous community.

**A711**

adj.—to be left alone or made lonely

Driving down the **desolate** road had Kelvin worried that he wouldn't reach a gas station in time.

# *Questions*

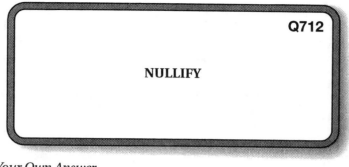

**Q712**

**NULLIFY**

*Your Own Answer*_____

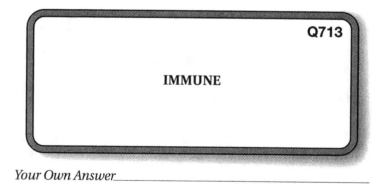

**Q713**

**IMMUNE**

*Your Own Answer*_____

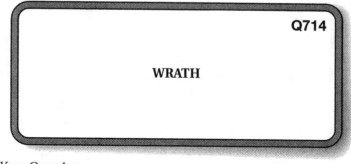

**Q714**

**WRATH**

*Your Own Answer*_____

# *Correct Answers*

**A712**

v.—to cancel; to invalidate
Drinking alcohol excessively will **nullify** the positive benefits of eating well and exercising daily.

**A713**

adj.—exempt from or protected against something
Doesn't everybody wish to be **immune** from the common cold?

**A714**

n.—violent or unrestrained anger; fury
Do not trespass on his property or you will have to deal with his **wrath**.

# *Questions*

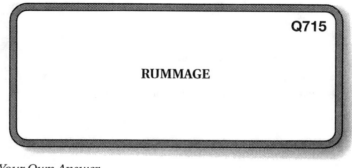

Q715

**RUMMAGE**

*Your Own Answer*_____

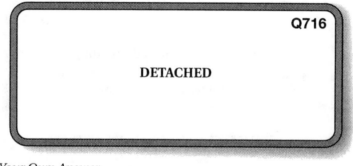

Q716

**DETACHED**

*Your Own Answer*_____

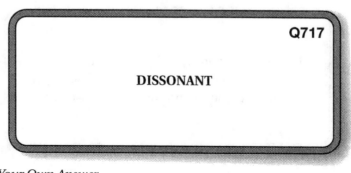

Q717

**DISSONANT**

*Your Own Answer*_____

# Correct Answers

**A715**

v.—to search thoroughly
Determined to find his college yearbook, he **rummaged** through every box in the garage.

**A716**

adj.—separated; not interested; standing alone
**Detached** from modern conveniences, the islanders live a simple, unhurried life.

**A717**

adj.—not in harmony; in disagreement
Despite several intense rehearsals, the voices of the choir members continued to be **dissonant**.

# *Questions*

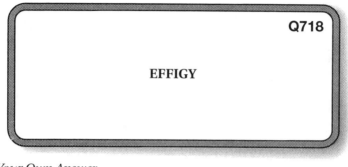

Q718

**EFFIGY**

*Your Own Answer*_____

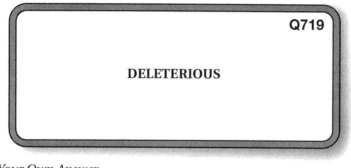

Q719

**DELETERIOUS**

*Your Own Answer*_____

Q720

**VULNERABLE**

*Your Own Answer*_____

# *Correct Answers*

**A718**

n.—the image or likeness of a person
Demonstrators carried **effigies** of the dictator they wanted overthrown.

**A719**

adj.—harmful; hurtful; noxious
**Deleterious** fumes were traced to the warehouse.

**A720**

adj.—open to attack; unprotected
Deer usually stay in the forest because they know they are **vulnerable** in open areas.

# *Questions*

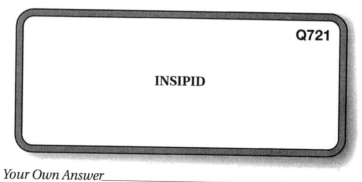

**Q721**

**INSIPID**

*Your Own Answer*_____

**Q722**

**DECISIVENESS**

*Your Own Answer*_____

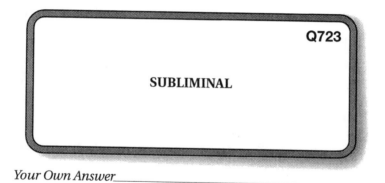

**Q723**

**SUBLIMINAL**

*Your Own Answer*_____

# Correct Answers

**A721**

adj.—uninteresting; bland
Declaring the offerings **insipid**, the critic grudgingly awarded the restaurant one star.

**A722**

n.—an act of being firm or determined
**Decisiveness** is one of the key qualities of a successful executive.

**A723**

adj.—below the level of consciousness
Critics of advertising say that it's loaded with **subliminal** messages.

# *Questions*

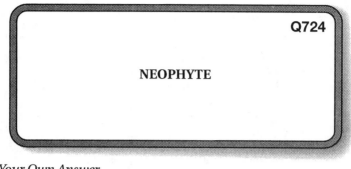

**Q724**

**NEOPHYTE**

*Your Own Answer*_____

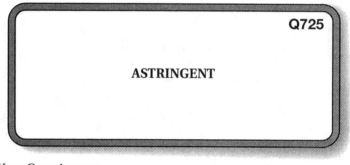

**Q725**

**ASTRINGENT**

*Your Own Answer*_____

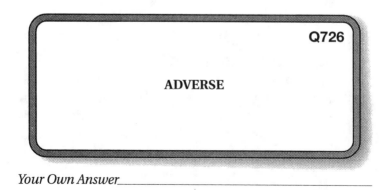

**Q726**

**ADVERSE**

*Your Own Answer*_____

# Correct Answers

**A724**

n.—beginner; newcomer

Critics applauded the **neophyte**'s success and speculated how much better he would get with age and experience.

**A725**

n.; adj.—1. a substance that contracts bodily tissues 2. causing contraction; tightening; stern; austere

1. After the operation, an **astringent** was used on his skin so that the stretched area would return to normal. 2. The downturn in sales caused the CEO to impose **astringent** measures.

**A726**

adj.—negative; hostile; antagonistic; inimical

Contrary to the ski resort's expectations, the warm weather generated **adverse** conditions for a profitable weekend.

# *Questions*

**Q727**

**RUFFIAN**

*Your Own Answer*_____

---

**Q728**

**CONTEMPORARY**

*Your Own Answer*_____

---

**Q729**

**DERISION**

*Your Own Answer*_____

---

# *Correct Answers*

n.—tough person or hoodlum

Contrary to popular opinion, **ruffians** are nothing new in the city.

adj.—living or happening at the same time; modern

**Contemporary** furniture will clash with your traditional sectional.

n.—the act of mocking; ridicule; mockery

Constant **derision** from classmates made him quit school.

# *Questions*

**Q730**

**OBSOLETE**

*Your Own Answer*_____

---

**Q731**

**DICTUM**

*Your Own Answer*_____

---

**Q732**

**CLOYING**

*Your Own Answer*_____

# Correct Answers

**A730**

adj.—out of date; passé

Computers have made many formerly manual tasks **obsolete**.

---

**A731**

n.—a formal statement of either fact or opinion

Computer programmers have a **dictum**: garbage in, garbage out.

---

**A732**

adj.—too sugary; too sentimental or flattering

Complimenting her on her weight loss, clothing, and hairstyle was a **cloying** way to begin asking for a raise.

# *Questions*

**Q733**

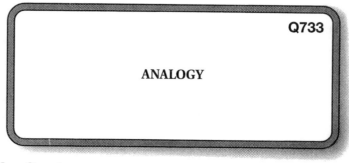

ANALOGY

*Your Own Answer*_____

---

**Q734**

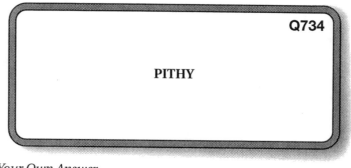

PITHY

*Your Own Answer*_____

---

**Q735**

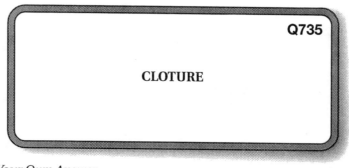

CLOTURE

*Your Own Answer*_____

# Correct Answers

**A733**

n.—similarity; correlation; parallelism; simile; metaphor

Comparing the newly discovered virus with one found long ago, the scientist made an **analogy** between the two organisms.

**A734**

adj.—terse and full of meaning

Columnist William Safire, a former presidential speech writer, has a way with words that often yields **pithy** comments.

**A735**

n.—a parliamentary procedure to end debate and begin to vote

**Cloture** was declared as the parliamentarians readied to register their votes.

# *Questions*

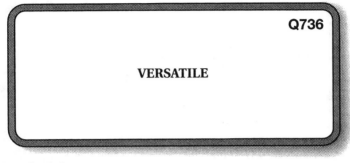

Q736

**VERSATILE**

*Your Own Answer*_____

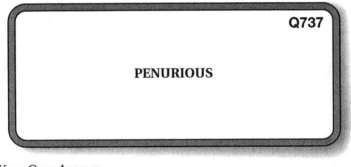

Q737

**PENURIOUS**

*Your Own Answer*_____

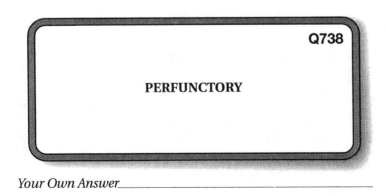

Q738

**PERFUNCTORY**

*Your Own Answer*_____

# Correct Answers

**A736**

adj.—having many uses; multifaceted

Clay is a **versatile** material since it can be shaped into so many different objects.

**A737**

adj.—stingy; miserly

Charles Dickens's Scrooge is the most **penurious** character in any of his tales.

**A738**

adj.—done in a routine, mechanical way, without interest

Change in career is a good cure for people who have become bored with their occupations and are currently performing their duties in a **perfunctory** fashion.

# *Questions*

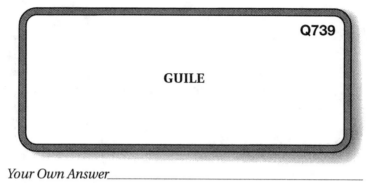

**Q739**

**GUILE**

*Your Own Answer_____*

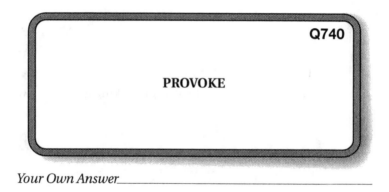

**Q740**

**PROVOKE**

*Your Own Answer_____*

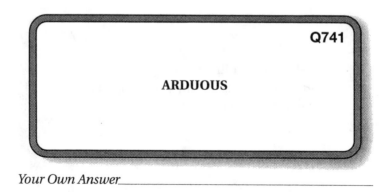

**Q741**

**ARDUOUS**

*Your Own Answer_____*

# Correct Answers

**A739**

n.—slyness; deceit

By using his **guile**, the gambler almost always won.

**A740**

v.—to stir action or feeling; to arouse

By calling him names, he was **provoking** a fight.

**A741**

adj.—laborious; difficult; strenuous

Building a house is **arduous** work, but the result is well worth the labor.

# *Questions*

**Q742**

HIATUS

*Your Own Answer*_____

**Q743**

RENEGADE

*Your Own Answer*_____

**Q744**

MINUTE

*Your Own Answer*_____

# *Correct Answers*

**A742**

n.—interval; break; period of rest

Between graduation and the first day of his new job, Tim took a three-month **hiatus** in the Caribbean.

**A743**

n.—a person who abandons something such as a religion, cause, or movement; a traitor

Benedict Arnold remains one of the most notorious **renegades** in American history.

**A744**

adj.—extremely small; tiny

Being on a sodium-restricted diet, he uses only a **minute** amount of salt in his dishes.

# Questions

**INCOMPATIBLE**

*Your Own Answer*_____

**KINDLE**

*Your Own Answer*_____

**TURMOIL**

*Your Own Answer*_____

# *Correct Answers*

**A745**

adj.—disagreeing; disharmonious; not compatible

Being **incompatible** with each other, the children were assigned to sit on opposite sides of the room.

**A746**

v.—to ignite; to arouse

Being around children **kindled** her interest in educational psychology.

**A747**

n.—unrest; agitation

Before the country recovered after the war, they experienced a time of great **turmoil**.

# *Questions*

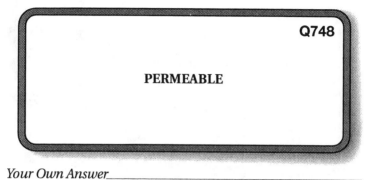

**Q748**

**PERMEABLE**

*Your Own Answer*_____

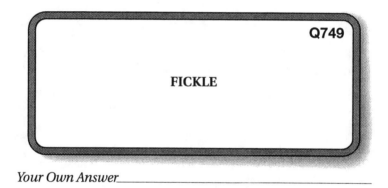

**Q749**

**FICKLE**

*Your Own Answer*_____

**Q750**

**JUDICIOUS**

*Your Own Answer*_____

# Correct Answers

**A748**

adj.—porous; allowing to pass through

Because the material was **permeable**, the water was able to drain.

**A749**

adj.—changeable; unpredictable

Because the man was **fickle**, he could not be trusted to make a competent decision.

**A750**

adj.—to have or show sound judgment

Because the elder was **judicious**, the tough decisions were left to him.

# Questions

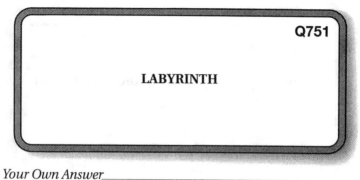

Q751

**LABYRINTH**

*Your Own Answer*_____

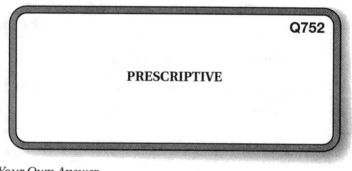

Q752

**PRESCRIPTIVE**

*Your Own Answer*_____

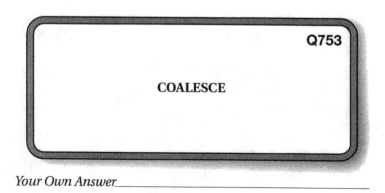

Q753

**COALESCE**

*Your Own Answer*_____

# Correct Answers

**A751**

n.—maze

Be careful not to get lost in the **labyrinth** of vegetation.

**A752**

adj.—done by custom; unbending

At the heart of the Australian aborigines' **prescriptive** coming-of-age rite for men is a walkabout.

**A753**

v.—to combine; to come together

At the end of the conference, the five groups **coalesced** in one room.

# Questions

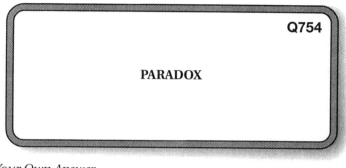

**Q754**

**PARADOX**

*Your Own Answer*_____

---

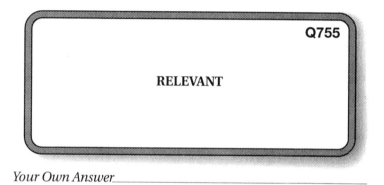

**Q755**

**RELEVANT**

*Your Own Answer*_____

---

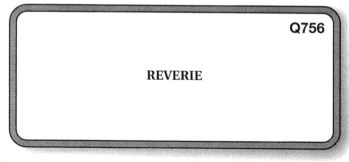

**Q756**

**REVERIE**

*Your Own Answer*_____

# *Correct Answers*

**A754**

n.—a tenet seemingly contradictory or false, but actually true

At first blush, the company's results were a **paradox**: sales were down, yet profits were up.

**A755**

adj.—of concern; significant

Asking applicants about their general health is **relevant** since much of the job requires physical strength.

**A756**

n.—the condition of being unaware of one's surroundings; trance; dreamy thinking or imagining, especially of agreeable things

As their anniversary neared, Liane fell into a **reverie** as she recalled all the good times she and Roscoe had had.

# *Questions*

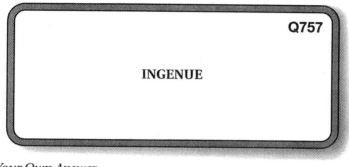

Q757

**INGENUE**

*Your Own Answer*_____

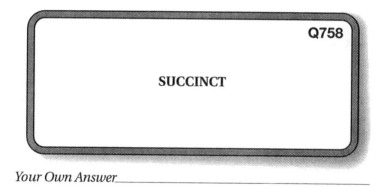

Q758

**SUCCINCT**

*Your Own Answer*_____

Q759

**LAGGARD**

*Your Own Answer*_____

# Correct Answers

**A757**

n.—an unworldly young woman

As an **ingenue**, Corky had no experience outside of her small town.

**A758**

adj.—consisting of few words; concise

Articles in *USA Today* are so **succinct** that some observers nicknamed the newspaper "McPaper."

**A759**

n.—a lazy person; one who lags behind

Anything can happen in a swim meet: last year's leader can become this year's **laggard**.

# *Questions*

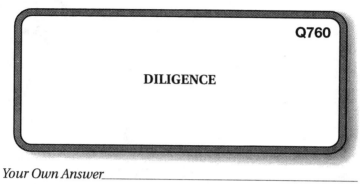

**Q760**

**DILIGENCE**

*Your Own Answer*_____

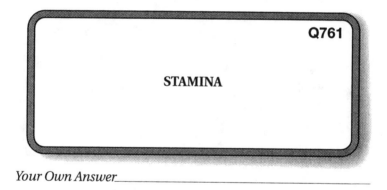

**Q761**

**STAMINA**

*Your Own Answer*_____

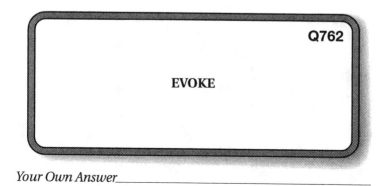

**Q762**

**EVOKE**

*Your Own Answer*_____

# Correct Answers

**A760**

n.—hard work
Anything can be accomplished with **diligence** and commitment.

**A761**

n.—endurance
Anybody who can finish the New York Marathon has lots of **stamina**.

**A762**

v.—to call forth; to elicit
Announcement of the results **evoked** a cheer from the crowd.

# *Questions*

Q763

**ANIMOSITY**

*Your Own Answer*_____

Q764

**INQUISITIVE**

*Your Own Answer*_____

Q765

**IMPLICATION**

*Your Own Answer*_____

# Correct Answers

**A763**

n.—a feeling of hatred or ill will

**Animosity** grew between the two feuding families.

**A764**

adj.—eager to ask questions in order to learn

An **inquisitive** youngster is likely to become a wise adult.

**A765**

n.—suggestion; inference

An **implication** was made that there might be trickery involved.

# *Questions*

**Q766**

**AUTHENTIC**

*Your Own Answer*_____

**Q767**

**BENEFACTOR**

*Your Own Answer*_____

**Q768**

**MANIFEST**

*Your Own Answer*_____

# Correct Answers

**A766**

adj.—real; genuine; trustworthy
An **authentic** diamond will cut glass.

**A767**

n.—one who helps others; a donor
An anonymous **benefactor** donated $10,000 to the children's hospital.

**A768**

adj.—obvious; clear
America's **manifest** destiny was to acquire all of the land between the Pacific and Atlantic Oceans.

# *Questions*

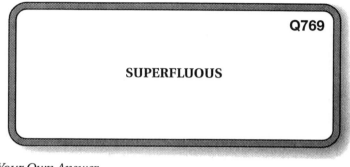

**Q769**

**SUPERFLUOUS**

*Your Own Answer*_____

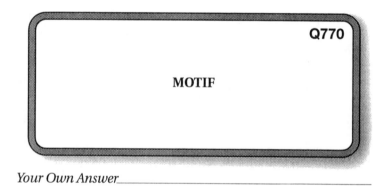

**Q770**

**MOTIF**

*Your Own Answer*_____

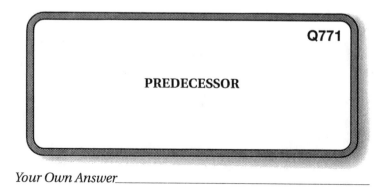

**Q771**

**PREDECESSOR**

*Your Own Answer*_____

# *Correct Answers*

**A769**

adj.—unnecessary; extra

Although the designer considered the piece **superfluous**, the woman wanted the extra chair in her bedroom.

**A770**

n.—theme

Although the college students lived in Alaska, they decided on a tropical **motif** for their dorm room.

**A771**

n.—one who has occupied an office before another

Although her **predecessor** did not accomplish any goals that would help the poor, the new mayor was confident that she could finally help those in need.

# *Questions*

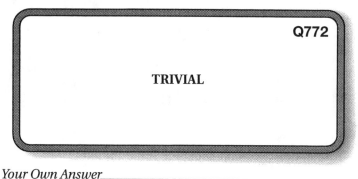

Q772

**TRIVIAL**

*Your Own Answer*_____

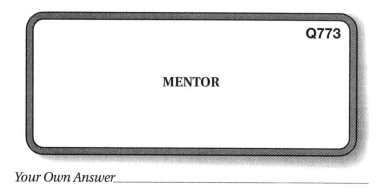

Q773

**MENTOR**

*Your Own Answer*_____

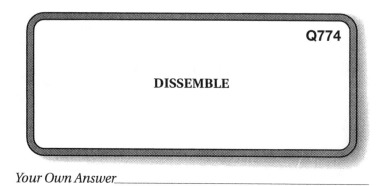

Q774

**DISSEMBLE**

*Your Own Answer*_____

# *Correct Answers*

**A772**

adj.—unimportant; small; worthless

Although her mother felt otherwise, she considered her dishwashing chore **trivial**.

**A773**

n.—teacher; wise and faithful advisor

Alan consulted his **mentor** when he needed critical advice.

**A774**

v.—to disguise and conceal

Agent 007 has a marvelous ability to **dissemble** his real intentions.

# *Questions*

Q775

**PHILANTHROPY**

*Your Own Answer*_____

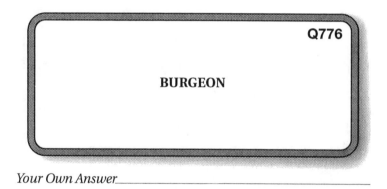

Q776

**BURGEON**

*Your Own Answer*_____

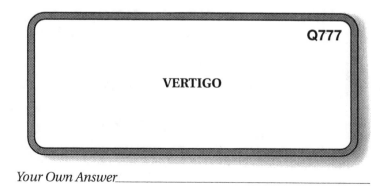

Q777

**VERTIGO**

*Your Own Answer*_____

# *Correct Answers*

**A775**

n.—charity; unselfishness

After years of donating time and money to the children's hospital, Mrs. Elderwood was commended for her **philanthropy**.

**A776**

v.—to grow or develop quickly

After the first punch was thrown, the dispute **burgeoned** into a brawl.

**A777**

n.—dizziness

After spinning around for five minutes, he experienced **vertigo**.

# *Questions*

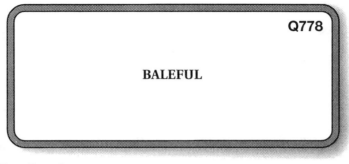

Q778

**BALEFUL**

*Your Own Answer*_____

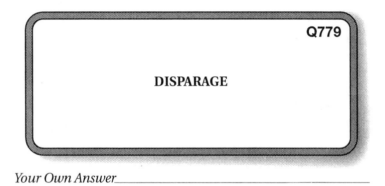

Q779

**DISPARAGE**

*Your Own Answer*_____

Q780

**SAVOR**

*Your Own Answer*_____

# Correct Answers

**A778**

adj.—harmful; malignant; detrimental

After she was fired, she realized it was a **baleful** move to point the blame at her superior.

**A779**

v.—to belittle; to undervalue

After she fired him, she realized that she had **disparaged** the value of his assistance.

**A780**

v.—to receive pleasure from; to enjoy with appreciation; to dwell on with delight

After several months without a day off, she **savored** every minute of her week-long vacation.

# Questions

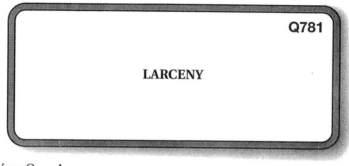

**Q781**

**LARCENY**

*Your Own Answer*_____

---

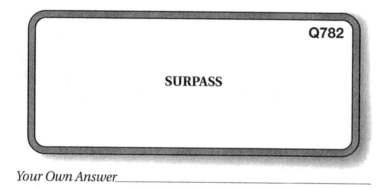

**Q782**

**SURPASS**

*Your Own Answer*_____

---

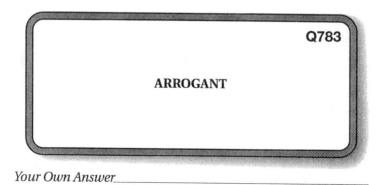

**Q783**

**ARROGANT**

*Your Own Answer*_____

# *Correct Answers*

n.—theft; stealing

After robbing the liquor store, she was found guilty of **larceny**.

v.—to go beyond; to outdo

After recovering from a serious illness, the boy **surpassed** the doctor's expectations by leaving the hospital two days early.

adj.—acting superior to others; conceited

After purchasing his new, expensive sports car, the **arrogant** doctor refused to allow anyone to ride with him to the country club.

# *Questions*

**Q784**

**INFAMOUS**

*Your Own Answer*_____

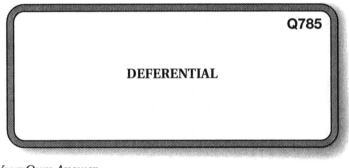

**Q785**

**DEFERENTIAL**

*Your Own Answer*_____

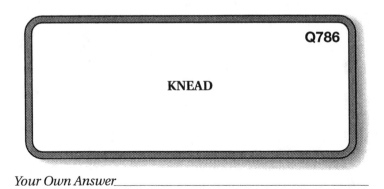

**Q786**

**KNEAD**

*Your Own Answer*_____

# *Correct Answers*

**A784**

adj.—having a bad reputation; notorious

After producing machines that developed many problems, the production company became **infamous** for poor manufacturing.

**A785**

adj.—yielding to the opinion of another

After months of debating students' needs in the Sixth Ward, the mayor's **deferential** statements indicated that he had found some common ground with them.

**A786**

v.—to mix; to massage

After mixing the ingredients, the baker **kneaded** the dough and set it aside to rise.

# Questions

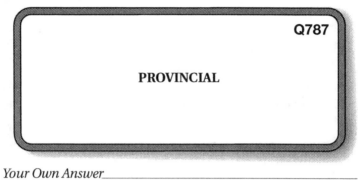

**Q787**

**PROVINCIAL**

*Your Own Answer*_____

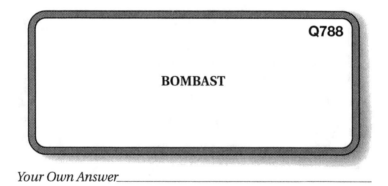

**Q788**

**BOMBAST**

*Your Own Answer*_____

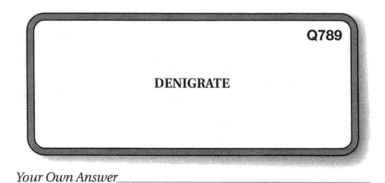

**Q789**

**DENIGRATE**

*Your Own Answer*_____

# *Correct Answers*

**A787**

adj.—regional; unsophisticated

After living in the city for five years, he found that his family back home on the farm was too **provincial** for his cultured ways.

**A788**

n.—pompous speech; pretentious words

After he delivered his **bombast** at the podium, he arrogantly left the meeting.

**A789**

v.—to defame; to blacken or sully; to belittle

After finding out her evil secret, he announced it to the council and **denigrated** her in public.

# *Questions*

Q790

**SCRUPULOUS**

*Your Own Answer*_____

---

Q791

**ABSOLVE**

*Your Own Answer*_____

---

Q792

**PESSIMISM**

*Your Own Answer*_____

---

# Correct Answers

**A790**

adj.—honorable; exact

After finding a purse with valuable items inside, the **scrupulous** Mr. Prendergast returned everything to its owner.

**A791**

v.—to forgive; to acquit

After feuding for many years, the brothers **absolved** each other for the many arguments they had.

**A792**

n.—seeing only the gloomy side; hopelessness

After endless years of drought, **pessimism** grew in the hearts of even the most dedicated farmers.

# Questions

Q793

**SCRUTINIZE**

*Your Own Answer*_____

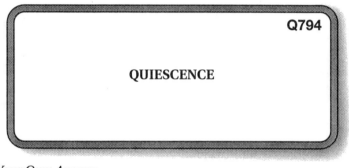

Q794

**QUIESCENCE**

*Your Own Answer*_____

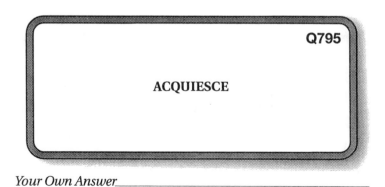

Q795

**ACQUIESCE**

*Your Own Answer*_____

# Correct Answers

**A793**

v.—to examine closely; to study

After allowing his son to borrow the family car, the father **scrutinized** every section for dents.

**A794**

n.—state of being at rest or without motion

After a tough day on the shipping dock, one needs **quiescence**.

**A795**

v.—to agree without protest

After a hard-fought battle, the retailers finally **acquiesced** to the draft regulations.

# *Questions*

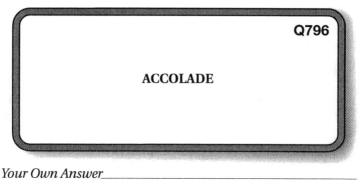

Q796

**ACCOLADE**

*Your Own Answer*_____

Q797

**DENOUNCE**

*Your Own Answer*_____

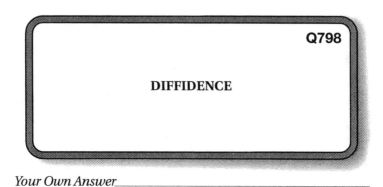

Q798

**DIFFIDENCE**

*Your Own Answer*_____

# *Correct Answers*

**A796**

n.—a sign of approval or respect

**Accolades** flowed into her dressing room following the opening-night triumph.

**A797**

v.—to speak out against; to condemn

A student rally was called to **denounce** the use of drugs on campus.

**A798**

n.—a hesitation in asserting oneself

A shy person may have great **diffidence** when faced with a problem.

# *Questions*

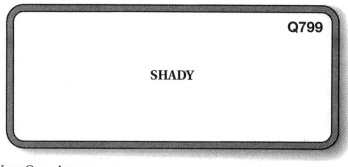

**Q799**

**SHADY**

*Your Own Answer*_____

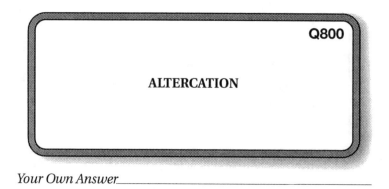

**Q800**

**ALTERCATION**

*Your Own Answer*_____

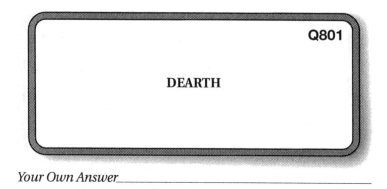

**Q801**

**DEARTH**

*Your Own Answer*_____

# *Correct Answers*

**A799**

adj.—a character of questionable honesty
A **shady** person would not be trusted with a sensitive secret.

**A800**

n.—controversy; dispute
A serious **altercation** caused the marriage to end in a bitter divorce.

**A801**

n.—scarcity; shortage
A series of coincidental resignations left the firm with a **dearth** of talent.

# *Questions*

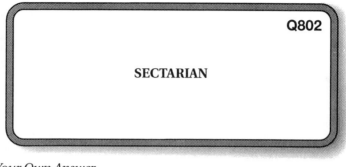

**Q802**

**SECTARIAN**

Your Own Answer_____

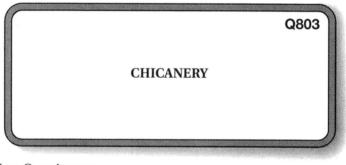

**Q803**

**CHICANERY**

Your Own Answer_____

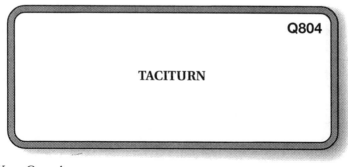

**Q804**

**TACITURN**

Your Own Answer_____

# Correct Answers

**A802**

adj.—to be narrow-minded or limited

A **sectarian** speaker precluded him from listening to the other side.

**A803**

n.—trickery or deception

A news broadcast is no place for **chicanery**.

**A804**

adj.—inclined to silence; speaking little; dour; stern

A mime may be **taciturn**, but his performance can speak volumes.

# *Questions*

**Q805**

APPEASE

*Your Own Answer*_____

---

**Q806**

METAMORPHOSIS

*Your Own Answer*_____

---

**Q807**

ANOINT

*Your Own Answer*_____

# Correct Answers

**A805**

v.—to satisfy; to calm
A milk bottle usually **appeases** a crying baby.

**A806**

n.—change of form
A **metamorphosis** caused the caterpillar to become a beautiful butterfly.

**A807**

v.—to crown; to ordain
A member of the monarchy was **anointed** by the king.

# *Questions*

Q808

**BENIGN**

*Your Own Answer*_____

---

Q809

**HYPOTHETICAL**

*Your Own Answer*_____

---

Q810

**EFFEMINATE**

*Your Own Answer*_____

# *Correct Answers*

**A808**

adj.—mild; harmless
A lamb is a **benign** animal, especially when compared with a lion.

**A809**

adj.—assumed; uncertain; conjectural
A **hypothetical** situation was set up so we could practice our responses.

**A810**

adj.—having qualities attributed to a woman; delicate
A high-pitched laugh made the man seem **effeminate**.

# *Questions*

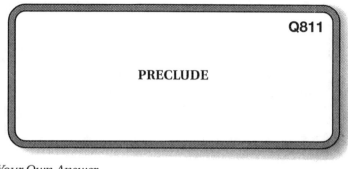

Q811

**PRECLUDE**

*Your Own Answer*_____

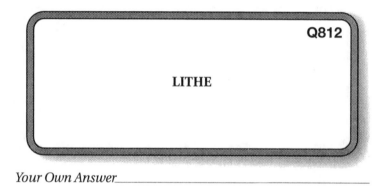

Q812

**LITHE**

*Your Own Answer*_____

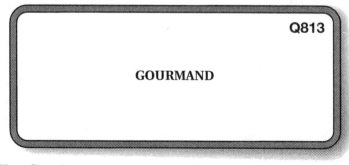

Q813

**GOURMAND**

*Your Own Answer*_____

# *Correct Answers*

---

**A811**

v.—to inhibit; to make impossible

A healthy diet and lifestyle will not **preclude** you from getting ill, although it improves your immune system.

---

**A812**

adj.—to be limber or supple

A gymnast needs to be **lithe** in order to do a split.

---

**A813**

n.—one who eats eagerly

A **gourmand** may eat several servings of entree.

# *Questions*

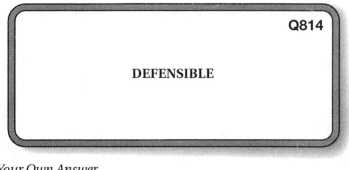

Q814

**DEFENSIBLE**

*Your Own Answer*_____

Q815

**FOSTER**

*Your Own Answer*_____

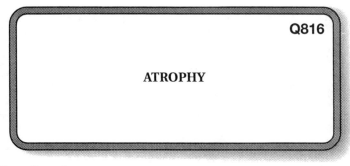

Q816

**ATROPHY**

*Your Own Answer*_____

# Correct Answers

**A814**

adj.—that which can be justified
A good strategy needs to be **defensible**.

**A815**

v.—to encourage; to nurture; to support
A good practice routine **fosters** success.

**A816**

v.—to waste away, as from lack of use; to wither
A few months after he lost his ability to walk, his
legs began to **atrophy**.

# *Questions*

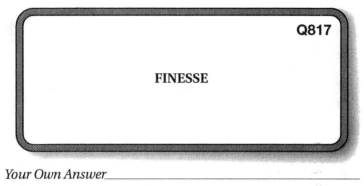

**Q817**

**FINESSE**

*Your Own Answer*_____

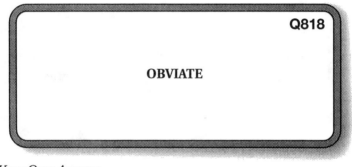

**Q818**

**OBVIATE**

*Your Own Answer*_____

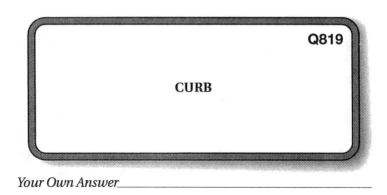

**Q819**

**CURB**

*Your Own Answer*_____

# Correct Answers

**A817**

n.—the ability to handle situations with skill and diplomacy

A diplomat with great **finesse**, Madeleine Albright was destined for high office.

**A818**

v.—to make unnecessary

A cure for the common cold would **obviate** the need for shelf after shelf of cold remedies.

**A819**

n.—a restraint or framework

A **curb** was put up along the street to help drainage.

# *Questions*

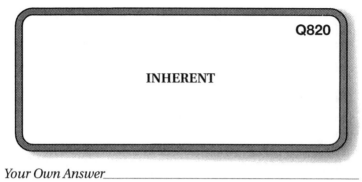

Q820

**INHERENT**

*Your Own Answer*_____

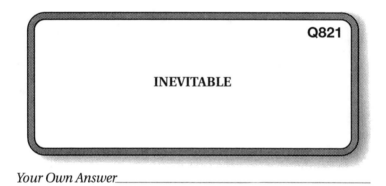

Q821

**INEVITABLE**

*Your Own Answer*_____

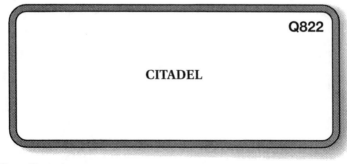

Q822

**CITADEL**

*Your Own Answer*_____

# Correct Answers

**A820**

adj.—part of the essential character; intrinsic

A constant smile is **inherent** in pageant competitors.

**A821**

adj.—sure to happen; unavoidable

A confrontation between the disagreeing neighbors seemed **inevitable**.

**A822**

n.—a fortress set up high to defend a city

A **citadel** sat on the hill to protect the city below.

# *Questions*

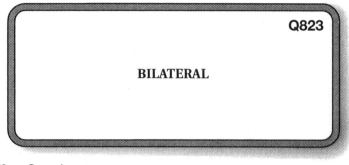

Q823

**BILATERAL**

*Your Own Answer*_____

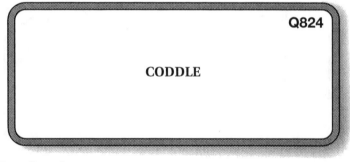

Q824

**CODDLE**

*Your Own Answer*_____

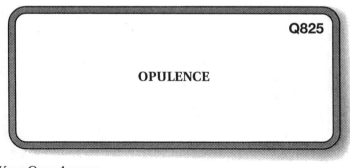

Q825

**OPULENCE**

*Your Own Answer*_____

# *Correct Answers*

**A823**

adj.—pertaining to or affecting both sides or two sides; having two sides

A **bilateral** decision was made so that both partners reaped equal benefits from the same amount of work.

**A824**

v.—to treat with tenderness

A baby needs to be **coddled**.

**A825**

n.—wealth; fortune

A 40-room mansion on 65 wooded acres is only the most visible sign of her **opulence**.

# *Questions*

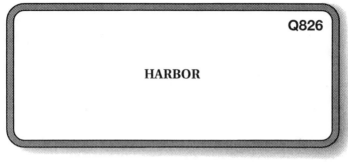

**Q826**

**HARBOR**

*Your Own Answer*_____

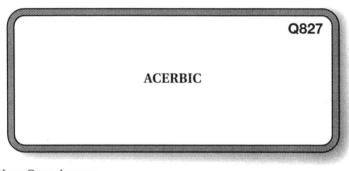

**Q827**

**ACERBIC**

*Your Own Answer*_____

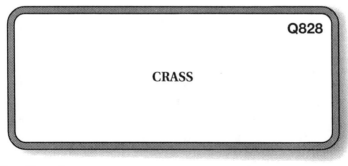

**Q828**

**CRASS**

*Your Own Answer*_____

# Correct Answers

**A826**

n.; v.—1. a place of safety or shelter 2. to give shelter or to protect

1. We stood at the dock as the ship sailed into the **harbor**.
2. The peasants were executed for **harboring** known rebels.

**A827**

adj.—1. tasting sour 2. harsh in language or temper

1. Too much bay leaf will make the eggplant **acerbic**.
2. The columnist's **acerbic** comments about the First Lady drew a strong denunciation from the President.

**A828**

adj.—1. stupid or dull; insensitive 2. materialistic

1. To make light of someone's weakness is **crass**.
2. They made their money the old-fashioned way, but still they were accused of being **crass**.

# *Questions*

**DOCUMENT**

*Your Own Answer*_____

**AFFINITY**

*Your Own Answer*_____

**EFFERVESCENCE**

*Your Own Answer*_____

# Correct Answers

**A829**

n.; v.—1. official paper containing information 2. to support; to substantiate; to verify

1. They needed a written **document** to prove that the transaction occurred.

2. Facing an audit, she had to **document** all her client contacts.

**A830**

n.—1. a connection 2. similarity of structure

1. There is a strong emotional **affinity** between the two siblings.

2. It turns out that the elements bear a strong **affinity** to each other.

**A831**

n.—1. liveliness; spirit 2. bubbliness

1. The woman's **effervescence** was a delightful change.

2. The cream soda's **effervescence** tickled my nose.

# *Questions*

Q832

**SPURN**

*Your Own Answer*_____

_____

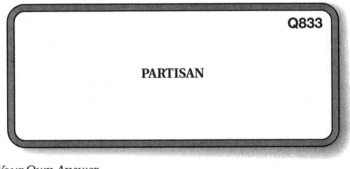

Q833

**PARTISAN**

*Your Own Answer*_____

_____

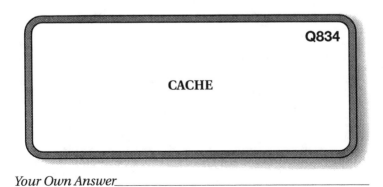

Q834

**CACHE**

*Your Own Answer*_____

_____

# Correct Answers

**A832**

v.; n.—1. to push away  2. a strong rejection

1. The woman **spurned** the advances of her suitor, saying she wasn't ready for a commitment.
2. Unlucky enough to be the ninth telemarketer to call Jane that evening, he caught her **spurn**.

**A833**

n.; adj.—1. supporter; follower 2. biased; one-sided

1. The union president is a **partisan** of minimum-wage legislation.
2. Republican U.S. Senator Alfonse D'Amato was accused by Democrats of having **partisan** motives in the zeal with which he pursued hearings on the Whitewater Affair.

**A834**

n.—1. stockpile  2. hiding place for goods

1. The town kept a **cache** of salt on hand to melt winter's snow off the roads.
2. Extra food is kept in the **cache** under the pantry.

# *Questions*

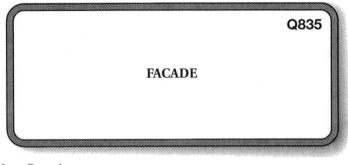

Q835

FACADE

*Your Own Answer*_____

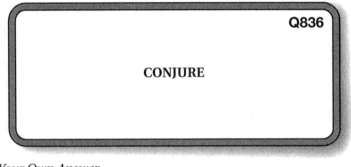

Q836

CONJURE

*Your Own Answer*_____

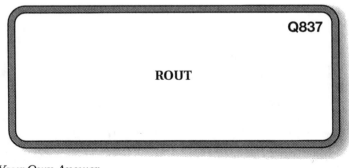

Q837

ROUT

*Your Own Answer*_____

# Correct Answers

**A835**

n.—1. false appearance 2. front view of a building

1. The smile on her face was only a **facade** for her true feelings of sorrow.
2. The building's **facade** was faded and aging.

**A836**

v.— 1. to call upon or appeal to 2. to cause to be, appear, or become

1. The smell of the dinner **conjured** images of childhood.
2. The magician **conjured** a rabbit out of a hat.

**A837**

n.; v.— 1. a noisy or disorderly crowd 2. a retreat or terrible defeat 3. to dig up

1. The **rout** kept the police busy all morning with crowd control.
2. The Scarlet Knights beat the Fighting Irish in a **rout**, 56-14.
3. I need to **rout** the backyard in order to put in the pipes.

# *Questions*

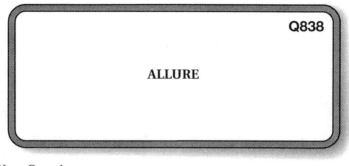

Q838

**ALLURE**

*Your Own Answer*_____

Q839

**CONFOUND**

*Your Own Answer*_____

Q840

**PONDEROUS**

*Your Own Answer*_____

# Correct Answers

**A838**

v.; n.— 1. to attract; to entice  2. attraction; temptation; glamour

1. The romantic young man **allured** the beautiful woman by preparing a wonderful dinner.
2. Singapore's **allure** is its bustling economy.

**A839**

v.—1. to lump together causing confusion  2. to damn

1. The problem **confounded** our ability to solve it.
2. **Confound** you, you scoundrel!

**A840**

adj.—1. unwieldy from weight 2. dull or labored

1. The **ponderous** piano posed a serious challenge to having it pulled up to the 16th floor.
2. As if being grainy wasn't bad enough, the film's **ponderous** story made it tough to get through.

# *Questions*

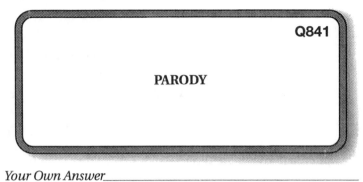

Q841

**PARODY**

*Your Own Answer*_____

---

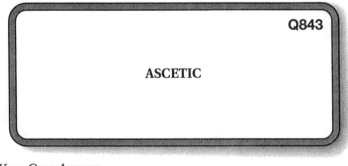

Q842

**DISPERSE**

*Your Own Answer*_____

---

Q843

**ASCETIC**

*Your Own Answer*_____

# *Correct Answers*

**A841**

n.—1. a piece of work imitating another in a satirical manner 2. a poor imitation

1. The play was a **parody** of the prince and princess's marital difficulties.
2. Ugh! This is a **parody** of a fashionable dress!

**A842**

v.—1. to scatter 2. to separate

1. The pilots **dispersed** the food drops over a wide area of devastation.
2. Tear gas was used to **disperse** the crowd.

**A843**

n.; adj.— 1. one who leads a simple life of self-denial 2. rigorously abstinent

1. The monastery is filled with **ascetics** who have devoted their lives to religion.
2. The nuns lead an **ascetic** life devoted to the Lord.

# *Questions*

**Q844**

INCLINED

*Your Own Answer*_____

**Q845**

OBTUSE

*Your Own Answer*_____

**Q846**

MACULATE

*Your Own Answer*_____

# Correct Answers

**A844**

adj.—1. apt to; likely 2. angled

1. The man's ear for music indicated he was **inclined** toward learning an instrument.
2. The hillside was **inclined** just enough to make for a fairly serious climb.

---

**A845**

adj.—1. dull 2. greater than 90° but less than 180° 3. slow to understand or perceive

1. The man was so **obtuse**, he even made the dog yawn.
2. The textbook problem asks the reader to solve for the **obtuse** angle.
3. He's **obtuse** when it comes to abstract art.

---

**A846**

adj.; v.—1. spotted; blotched; defiled; impure (opposite: immaculate) 2. to stain; to spot; to defile

1. The **maculate** rug could not be cleaned.
2. Grape juice **maculated** the carpet.

# Questions

Q847

**LUCID**

*Your Own Answer*_____

Q848

**AGHAST**

*Your Own Answer*_____

Q849

**REND**

*Your Own Answer*_____

# Correct Answers

---

**A847**

adj.—1. shining 2. easily understood

1. The **lucid** quarter was easily spotted.
2. Lincoln's Gettysburg Address was artful, yet **lucid**.

---

**A848**

adj.—1. astonished; amazed 2. horrified; terrified; appalled

1. The landlord was **aghast** at his water bill.
2. The children's **aghast** expressions were indicative of the frightening experience they had on the amusement ride.

---

**A849**

v.— 1. to rip or pull from 2. to split with violence 3. to disturb with a sharp noise

1. The kidnapper **rent** the newborn baby from the arms of its mother as she was leaving the hospital.
2. A freakish water spout **rent** the fishing boat in half.
3. Every morning, the 5:47 local out of New Brunswick **rends** the dawn's silence with its air horn.

# *Questions*

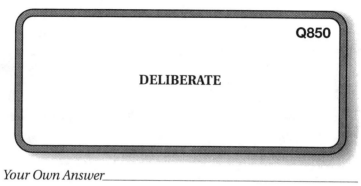

Q850

**DELIBERATE**

*Your Own Answer*_____

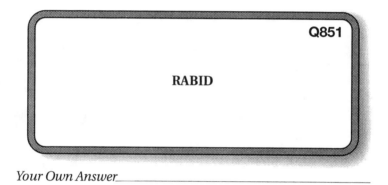

Q851

**RABID**

*Your Own Answer*_____

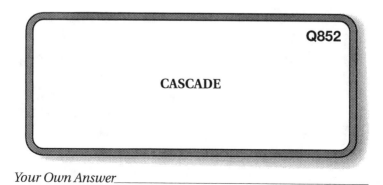

Q852

**CASCADE**

*Your Own Answer*_____

# Correct Answers

**A850**

v.; adj.—1. to consider carefully; weigh in the mind 2. intentional

1. The jury **deliberated** for three days before reaching a verdict.
2. The brother's **deliberate** attempt to get his sibling blamed for his mistake was obvious to all.

**A851**

adj.; n.— 1. furious; with extreme anger 2. a disease affecting animals

1. The insult made him **rabid**.
2. Discovering that the dog was **rabid**, the mail carrier knew he'd have to get a shot after he was bitten.

**A852**

n.; v.—1. waterfall 2. to pour; to rush; to fall

1. The hikers stopped along the path to take in the beauty of the rushing **cascade**.
2. The water **cascaded** down the rocks into the pool.

# Questions

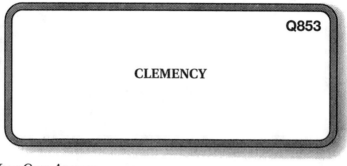

Q853

**CLEMENCY**

*Your Own Answer*_____

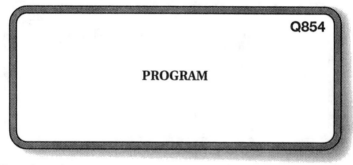

Q854

**PROGRAM**

*Your Own Answer*_____

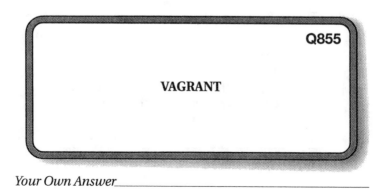

Q855

**VAGRANT**

*Your Own Answer*_____

# Correct Answers

## A853

n.— 1. mercy toward an offender 2. mildness

1. The governor granted the prisoner **clemency**.
2. The weather's **clemency** made for a perfect picnic.

## A854

n.— 1. the parts of entertainment 2. a plan for dealing with a matter 3. coded instructions

1. The free-form music **program** on Sunday nights is virtually unique in commercial radio.
2. The **program** for better health is to eat more vegetables and fruits.
3. The store's computer **program** allows sale information to prompt at the register for certain items at certain hours.

## A855

n.; adj.— 1. homeless person 2. rambling; wandering; transient

1. The first thing the shop owner did every morning was chase a **vagrant** from her doorstep.
2. Circus performers, with nary an opportunity to put down roots, typically lead a **vagrant** life.

# Questions

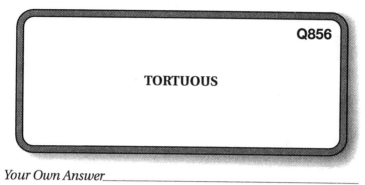

**Q856**

**TORTUOUS**

*Your Own Answer*_____

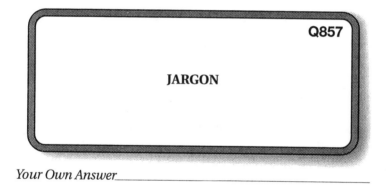

**Q857**

**JARGON**

*Your Own Answer*_____

**Q858**

**INUNDATE**

*Your Own Answer*_____

# Correct Answers

**A856**

adj.—1. full of twists and turns 2. deceitful

1. The course for the 10K race proved **tortuous**, with most of the turns keeping the runners within view of the shoreline.
2. Emilio gave a **tortuous** explanation for his whereabouts the night before, and his wife furrowed her brow in disbelief.

**A857**

n.—1. incoherent speech 2. specialized vocabulary in certain fields

1. The conversation was nothing but **jargon**, but then the speakers were nothing but cartoon characters who specialize in an oddly bracing form of gibberish.
2. The engineers' **jargon** is indecipherable to a layperson.

**A858**

v.—1. to flood 2. to overwhelm with a large amount of

1. The broken water main **inundated** the business district with water.
2. Surfing the Internet can **inundate** you with information, which is why a Web browser comes in handy.

# *Questions*

Q859

**LAMENT**

*Your Own Answer*_____

Q860

**BLATANT**

*Your Own Answer*_____

Q861

**BIENNIAL**

*Your Own Answer*_____

# Correct Answers

**A859**

v.; n.—1. to mourn or grieve 2. expression of grief or sorrow

1. The boy is **lamenting** the loss of his pet.
2. Pedro's only **lament** was that his wife didn't out-live him.

**A860**

adj.—1. obvious; unmistakable 2. crude; vulgar

1. The **blatant** foul was reason for ejection.
2. The defendant was **blatant** in his testimony.

**A861**

adj.; n.— 1. happening every two years 2. a plant which blooms every two years

1. The **biennial** journal's influence seemed only magnified by its infrequent publication.
2. She has lived here for four years and has seen the **biennials** bloom twice.

# Questions

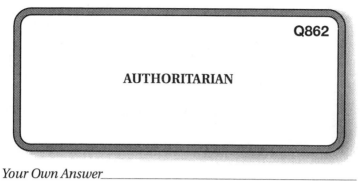

Q862

**AUTHORITARIAN**

*Your Own Answer*_____

_____

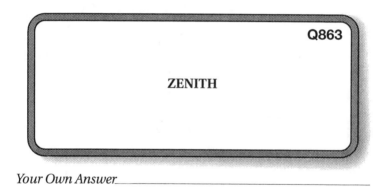

Q863

**ZENITH**

*Your Own Answer*_____

_____

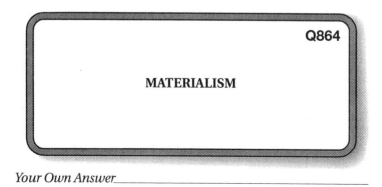

Q864

**MATERIALISM**

*Your Own Answer*_____

_____

# Correct Answers

**A862**

n.; adj.— 1. acting as a dictator  2. demanding obedience

1. The **authoritarian** made all of the rules but did none of the work.
2. Fidel Castro is reluctant to give up his **authoritarian** rule.

**A863**

n.—1. point directly overhead in the sky  2. highest point

1. The astronomer pointed her telescope straight up toward the **zenith**.
2. The Broncos seemed to be at the **zenith** of their power just as their rivals on the turf were flagging.

**A864**

n.— 1. the belief that everything in the universe is explained in terms of matter 2.the belief that worldly possessions are the be-all and end-all in life

1. Spiritualists will tell you that **materialism** is only half the story.
2. Some said that the prince's profligacy gave **materialism** a bad name.

# Questions

**DISDAIN**

*Your Own Answer*_____

**DEMUR**

*Your Own Answer*_____

**TEMPER**

*Your Own Answer*_____

# Correct Answers

**A865**

n.; v.— 1. intense dislike 2. to look down upon; to scorn

1. She showed great **disdain** toward anyone who did not agree with her.
2. She **disdains** the very ground you walk upon.

**A866**

v.; n.— 1. to object 2. objection; misgiving

1. She hated animals, so when the subject of buying a cat came up, she **demurred**.
2. She said yes, but he detected a **demur** in her voice.

**A867**

v.—1. to moderate, as by mingling with something else 2. to bring to the proper condition by treatment

1. She drew a hot bath, but then realized she'd have to **temper** it with a little cool water or end up scalded.
2. The craftsman **tempered** the steel before being able to twist it to form a table leg.

# Questions

**DITHER**

*Your Own Answer*_____

**AMISS**

*Your Own Answer*_____

**DIDACTIC**

*Your Own Answer*_____

# *Correct Answers*

**A868**

v.; n.— 1. to act indecisively 2. a confused condition

1. She **dithered** every time she had to make a decision.
2. Having to take two tests in one day left the student in a **dither**.

**A869**

adj.; adv.—1. wrong; awry 2. wrongly; in a defective manner

1. Seeing that his anorak was gone, he knew something was **amiss**.
2. Its new muffler aside, the car was behaving **amiss**.

**A870**

adj.—1. instructive 2. dogmatic; preachy

1. Our teacher's **didactic** technique boosted our scores.
2. The **didactic** activist was not one to be swayed.

# *Questions*

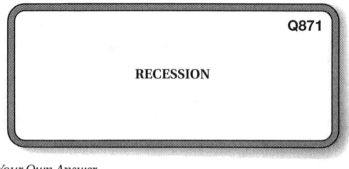

Q871

**RECESSION**

*Your Own Answer*_____

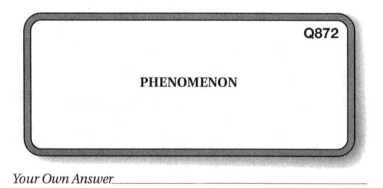

Q872

**PHENOMENON**

*Your Own Answer*_____

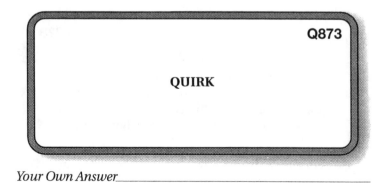

Q873

**QUIRK**

*Your Own Answer*_____

# *Correct Answers*

**A871**

n.—1. withdrawal 2. economic downturn

1. Oscar's gum **recession** left him with sensitive teeth.
2. Soaring unemployment in the nation's industrial belt triggered **recession**.

**A872**

n.—1. exceptional person 2. unusual occurrence

1. They call Yankee Stadium "The House that Ruth Built" because the Babe was a **phenomenon**.
2. The northern lights are a rare **phenomenon** for those not living near the Arctic Circle.

**A873**

n.—1. peculiar behavior 2. startling twist

1. Nobody's perfect—we all have our **quirks**.
2. Our vacation went smoothly save for one **quirk**—a hurricane that came barreling into the coastline as we were preparing to head home.

# Questions

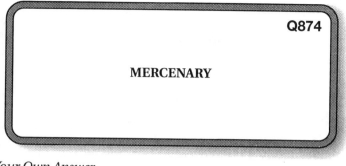

Q874

**MERCENARY**

*Your Own Answer*_____

_____

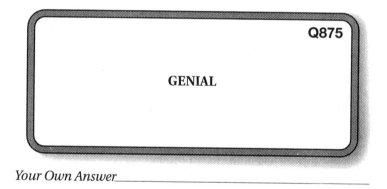

Q875

**GENIAL**

*Your Own Answer*_____

_____

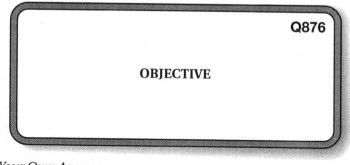

Q876

**OBJECTIVE**

*Your Own Answer*_____

_____

# Correct Answers

**A874**

adj.; n.— 1. working or done for payment only
2. hired (soldier)

1. Lila was suspicious that Joe had jumped at the chance only for **mercenary** reasons.
2. A **mercenary** was hired for a hundred dollars a month, good money in those days even if you had to fight a war to get it.

**A875**

adj.— 1. contributing to life 2. amiable

1. Key West's **genial** climate is among its many attractive aspects.
2. Her **genial** personality made her a favorite party guest.

**A876**

adj.; n.— 1. open-minded; impartial 2. goal

1. It's hard to set aside your biases and be **objective**.
2. The law student decided that her primary **objective** after graduation was to pass the Bar examination.

# *Questions*

**Q877**

**ARTICULATE**

*Your Own Answer*_____

**Q878**

**RAZE**

*Your Own Answer*_____

**Q879**

**VIABLE**

*Your Own Answer*_____

# Correct Answers

**A877**

v.; adj.—1. to utter clearly and distinctly 2. clear; distinct; expressed with clarity; skillful with words

1. It's even more important to **articulate** your words when you're on the phone.
2. You didn't have to vote for him to agree that Adlai Stevenson was **articulate**.

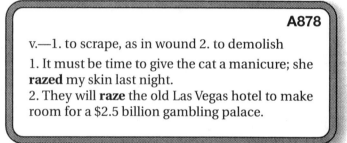

**A878**

v.—1. to scrape, as in wound 2. to demolish

1. It must be time to give the cat a manicure; she **razed** my skin last night.
2. They will **raze** the old Las Vegas hotel to make room for a $2.5 billion gambling palace.

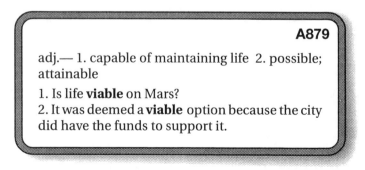

**A879**

adj.— 1. capable of maintaining life 2. possible; attainable

1. Is life **viable** on Mars?
2. It was deemed a **viable** option because the city did have the funds to support it.

# Questions

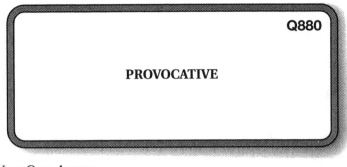

Q880

**PROVOCATIVE**

*Your Own Answer*_____

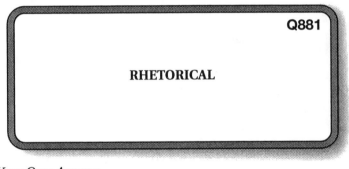

Q881

**RHETORICAL**

*Your Own Answer*_____

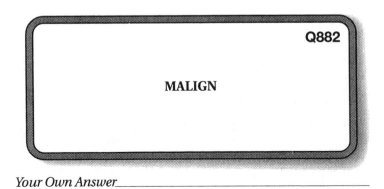

Q882

**MALIGN**

*Your Own Answer*_____

# Correct Answers

**A880**

adj.—1. tempting  2. irritating

1. In the movie *Roger Rabbit*, the animated Jessica Rabbit demurs when she's told she's **provocative**, saying that she's only drawn that way.
2. The U.S. considered the invasion of Kuwait a **provocative** action.

**A881**

adj.—1. having to do with verbal communication 2. artificial eloquence

1. In posing a **rhetorical** question, he hoped to get people thinking.
2. The perception that Gary Hart was spouting **rhetorical** flourishes enabled fellow Democrat Walter Mondale to score debate points by asking, "Where's the beef?"

**A882**

v.; adj.—1. to speak evil of  2. having an evil disposition toward others (opposite: benign)

1. In her statement to the judge, she **maligned** her soon-to-be ex-husband.
2. She had such a **malign** personality that no one even tried to approach her, mostly out of fear.

# Questions

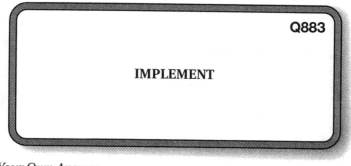

**Q883**

**IMPLEMENT**

*Your Own Answer*_____

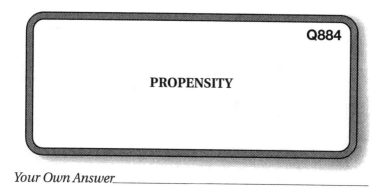

**Q884**

**PROPENSITY**

*Your Own Answer*_____

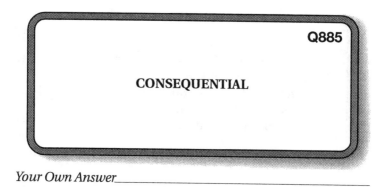

**Q885**

**CONSEQUENTIAL**

*Your Own Answer*_____

# Correct Answers

**A883**

v.; n.—1. to carry into effect 2. something used in a given activity

1. In case of emergency, **implement** the evacuation plan immediately.
2. The rack is an **implement** of torture.

**A884**

n.—1. a natural tendency towards 2. bias

1. I have a **propensity** to talk too fast.
2. She has a **propensity** to hire men over women.

**A885**

adj.—1. following as an effect 2. important

1. His long illness and **consequential** absence set him behind in his homework.
2. The decision to move the company will be **consequential** to its success.

# Questions

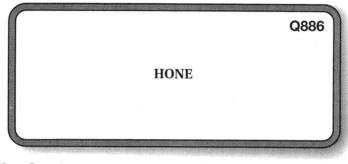

**Q886**

**HONE**

*Your Own Answer*_____

**Q887**

**RESIGNATION**

*Your Own Answer*_____

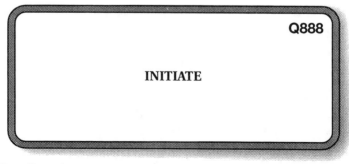

**Q888**

**INITIATE**

*Your Own Answer*_____

# *Correct Answers*

**A886**

v.—1. to sharpen, as with a stone 2. to long or yearn for

1. He's still **honing** his skills at the potter's wheel.
2. The traveler **hones** for his homeland.

**A887**

n.—1. quitting 2. submission

1. He submitted his **resignation** because he found a new job.
2. You could see the **resignation** on his face: Things just weren't working out as he had expected.

**A888**

v.; n.—1. to begin; to admit into a group 2. a person who is in the process of being admitted into a group

1. He **initiated** the dinner discussion by asking his father to borrow the car.
2. As an **initiate** to the Explorers, George was expected to have a taste for the outdoor life.

# Questions

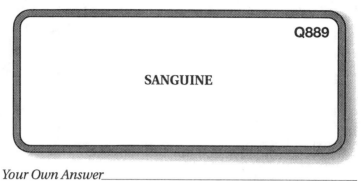

Q889

**SANGUINE**

*Your Own Answer*_____

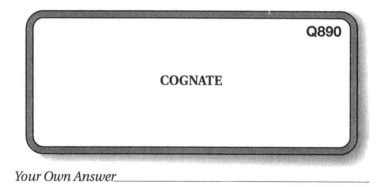

Q890

**COGNATE**

*Your Own Answer*_____

Q891

**NOTORIOUS**

*Your Own Answer*_____

# Correct Answers

**A889**

adj.—1. optimistic; cheerful 2. red

1. Even when victory seemed impossible, the general remained **sanguine**.

2. The dress was **sanguine** with a bright green border stripe.

**A890**

adj.; n.— 1. having the same family 2. a person related through ancestry

1. English and German are **cognate** languages.

2. The woman was a **cognate** to the royal family.

**A891**

adj.—1. infamous; renowned 2. having an unfavorable connotation

1. Discovering that her new neighbor was **notorious** for thievery, she decided to purchase an alarm system for her home.

2. The criminal had a **notorious** reputation.

# *Questions*

Q892

**PAROCHIAL**

*Your Own Answer*_____

Q893

**IMPETUOUS**

*Your Own Answer*_____

Q894

**WRETCHED**

*Your Own Answer*_____

# *Correct Answers*

**A892**

adj.—1. religious 2. narrow-minded

1. Devout Christians, the Chesterfields enrolled their children in a **parochial** school.
2. Governor Kean urged Republicans to rise above **parochial** interests and be the party of inclusion.

**A893**

adj.—1. rash; impulsive 2. forcible; violent

1. Dagmar came to regret his **impetuous** actions, once he realized what he'd done.
2. The pirate's men boarded the ship with **impetuous** matter-of-factness.

**A894**

adj.—1. miserable or unhappy 2. causing distress

1. Brought up in an orphanage, Annie led a **wretched** existence.
2. The continual rain made for a **wretched** vacation.

# *Questions*

**Q895**

**PIQUE**

*Your Own Answer*_____

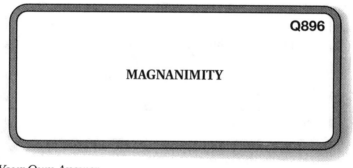

**Q896**

**MAGNANIMITY**

*Your Own Answer*_____

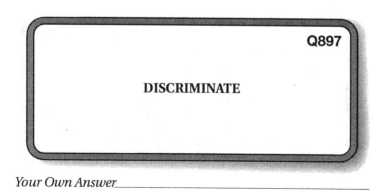

**Q897**

**DISCRIMINATE**

*Your Own Answer*_____

# Correct Answers

n.; v.—1. resentment at being slighted 2. to provoke

1. Being passed over for the promotion aroused his **pique**.
2. The more he **piqued** her, the redder she grew.

n.; adj.—1. a quality of nobleness of mind, disdain of meanness or revenge 2. forgiving; unselfish

1. Being full of **magnanimity**, he asked the thief only for an apology and set him free.
2. The **magnanimous** store owner did not press charges once an apology was given.

v.; adj.—1. to distinguish 2. demonstrating bias

1. Being a chef, he **discriminated** carefully among ingredients.
2. Reeling from the fact that senior managers had been caught on tape making offensive remarks, the CEO said he would not tolerate any of his firm's employees **discriminating** against anyone for any reason.

# Questions

Q898

**ADVOCATE**

*Your Own Answer*_____

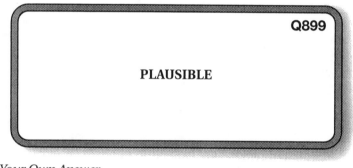

Q899

**PLAUSIBLE**

*Your Own Answer*_____

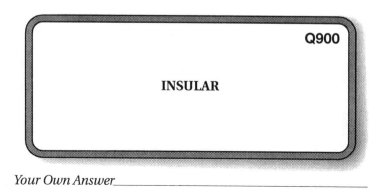

Q900

**INSULAR**

*Your Own Answer*_____

# Correct Answers

**A898**

v.; n.—1. to plead in favor of 2. supporter; defender

1. Amnesty International **advocates** the cause for human rights.
2. Martin Luther King, Jr. was a great **advocate** of civil rights.

**A899**

adj.—1. probable 2. feasible
1. After weeks of trying to determine what or who was raiding the chicken coop, the farmer came up with a **plausible** explanation.
2. After scrimping and saving for a decade, it was now **plausible** to send his daughter to college.

**A900**

adj.—1. having the characteristics of an island 2. narrow-minded, provincial
1. After walking along the entire perimeter and seeing that the spit of land was actually **insular**, we realized it was time to build a boat.
2. His **insular** approach to education makes him a pariah among liberals.

# BLANK CARDS
## *To Make Up Your Own Questions*

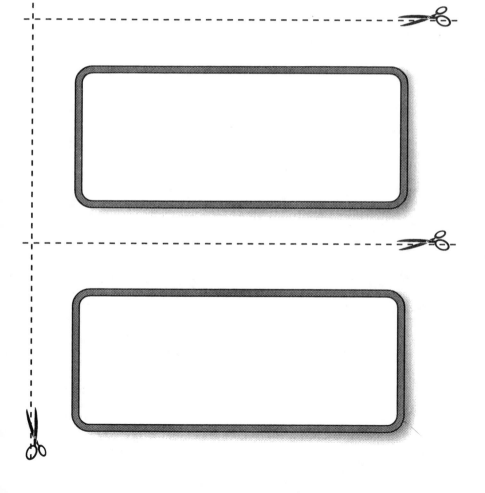

# CORRECT ANSWERS

## *for*

# *Your Own Questions*

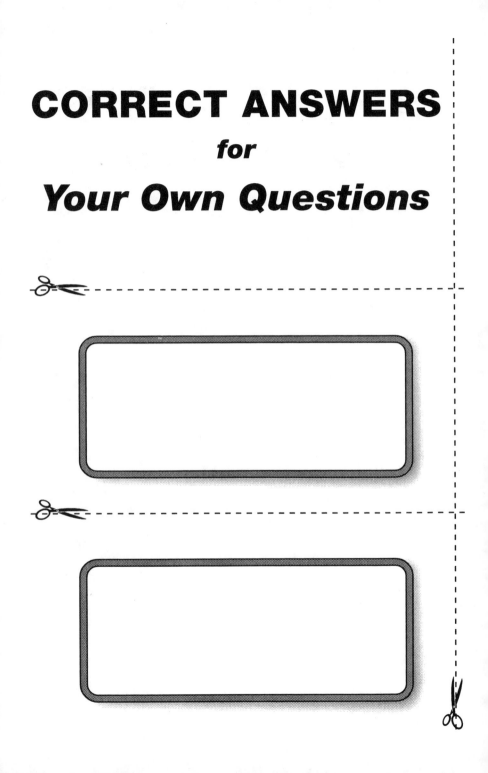

# Blank Cards for
## *Your Own Questions*

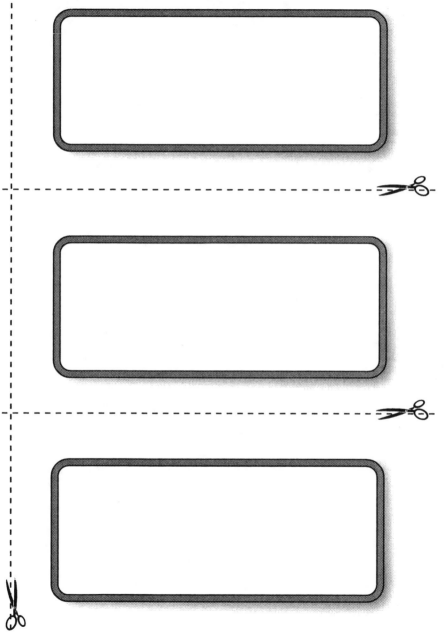

# Correct Answers

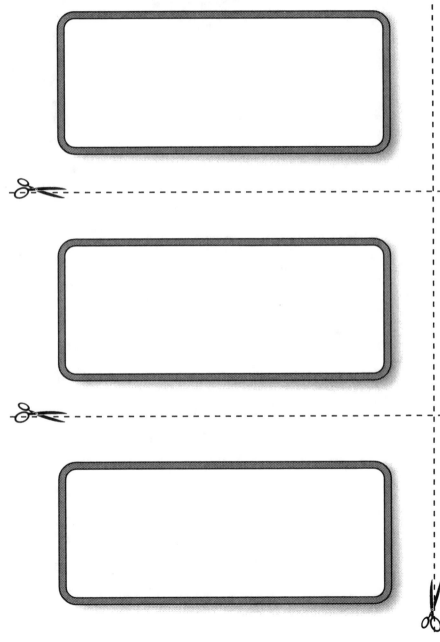

# Blank Cards for
# *Your Own Questions*

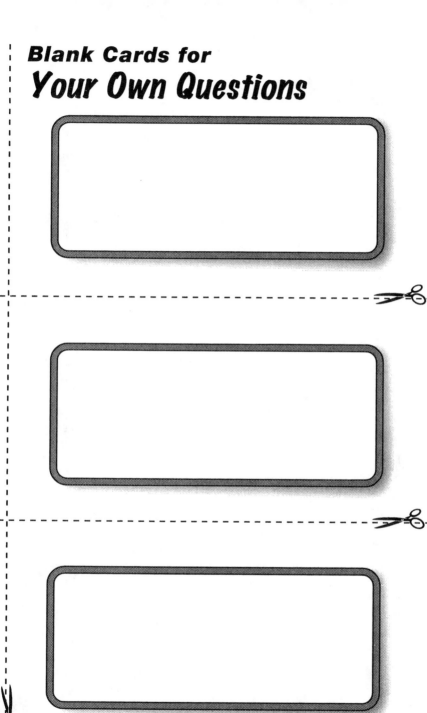

# Correct Answers

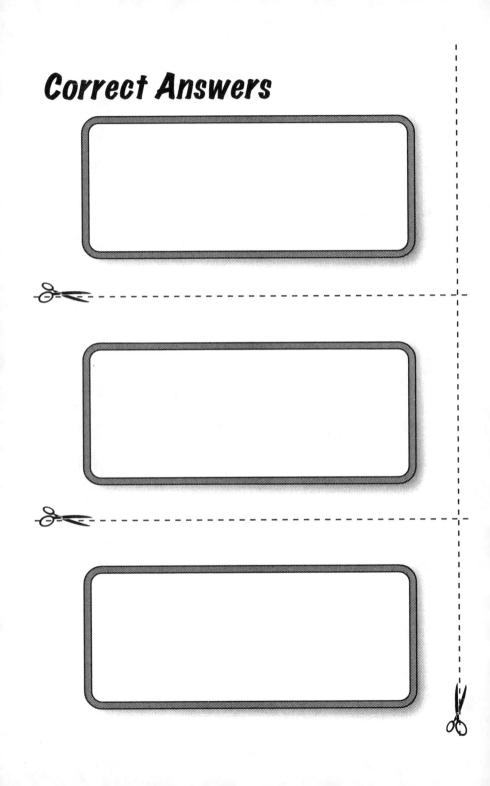

# Blank Cards for *Your Own Questions*

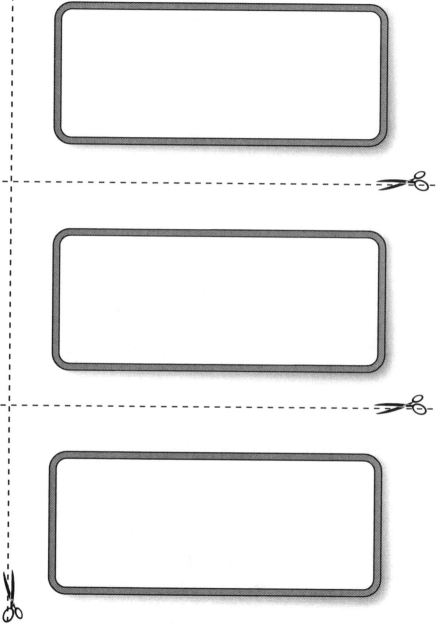

# Correct Answers

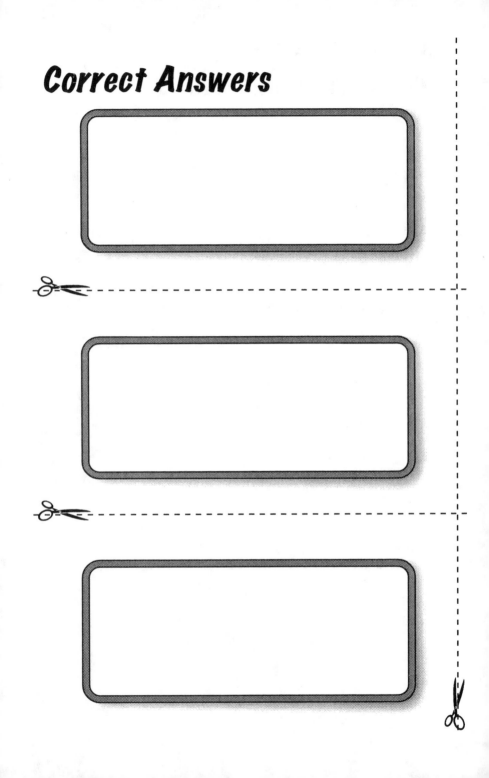

# Blank Cards for *Your Own Questions*

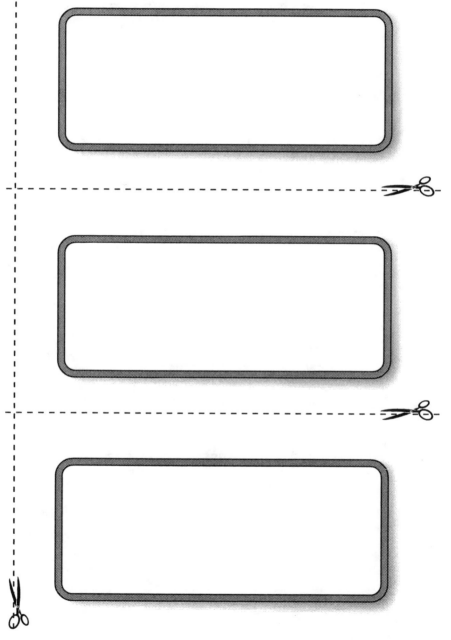

# Correct Answers

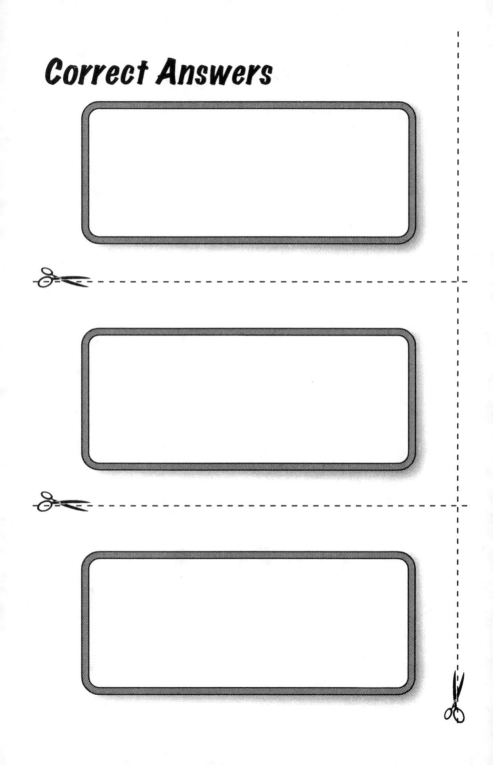

# Blank Cards for
# *Your Own Questions*

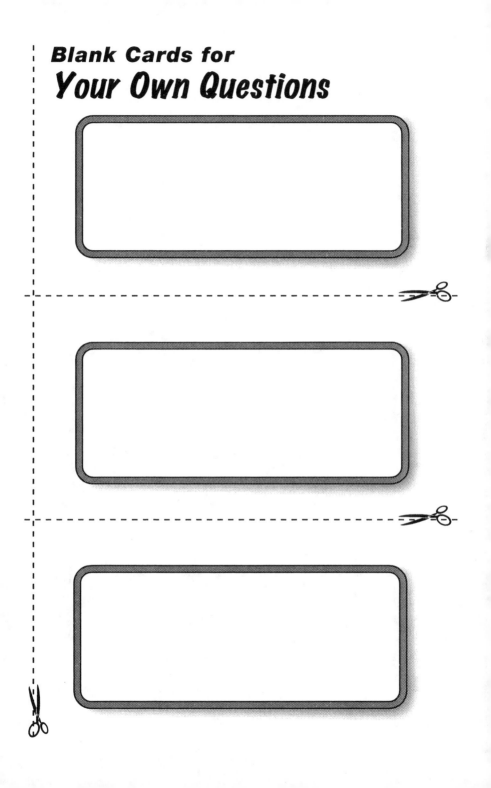

# Correct Answers

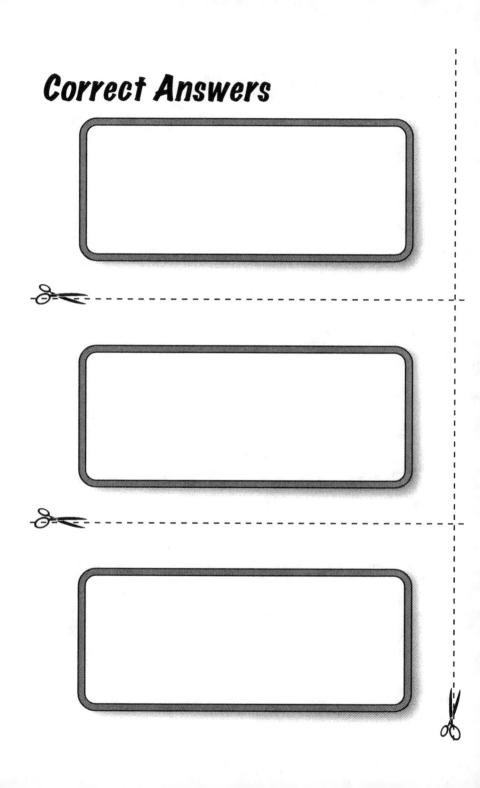

## Blank Cards for *Your Own Questions*

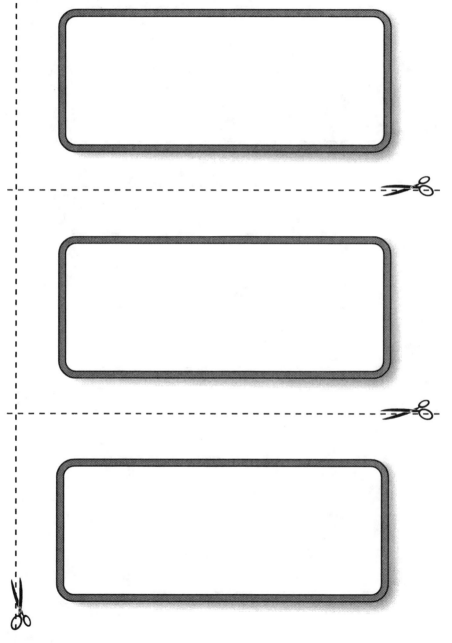

# Correct Answers

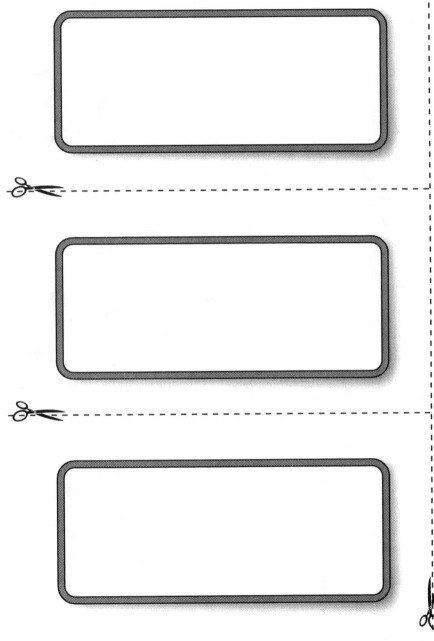

# Blank Cards for
# Your Own Questions

# Correct Answers

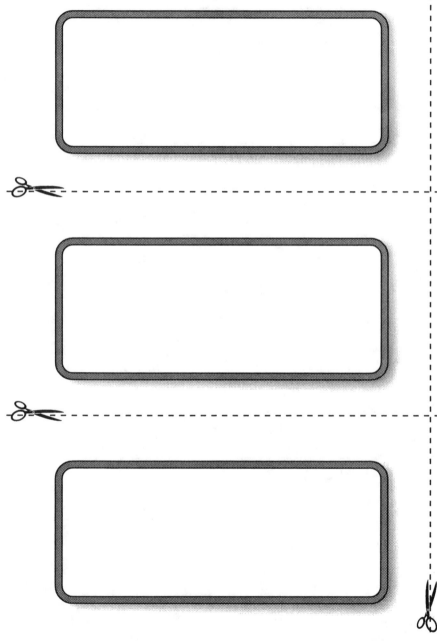

# Blank Cards for *Your Own Questions*

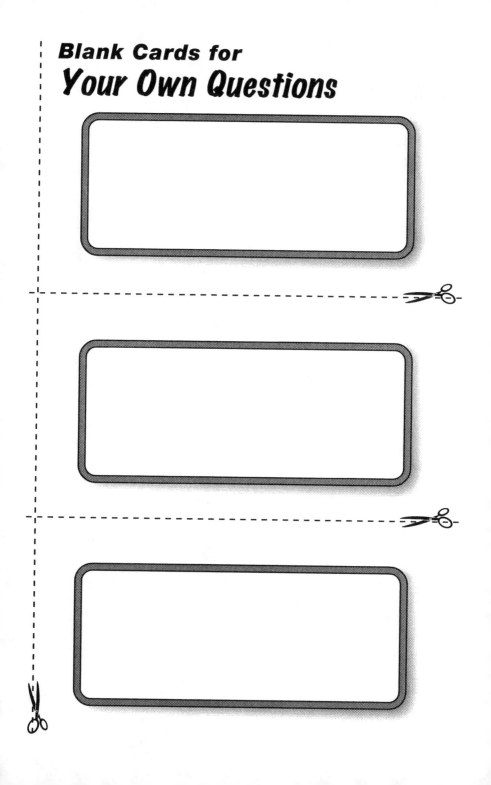

# Correct Answers

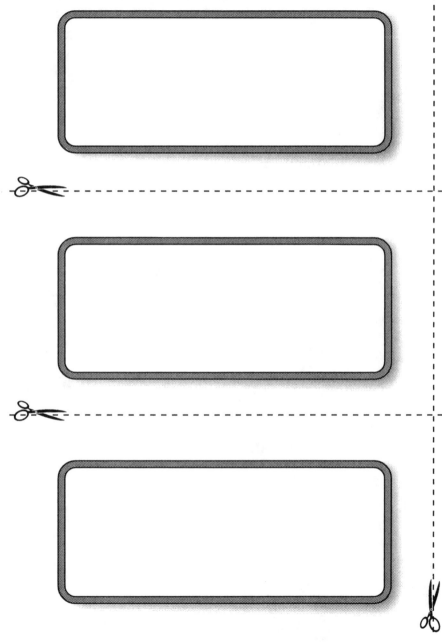

# Blank Cards for *Your Own Questions*

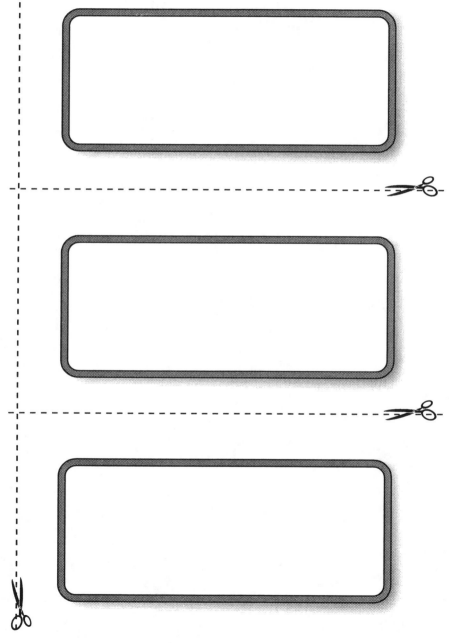

# *Correct Answers*

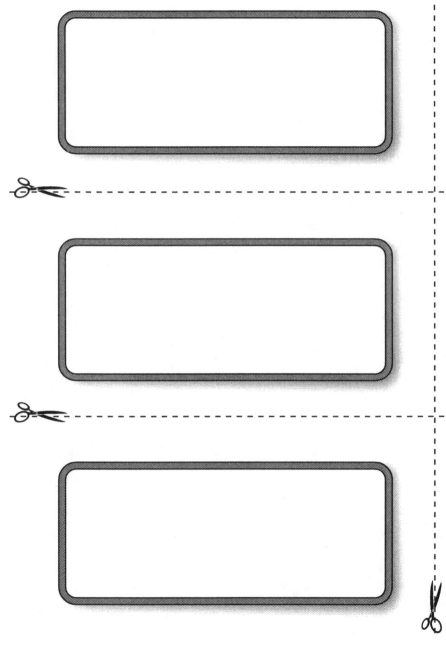

# Blank Cards for
## *Your Own Questions*

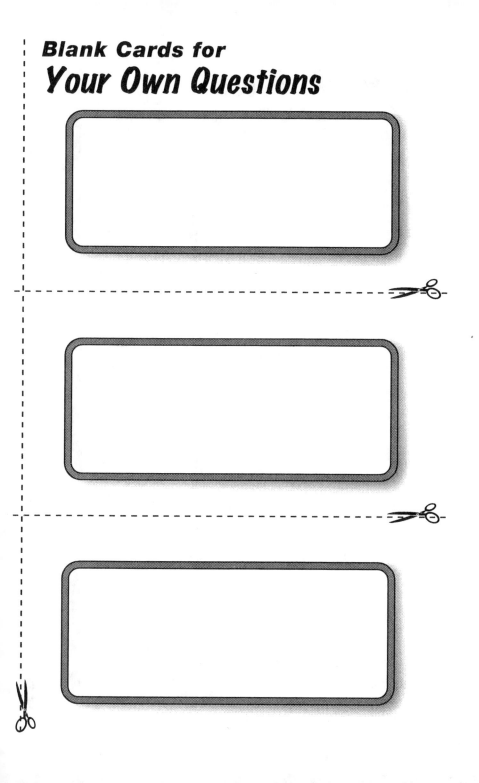

# Correct Answers

# Blank Cards for *Your Own Questions*

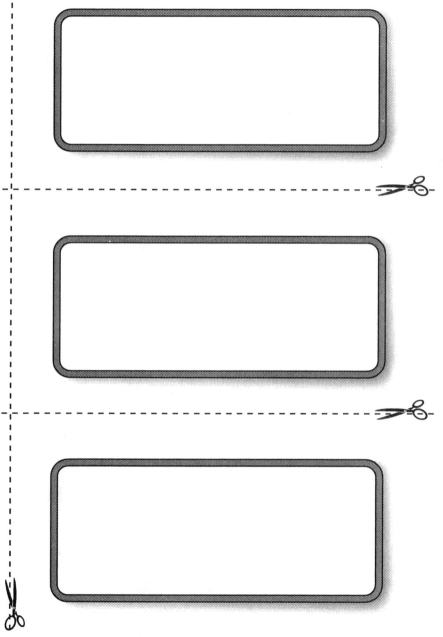

# Correct Answers

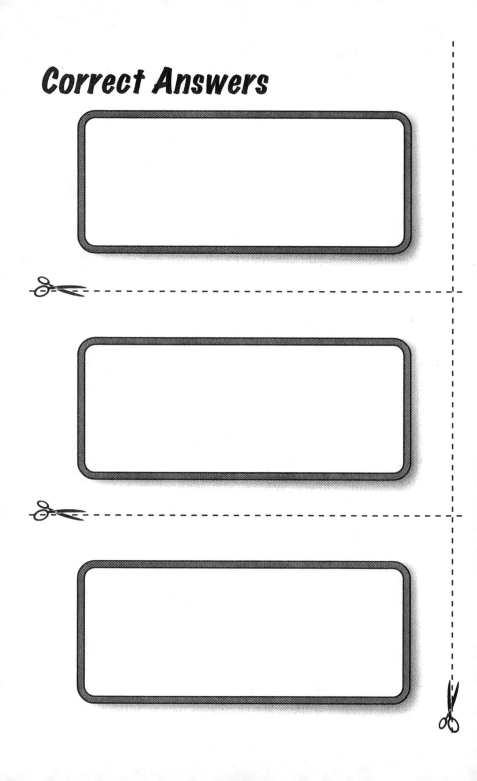

# Blank Cards for
## *Your Own Questions*

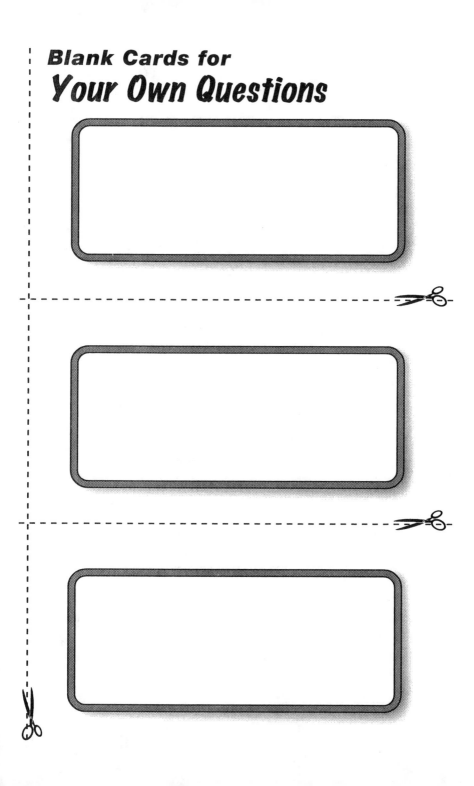

# Correct Answers

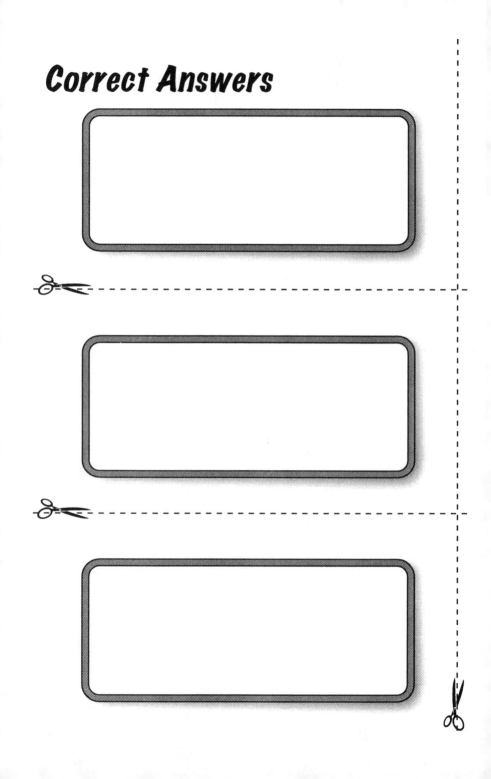

# Blank Cards for
# *Your Own Questions*

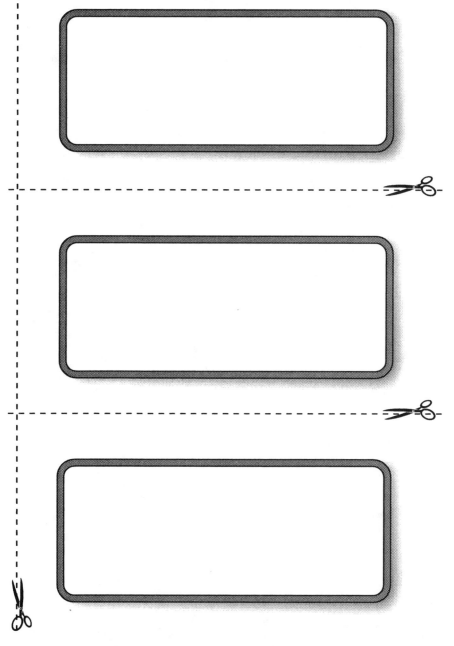

# Correct Answers

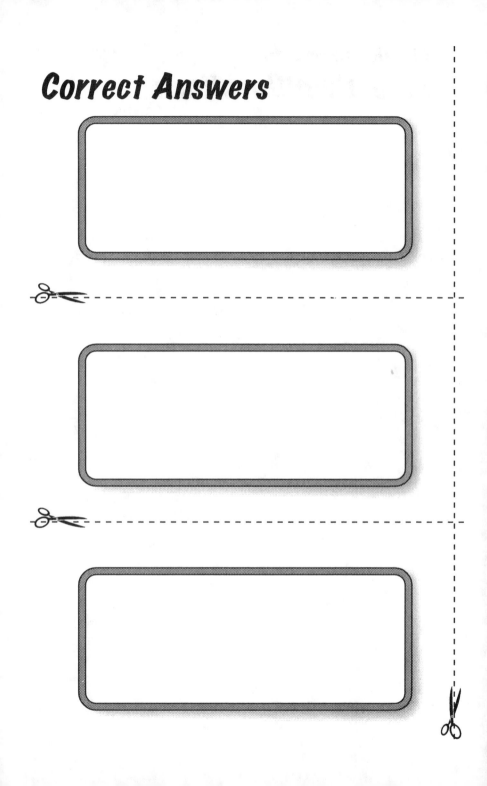

# Blank Cards for
# *Your Own Questions*

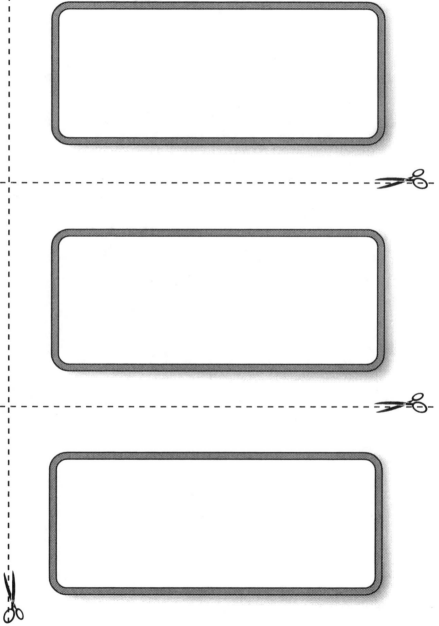

# Correct Answers

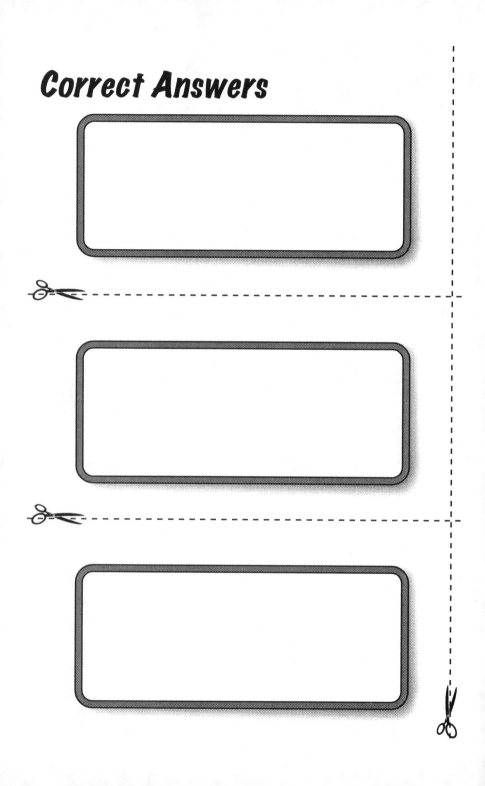

# Blank Cards for
# *Your Own Questions*

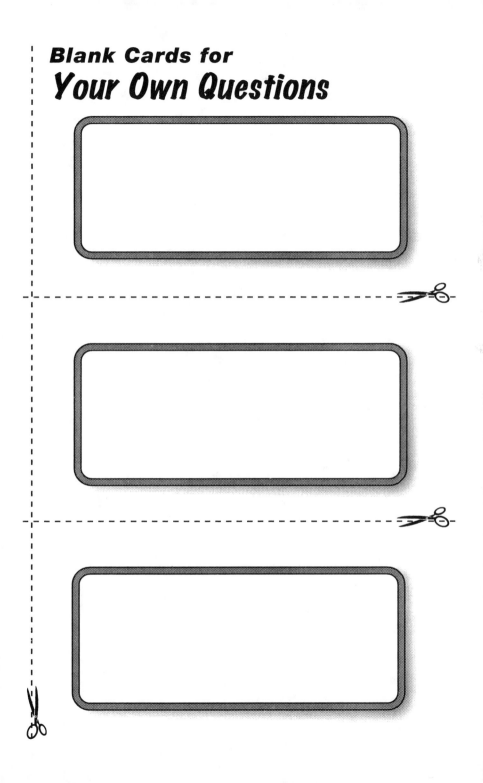

# *Correct Answers*

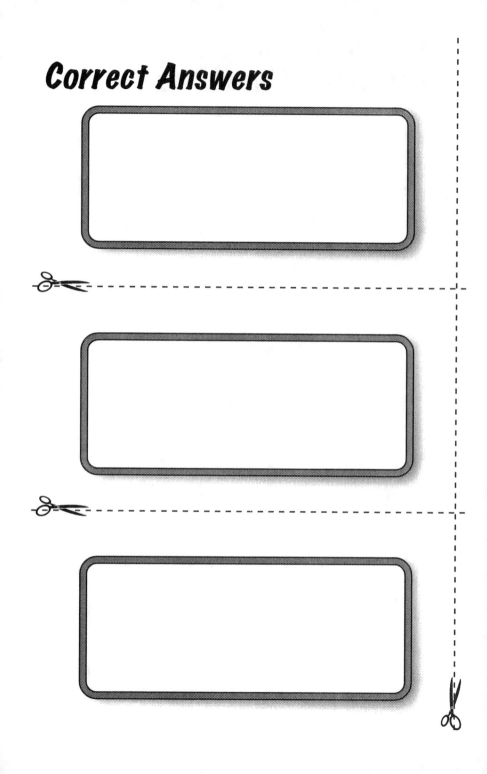

# Blank Cards for
## *Your Own Questions*

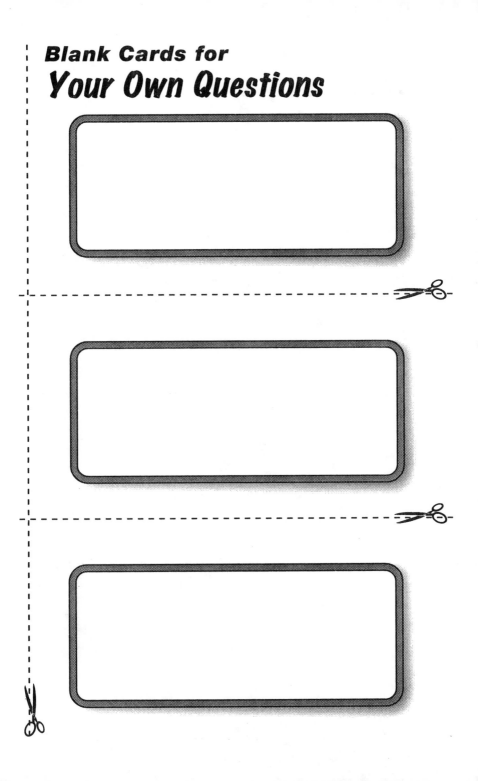

# Correct Answers

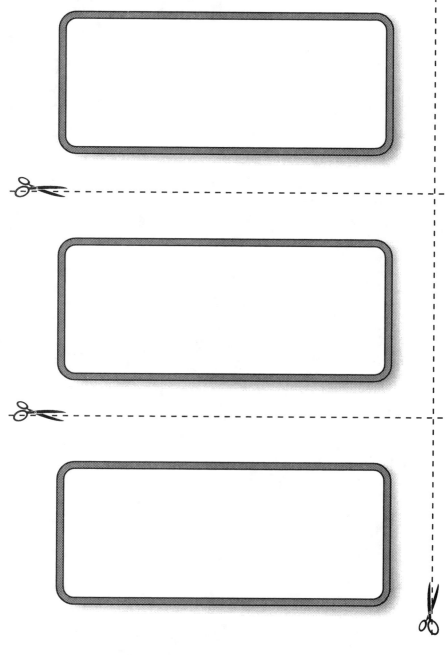

# Blank Cards for
# *Your Own Questions*

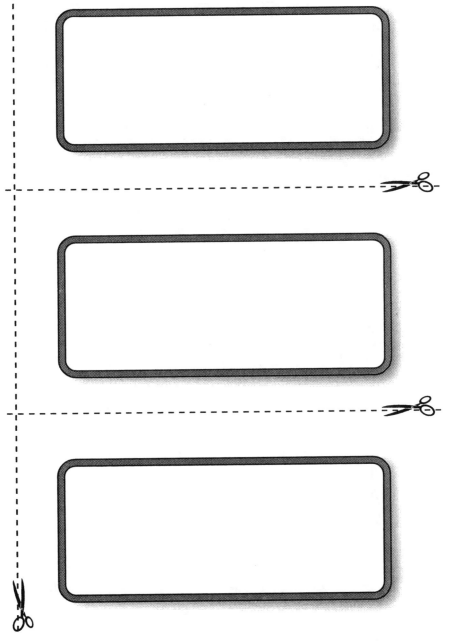

# Correct Answers

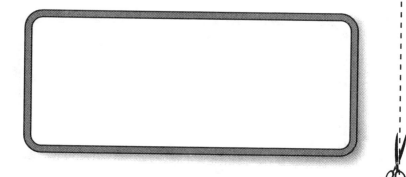

## Blank Cards for *Your Own Questions*

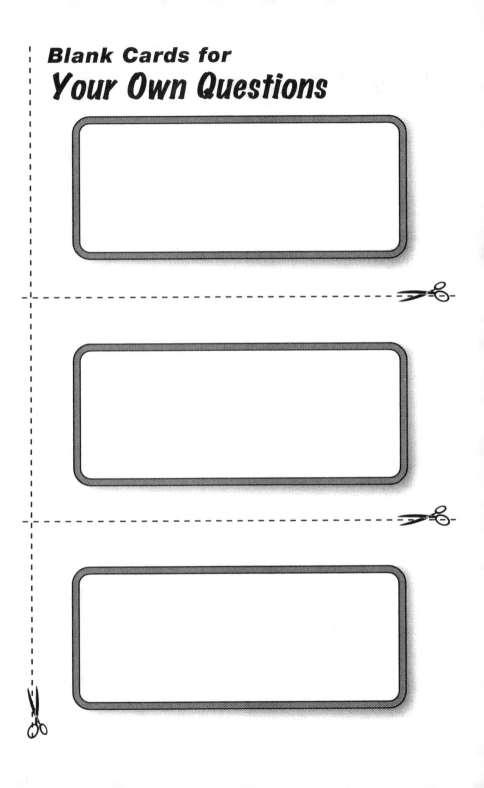

# Correct Answers

# Blank Cards for
# *Your Own Questions*

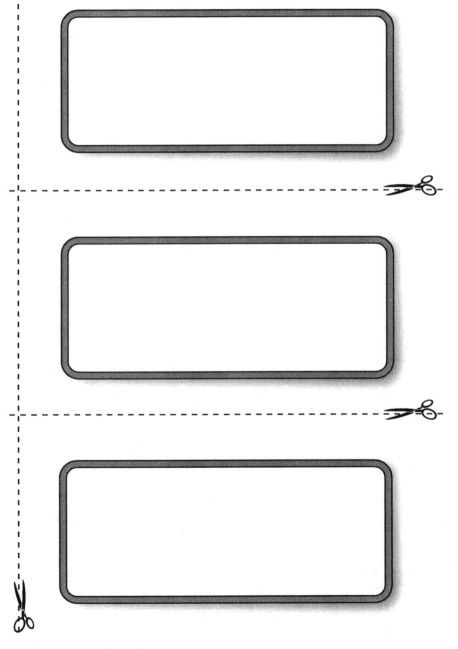

# Correct Answers

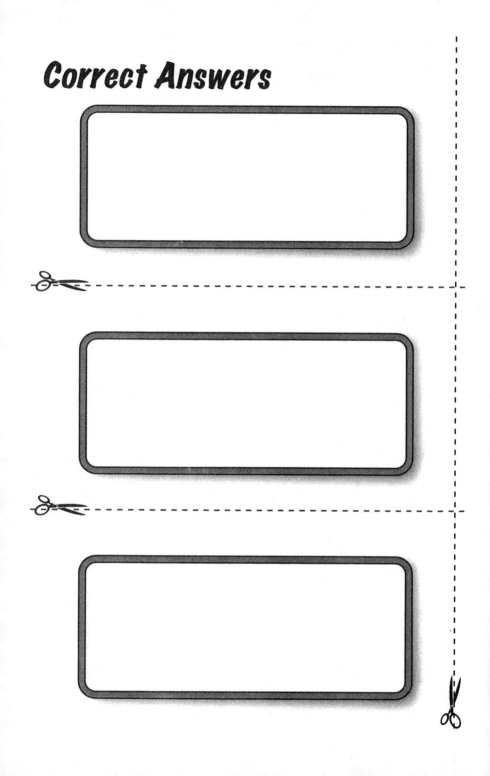

# INDEX

abase, 289
abbreviate, 596
aberrant, 613
abhor, 335
abject, 298
abominate, 493
abridge, 332
abrupt, 429
absolve, 791
abstemious, 577
abstinence, 574
abstract, 683
abstruse, 107
accede, 13
acclaim, 705
accolade, 796
accomplice, 398
accrue, 707
acerbic, 827
acquiesce, 795
acrid, 319
adage, 426
adamant, 307
adept, 155
adroit, 333
adulation, 425
adversary, 207
adverse, 726
advocate, 898
aesthetic, 597
affable, 629
affiliate, 295
affinity, 830
aghast, 848
alacrity, 512
alchemist, 423
alleviate, 424
allocate, 323
allude, 3
allure, 838

allusion, 576
aloof, 378
altercation, 800
altruism, 475
altruistic, 420
amalgam, 433
amalgamate, 111
amass, 77
ambiguous, 419
ambivalent, 418
ameliorate, 37
amendment, 417
amiable, 416
amiss, 869
amity, 415
amorphous, 167
anachronism, 657
analogy, 733
anarchist, 414
anchorage, 539
anecdote, 141
animosity, 763
anoint, 807
anomaly, 578
anonymous, 514
antagonism, 182
antipathy, 90
apathy, 336
apocryphal, 253
appease, 805
apposite, 4
apprehensive, 232
approbatory, 278
arable, 21
arbiter, 345
arbitrary, 489
arcane, 79
archetype, 166
ardent, 324
arduous, 741
arid, 68
aromatic, 412

arrogant, 783
articulate, 877
ascetic, 843
aseptic, 128
asperity, 410
aspersion, 675
aspirant, 409
assess, 479
assiduous, 671
assuage, 250
astringent, 725
astute, 408
atrophy, 816
attenuate, 370
atypical, 406
audacious, 405
augment, 47
august, 212
austere, 403
authentic, 766
authoritarian, 862
autocracy, 453
autocrat, 401
avarice, 400
aviary, 391
awry, 632
azure, 399
baleful, 778
banal, 562
baneful, 515
baroque, 396
bastion, 136
behoove, 547
belittle, 94
bemuse, 308
benefactor, 767
beneficent, 666
benevolent, 189
benign, 808
berate, 368
bereft, 80
biased, 91

biennial, 861
bilateral, 823
blasphemous, 93
blatant, 860
blithe, 82
bombast, 788
bombastic, 388
breadth, 125
brevity, 511
bungler, 216
burgeon, 776
burly, 260
cache, 834
cacophonous, 379
cacophony, 394
cajole, 42
calamity, 317
callow, 11
candid, 502
cant, 114
caprice, 275
capricious, 376
cascade, 852
catalyst, 261
catharsis, 670
caustic, 611
censor, 366
censure, 620
ceremonious, 390
chagrin, 458
charisma, 467
charlatan, 552
chastise, 133
cherish, 384
chicanery, 803
chimera, 501
choleric, 487
chortle, 365
churlishness, 316
circumlocution, 369
circumlocutory, 560
citadel, 822

clemency, 853
cloture, 735
cloying, 732
coagulate, 267
coalesce, 753
coda, 404
coddle, 824
codify, 287
coffer, 361
cogent, 660
cogitate, 171
cognate, 890
cognitive, 510
cognizant, 555
coherent, 585
cohesion, 360
collaborate, 101
colloquial, 69
comeliness, 628
commiserate, 293
commodious, 48
communal, 357
compatible, 25
complacent, 373
complaisance, 356
compliant, 154
comprehensive, 544
compromise, 538
concede, 300
conceit, 252
conciliation, 407
concise, 355
condescend, 411
condone, 263
confluence, 681
confound, 839
conglomeration, 143
conjure, 836
connoisseur, 57
connotative, 353
consecrate, 41
consequential, 885

conspicuous, 338
consternation, 265
constrain, 132
consummation, 690
contemporary, 728
contempt, 301
contentious, 51
contest, 586
contiguous, 66
contravene, 96
contrite, 491
conundrum, 268
conventional, 383
converge, 550
convoke, 124
copious, 610
corpulence, 352
correlate, 158
coterie, 700
cower, 119
crass, 828
craven, 17
curb, 819
cynic, 347
dearth, 801
debacle, 161
debase, 315
debilitate, 202
decisiveness, 722
decorous, 45
defamation, 374
defensible, 814
deferential, 785
deign, 655
deleterious, 719
deliberate, 850
delineate, 476
demise, 342
demur, 866
denigrate, 789
denounce, 797
depict, 239

deplete, 678
depravity, 710
deprecate, 329
deride, 519
derision, 729
derogatory, 637
desecrate, 121
desist, 279
desolate, 711
destitute, 508
detached, 716
deter, 673
determinate, 230
devoid, 142
diatribe, 387
dichotomy, 340
dictum, 731
didactic, 870
diffidence, 798
diffident, 627
diffuse, 601
digress, 564
diligence, 760
din, 337
dirge, 241
disapprobation, 626
disarray, 113
disavow, 428
discerning, 669
discord, 62
discourse, 165
discrete, 364
discriminate, 897
disdain, 865
disentangle, 35
disheartened, 694
disingenuous, 676
disinterested, 658
disparage, 779
disparate, 59
disparity, 64
dispassionate, 454

disperse, 842
disputatious, 608
dissemble, 774
disseminate, 643
dissent, 58
dissonance, 523
dissonant, 717
distant, 486
distention, 382
dither, 868
diverge, 208
diverse, 351
docile, 34
document, 829
dogma, 334
dogmatic, 584
dubious, 529
duplicity, 473
duress, 271
eccentric, 33
economical, 12
effeminate, 810
effervescence, 831
effigy, 718
epitome, 78
erratic, 607
ethnic, 703
euphony, 310
evoke, 762
exemplary, 704
exonerate, 594
exorbitant, 503
exotic, 528
facade, 835
facilitate, 494
fatuous, 322
fealty, 397
feasible, 569
fervor, 348
fickle, 749
finesse, 817
finite, 320

flaccid, 221
fledgling, 350
fluency, 367
foible, 522
foist, 149
fortuitous, 116
foster, 815
frugality, 606
fulminate, 481
gainsay, 638
garbled, 288
garrulous, 518
gauntlet, 311
generic, 18
genial, 875
germane, 625
gibber, 55
gloat, 471
glutton, 306
gourmand, 813
grandiose, 605
gravity, 303
guffaw, 6
guile, 739
guise, 98
gullible, 680
hackneyed, 542
haggard, 543
halcyon, 220
hamper, 173
haphazard, 674
harbor, 826
harmonious, 372
haughty, 297
hedonistic, 300
heed, 583
hefty, 99
heresy, 571
hiatus, 742
hierarchy, 587
hindrance, 612
homage, 195

hone, 886
humility, 684
hyperbole, 327
hypocritical, 524
hypothetical, 809
iconoclast, 520
ideology, 663
ignoble, 551
illuminate, 589
illusory, 640
imbue, 231
immune, 713
immutable, 109
impale, 273
impartial, 697
impassive, 701
impecunious, 302
impede, 184
imperturbable, 291
impervious, 88
impetuous, 893
implacable, 100
implement, 883
implication, 765
impromptu, 623
impugn, 343
inadvertent, 556
inanimate, 386
inarticulate, 639
inaudible, 156
incessant, 570
inchoate, 214
incidental, 344
incisive, 602
inclined, 844
incognito, 321
incoherent, 691
incompatible, 745
incompetence, 422
inconclusive, 175
incredulous, 176
indecipherable, 164

indelible, 201
indict, 304
indifferent, 65
indigence, 325
indigenous, 499
indolent, 582
indulgent, 667
inept, 447
inert, 568
inevitable, 821
infamous, 784
infamy, 106
infer, 685
ingenue, 757
ingenuous, 290
ingratiate, 254
ingratitude, 24
inherent, 820
initiate, 888
innate, 616
innocuous, 120
innovate, 466
innuendo, 222
inquisitive, 764
insinuate, 635
insipid, 721
instigate, 549
insubordinate, 385
insular, 900
intangible, 567
intercede, 131
intermittent, 531
intractable, 699
intransigent, 395
intrepid, 286
inundate, 858
inveterate, 285
invoke, 211
iota, 60
irascible, 540
ironic, 566
irrational, 546

irreparable, 296
irreproachable, 294
itinerary, 67
jargon, 857
jeopardy, 377
jester, 284
jocund, 185
jollity, 280
jovial, 456
judicious, 750
juncture, 22
juxtapose, 402
kindle, 746
kinship, 533
knavery, 122
knead, 786
knotty, 238
labyrinth, 751
laconic, 205
laggard, 759
lament, 859
languid, 708
larceny, 781
lascivious, 654
lassitude, 537
laud, 661
lax, 450
lecherous, 269
lethal, 234
lethargic, 692
levity, 535
liaison, 134
liberalism, 581
limber, 346
lithe, 812
livid, 530
loiter, 526
loquacious, 452
lucid, 847
lucrative, 474
luminous, 54
lunge, 213

lustrous, 434
luxuriant, 259
macerate, 46
maculate, 846
magnanimity, 896
malediction, 236
malefactor, 257
malevolent, 469
malicious, 256
malign, 882
malinger, 634
malleable, 163
mandate, 229
manifest, 768
mar, 137
materialism, 864
meander, 49
melancholy, 313
melodious, 249
menagerie, 534
mentor, 773
mercenary, 874
mercurial, 248
mesmerize, 127
metamorphosis, 806
meticulous, 272
mimicry, 359
minute, 744
mire, 375
misanthrope, 247
miser, 246
mitigate, 459
molten, 439
morose, 636
motif, 770
mundane, 152
munificent, 240
muse, 588
myriad, 682
narcissistic, 237
nautical, 362
nefarious, 233

negligence, 521
neologism, 437
neophyte, 724
nettle, 72
neutral, 243
nostalgic, 464
nostrum, 226
notorious, 891
novel, 559
noxious, 225
nullify, 712
obdurate, 224
objective, 876
obligatory, 575
obliterate, 498
obscure, 215
obsequious, 190
obsolete, 730
obstinate, 624
obtuse, 845
obviate, 818
occult, 490
ominous, 482
opaque, 517
optimist, 633
opulence, 825
ornate, 349
orthodox, 309
ossify, 505
ostentatious, 436
oust, 339
pagan, 525
painstaking, 630
pallid, 603
pallor, 244
palpable, 513
panegyric, 599
paradigm, 251
paradox, 754
paraphernalia, 465
parochial, 892
parody, 841

parsimonious, 210
parsimony, 209
partisan, 833
passive, 664
pavilion, 83
pedantic, 496
pedestrian, 36
pejorative, 206
penitent, 381
pensive, 451
penurious, 737
perceptive, 203
percussion, 264
perfunctory, 738
peripheral, 44
perjury, 421
permeable, 748
pernicious, 440
perpetual, 500
pertinent, 709
pervade, 618
pessimism, 792
petty, 15
petulant, 108
phenomenon, 872
philanthropy, 775
phlegmatic, 198
phobia, 693
pious, 178
pique, 895
pithy, 734
pittance, 266
placate, 16
plaintive, 595
plausible, 899
plethora, 63
polemicist, 196
ponderous, 840
potable, 483
potent, 650
pragmatic, 446
preclude, 811

predecessor, 771
premise, 187
prescriptive, 752
prevalent, 495
prevaricate, 600
pristine, 468
privy, 641
prodigal, 427
prodigious, 330
profound, 548
profusion, 81
progeny, 563
program, 854
promontory, 389
propensity, 884
prosaic, 647
proverbial, 541
provincial, 787
provocative, 880
provoke, 740
prudent, 617
pulchritude, 186
pungent, 20
putrefaction, 413
putrefy, 218
quaint, 507
qualified, 448
quandary, 40
quarantine, 43
quiescence, 794
quiescent, 393
quirk, 873
quixotic, 470
rabid, 851
rancid, 536
rancor, 435
rant, 672
rarefy, 590
ratify, 159
rationalize, 609
raucous, 183
raze, 878

realm, 572
rebuff, 181
rebuttal, 270
recalcitrant, 180
recession, 871
reciprocal, 615
recluse, 591
recondite, 527
rectify, 157
redundant, 9
refurbish, 227
refute, 656
regal, 179
reiterate, 485
relegate, 10
relevant, 755
relinquish, 592
remorse, 188
rend, 849
render, 73
renegade, 743
repast, 177
replete, 274
replica, 328
reprehensible, 444
reproach, 258
reproof, 688
repudiate, 223
rescind, 480
resignation, 887
resilient, 331
resolution, 686
respite, 74
resplendent, 621
reticent, 174
retract, 509
retroaction, 392
reverent, 354
reverie, 756
rhapsodize, 631
rhetorical, 881
ribald, 443

rigor, 477
rout, 837
ruffian, 727
ruminate, 695
rummage, 715
rustic, 191
saga, 168
sagacious, 219
salient, 31
salubrious, 696
salvage, 326
sanguine, 889
sarcasm, 123
satire, 228
saturate, 461
saunter, 262
savor, 780
scanty, 255
scrupulous, 790
scrutinize, 793
sectarian, 802
sedition, 160
seethe, 653
sequester, 276
serrated, 19
servile, 662
shady, 799
shoddy, 138
sinuous, 445
skeptic, 702
skulk, 112
slander, 506
slothful, 153
sojourn, 299
solace, 28
solemnity, 147
solicit, 282
soliloquy, 579
solubility, 146
somber, 169
soporific, 145
sordid, 144

sovereign, 192
specious, 277
sporadic, 573
spurious, 441
spurn, 832
squalid, 659
stagnant, 139
stamina, 761
stanza, 197
static, 86
steadfast, 162
stigma, 430
stipend, 462
stoic, 148
stoke, 5
stridency, 135
stupor, 642
suave, 455
subjugate, 170
subliminal, 723
subsidiary, 677
subtlety, 61
succinct, 758
succumb, 30
sunder, 363
superficial, 87
superfluous, 769
superlative, 305
suppress, 292
surmise, 652
surpass, 782
susceptible, 472
sycophant, 488
symmetry, 172
synthetic, 126
table, 105
tacit, 235
taciturn, 804
tantalize, 341
tarry, 460
taut, 50
tedious, 8

temper, 867
tenacious, 604
tensile, 200
tentative, 516
tenuous, 140
tepid, 118
terse, 478
thrifty, 110
thwart, 70
timorous, 614
torpid, 217
tortuous, 856
toxic, 545
tractable, 679
tranquillity, 104
transmutation, 442
transpire, 14
traumatic, 558
trek, 52
trepidation, 622
tribute, 619
trite, 358
trivial, 772
truculent, 103
truncate, 7
tumid, 102
turbulence, 698
turmoil, 747
tycoon, 380
tyranny, 204
ubiquitous, 38
ulterior, 449
uncanny, 432
undermine, 129
unequivocal, 598
ungainly, 97
uniform, 504
unique, 283
universal, 497
unobtrusive, 553
unprecedented, 32
unpretentious, 645

unruly, 95
unwonted, 371
upshot, 92
urbane, 312
usurpation, 706
usury, 532
utopia, 39
vacillation, 554
vacuous, 689
vagabond, 484
vagrant, 855
valance, 56
valiant, 318
valid, 580
valor, 463
vantage, 242
vaunted, 27
vehement, 687
velocity, 130
vendetta, 115
venerate, 245
venue, 53
veracious, 193
verbatim, 646
verbose, 89
versatile, 736
vertigo, 777
vex, 644
viable, 879
vigor, 651
vilify, 117

vindicate, 648
virtuoso, 431
virulent, 492
viscous, 85
vital, 26
vivacious, 665
vogue, 2
volatile, 557
voluble, 84
vulnerable, 720
waft, 150
waive, 457
wane, 314
wanton, 565
warrant, 194
welter, 23
wheedle, 649
whet, 151
whimsical, 438
wither, 199
wooden, 76
workaday, 75
wrath, 714
wretched, 894
wry, 668
xenophobia, 1
yoke, 281
yore, 29
zealot, 71
zenith, 863
zephyr, 561